Every Other Day

Letters from the Pacific

GEORGE B. LUCAS

Every Other Day

Naval Institute Press / *Annapolis, Maryland*

Library of Congress Cataloging-in-Publication Data
Lucas, George Blanchard.
    Every other day : letters from the Pacific / George B. Lucas.
        p.   cm.
    ISBN 1-55750-528-4 (acid-free paper)
    1. Lucas, George Blanchard—Correspondence.   2. Lucas, Betty, d.
1950—Correspondence.   3. Tern (Tugboat)   4. World War, 1939–1945—
Naval operations, American.   5. Sailors—United States—
Correspondence.   6. United States Navy—Biography.   I. Title.
D774.T37L83   1995
940.54'5973'092—dc20   95-8682
                                                                           CIP

Printed in the United States of America on acid-free paper ⊗

02   01   00   99   98   97   96   95   9   8   7   6   5   4   3   2
First printing

All illustrative materials appear courtesy of the author.

Preface

This book is a fictionalized version of a true story. All of the names except mine and my wife's have been changed and some scenarios altered; dates and explanatory phrases have been added for clarity. However, all in all it is an accurate record of what a young U.S. naval officer saw and did and felt during his two-year tour of duty in World War II in the Pacific theater from May 16, 1943, to April 26, 1945.

Before our ship sailed from Long Beach, California, that morning in May, I told my wife, Betty, I would try to write her every other day. I kept my word pretty well; I wrote 324 letters. Unbeknownst to me, she kept the letters, every one. This is an edited collection of many of them.

I met Betty at Penn State University in September 1939. She was a freshman, 18 years old. I received my B.S. degree in June 1940 and went to Louisiana State University, where

I had a research assistantship. At Christmastime I returned home by bus to Philipsburg, Pennsylvania, where Betty and I were secretly married on December 27, 1940. She finished her freshman year and came to Baton Rouge in June 1941.

My graduate studies were interrupted in November 1942, when I enlisted in the U.S. Navy. After attending officers' training school for four months at Northwestern University in Chicago, I received my ensign's commission early in 1943 in the U.S. Navy and was assigned to a seagoing tug. It was a member of the class of tugs named after birds. Those stalwart tugs had names like the *Kingfisher,* the *Oriole,* the *Robin,* and the *Bobolink.* My ship was the U.S.S. *Tern,* ATO 142. The ship left California for the mid-Pacific in May 1943. I had never been to sea before. My wife and I had been married less than three years, and I didn't see her again until 24 months later.

After I was mustered out of the Navy in September 1945 I completed my Ph.D. at Louisiana State University in July 1946. We put the letters I had written Betty in a large cardboard box and took them with us to North Carolina, where I had accepted a position as assistant professor at North Carolina State University.

My wife and I had a happy marriage. Unfortunately, she died of leukemia on November 5, 1950. We had three children, all boys. The oldest was 4½ years old and the twins were 18 months old. Irvin, Glenn, Guy, and I are still a close family.

To assuage my grief and try to kill some of the pain, a few months after Betty's death I began to reread and edit the letters I had written her. Off and on this secret task has occupied my spare time for more than 40 years as I built this hymn to her memory.

Our tug belonged to the Third Service Fleet. We were not a fighting ship, although it was equipped with a 3-inch cannon, four 20-mm machine guns, depth charges, and small arms. Mostly we were a working ship. We towed barges and injured ships, pulled targets for dive-bombers, and recovered torpedoes for submarines and destroyers during practice drills. Our primary duty was to serve the fighting ships, and we followed the task forces at a safe distance. After a landing had been completed, we would drag landing craft off the beach and assist those that were disabled so they could be used again.

From May 1943 through June 1944 the ship was stationed at Pearl Harbor, where we performed the endless tasks needed to prepare fighting ships for battle. We towed barges and targets; we rescued an observation plane; with another tug we towed a disabled aircraft carrier for three days; we performed picket duty off the entrance to Pearl Harbor.

With the fall of Germany in 1944, the war effort increased in the Pacific. Our ship left Pearl Harbor in July 1944 towing a barge loaded with supplies to Eniwetok, an atoll in the Marhsall Islands that was being used by our task forces as an anchorage and staging area.

We operated out of Eniwetok and Kwajalein atolls (in the Gilbert Islands), where we helped rearm, refuel, and reprovision fighting ships of various task forces until October 1944. In August 1944, we towed (at six knots) a large concrete ship to Manus Island in the Admiralty Islands, down near New Guinea. This ship had no engine, the forward storage tanks were filled with oil, and the aft storage tanks were filled with drinking water. Upon our return to Eniwetok we towed some barges to Tarawa and then worked there a week or so cleaning up some of the debris left over from the Tarawa campaign. I got to go ashore on Tarawa. The wreckage and destruction of the battle there left a deep impression on me.

In October we left the Gilbert Islands and towed a barge to the Palau Islands. We stayed there a week or so, then moved to Ulithi atoll, a secret anchorage for the U.S. fleet 300 miles south of Guam. Around Thanksgiving we towed a barge loaded with spare radio parts to Guam and another barge to Saipan in the Mariana Islands. After a week or so we returned to Palau, where we were stationed until I left the ship in April 1945 and returned to the good ol' USA.

In 1955 I married Vernelle Vaughan, a divorcée with two young sons, Woodson and Lee. We had two more children, Candace and George B., Jr. Ours was a busy family during their growing-up years.

But then Vernelle died of lung cancer on November 2, 1987.

In 1993 I married Mary Elizabeth Wood, a widow with three grown children—Beth, Jane, and Robert—and eight grandchildren. Our wedding was a family affair, with lots of children.

Acknowledgments

I am indebted to Joseph P. Hobbs, Professor of History, North Carolina State University, who graciously helped me "build" this book. Also I am grateful to Polly Carlsen, who did the typing and provided friendship, moral support, and frequent suggestions during the past 30 years.

Finally, I thank Mrs. Linda Lombroso, who shortened and edited the entire text, and Anne Collier, who shepherded this manuscript through its many changes.

Every Other Day

5/16/43

Dearest Betty,

How odd it feels to be writing this first letter to you, not knowing how many I shall write before we can touch each other again. After all, though, it could be a lot worse. When I think how much some people sacrifice, ours does not assume such overwhelming proportions. Anyway, we must bear it the best we can. If we brood on it too much, it will make it that much worse. I am just going to keep my mind fixed on the day when we can be together again.

Whenever I think back to the happy days we knew, I sure feel forlorn. Incidentally, I must not look back, but look ahead. To dwell on the past is fatal indeed. Help me to look ahead. Carry your heart on your sleeve for Luke. Only don't show it to anyone but me.

When we put to sea from Long Beach the wind was brisk and the waves were choppy. Our ship bobbed and rolled. I did fine till we sat down to supper that night. We had avocado salad. About the third bite, I hurriedly pushed back my chair and bolted for the door. It was only two steps to the rail, and I let go. From then on I was seasick for about three days. But I still had to go on watch. The nights were cool and I wore my overcoat with the collar turned up. One night on watch I felt bad. I leaned over the windscreen to vomit and the wind blew the green, wet excrement back in my face and onto my collar. I was too sick to wipe it away. I didn't even care.

When off watch I would immediately hit the sack. I didn't even bother to take off my clothes or shave for three days. My clothes were rumpled and I looked awful, but I didn't care. Most of the crew had never been to sea before so we had plenty of seasick sailors with us. We were a sorry looking outfit. If we had sighted a Jap sub we would have been a pitiful opponent.

5/18/43

Dear Gretchen,*

I am completely over my seasickness, but even yet the peculiar odors about the ship make my stomach queasy. I eat lots of pickles and celery. I have a voracious appetite for them. But I have lost all desire for coffee. It certainly is queer how the stomach acts up. Boy, the guy who discovers a cure for seasickness will certainly be a rich man!

---

*Gretchen was a favorite nickname for Betty. The author used several different salutations in letters to his wife.

Emersin is worried because I write so often. But I told him I would write enough for both of us. Since you and Madeline are sharing the same apartment, we can consider them family letters. I tell you one thing, it was nice of them to take us in when we came to LA to report to the *Tern*!

5/20/43

Dearest spouse,

The first time I saw the *Tern,* she was in a shipyard at Long Beach, California, being overhauled. She had just come back from the Society Islands by way of Pearl Harbor after 18 months' duty in the South Pacific. She accompanied one of our cruisers, the *Pensacola,* that had been hit by a torpedo. The *Tern* followed close by in case the big ship foundered, but now the *Tern* was sitting up on blocks in drydock. Most of her crew were on leave and only one officer was aboard. The men were using every available moment of their precious days in the States, for they knew they soon must go back "out there" again. I had the duty my first night. But there wasn't anything to do, and even if there had been I couldn't have done much. I was a new ensign just out of midshipman school, and I didn't know much about ships. In fact I had never been to sea before.

5/22/43

Faithful spouse,

Last night there was a big yellow moon floating over the calm sea. We must darken ship each night at sundown. We close all hatches and ports and leave only a few dim, red lights burning. It gets stuffy in the cabins, so after dark we sit outside on the benches that line the rail and talk. On such a little ship the officers and crew are more intimate than on a battleship. (The captain keeps to himself, though.) It's surprising what the sailors bull about. Most of them are reliving and retelling their Long Beach experiences.

One of the messboys is called Isaiah Izzle. He surely is funny, and last night I read a letter he wrote to his girl. He misspelled words and his construction was not perfect, but at the end he wrote, "I will close this letter, but never my heart." I thought that was a beautiful, sincere thing to say, so quite shamelessly I am copying the words from him and say them to you. I love you so.

The other ships in our convoy are silhouettes off to our left, and the boss ship is a destroyer. It certainly has been busy on this trip keeping the ships on station. It is always on the go, back and forth, up and down. Once we had a submarine scare and that destroyer took off like a jackrabbit! Destroyers really go fast. Their bow waves at high speed are beautiful.

We expect to make land tomorrow. It's a big famous place that you have heard much about.

5/23/43

Dearest Gretchen,

How can I tell you, how can I convey to you the impact of the sea on me, a landsman? How can I describe the colors, the motions, the vastness? What shall I write you of the loneliness, the vague disquiet, the awe, the insignificance it creates in me? To watch the sun come up out of the water and roll across the tall empty heaven and disappear back into the western waves at night; to observe this day after day; to sail toward the curve of the horizon, meeting the curve of the heaven with the empty, masterless wilderness of ocean spread all around to and beyond the limits of sight; to see the endless parade of waves in cadence governed by the ever-present wind; to feel afraid and alone, and lost, and perplexed, and full of awe.

What will this mysterious Pacific Ocean do to me?

Last night we went to the movies on a nearby ship. As the weather is always warm here, the movie screen is rigged on the stern of a ship or the boat deck, wherever there is enough horizontal space for the crew to bring folding chairs, cots or anything on which to sit. Sometimes they sprawl on the deck or sit on the rail or in a coil of line or just squat, or climb in the riggin'. Everybody has his favorite spot. Our ship has no movie projector so we visit another ship or go to one of the nearby movie shows at the various headquarters located around the harbor. Of course movies are free. All movies are shown outside. The projector is protected from rain and the screen has a roof over it. If it begins to rain very few leave. They break out ponchos, raincoats or tarpaulins and the movie goes on. Movies are a favorite recreation of ship crews.

5/26/43

Dearest wife,

Probably one reason the sea doesn't appeal to me is because I get sick so easy. It's more of a nuisance than anything else, but just the same it is a lousy feeling. I must drive myself to do anything and the half-sick headache is exasperating. One pleasant thing, however: as soon as the sea calms and we get back to land, I feel 100 percent better.

The restless, changing sea slaps the side of the ship and whispers and gurgles. The insistent ocean becomes a part of all men at sea. It pervades their being. It is always there. And its restless changing dictates their moves and actions.

There is no foolishness about the ocean. It knows who is boss, and the little ships and the big ships just better be careful.

One thing I have noticed among all the men I have met: they want to get it over with and get home. Everyone jokes and laughs, but underneath the seriousness is there.

Mosquitoes aren't so bad here, but one boy wrote they were so big we used chicken wire to keep them out. And one mosquito took so much blood he must have been working for the Red Cross.

Boisee, our chief pharmacist's mate who is a short Frenchman with an Adolph Menjou moustache, told me the other day that when he gets home, he will never have a cross word with his wife again. He told me that "when I get back, I will appreciate anything I ever had, like a soft bed, the smell of flowers, wife's cooking, a morning newspaper, room to run in, and freedom to come and go."

I hate to think I am homesick, but my mind is continually filled with visions of land and tree-lined streets and the smell of grass and flowers. The sun on the sea makes such a glare. The colors seem so brash and hard.

The other day I went into town to visit the university. It sure is pretty up around the campus. The mountains are lovely and you can see the ocean; palm trees everywhere. The university seems a little run down. They have slit trenches and bomb shelters everywhere. I talked to one of the horticulture teachers. He said they have very few men students left, and they are just marking time till the war ends.

I was standing on the library steps when three soldiers passed by. They stopped and one of them turned out to be Ben Overholts, Dr. Overholts's son from Penn State Botany Department. He sure was glad to see me and I him. He is a sergeant in the signal corps and may be here for the duration of the war. I asked him why he didn't bring his wife out. He said, "No, too many men here. They say the ratio is 100 to 1 and I sure believe it."

Yesterday I walked from our pier to one of the offices to get some communication papers. On the way back, I passed a baseball field where some sailors were playing ball. I sat down awhile and watched them. I was tired from walking because the buildings here are far apart. The sun was warm, so the shade felt good. It was nice to sit there and smell the earth and grass. I never realized how good they could smell! And someone was burning leaves somewhere nearby. The faint, acrid smell of smoke had a fine essence. In the background were the green-brown jagged hills. I didn't know what a nice color green is until after I had made this sea trip. I guess I am just a landsman at heart.

5/29/43

Gretchen, sweet:

Few people realize that when you are cooped up on a ship 24 hours a day, day after day, the ship becomes your world. And the boundaries of the ship are the limits of your world. You are confined by its dimensions, you are limited and restricted. For instance, when I take a walk, I step out the port door of the wardroom, walk 10 steps toward the bow, then 6 steps across the bow, then turn and walk aft down the starboard side 58 steps, then 10 steps across the fantail, then 48 steps back to my cabin.

Also, if we run out of toothpaste or other necessities, we do without till we get to the next port where they are available.

And the way you spend your spare time, your leisure time, aboard ship is determined by the ship itself. It isn't like working in an office or factory, where you jump in your car and ride home or else enjoy a delightful walk to your house. On a ship, when you are done with your watch, you stay right on the ship. You are either on the bridge, in the wardroom, in the bunk, visiting the engine room, inspecting crew's quarters, or walking 10–6–58–10–48 steps.

So in my leisure time I read books. With 66 men and six officers, we have a collection of tastes. And the Navy is good about supplying us with paperbound Armed Forces pocket editions. Of course, I could sleep all the time like Sankin does, or just sit and shoot the breeze or stand at the rail and watch the ocean, and I do all these things, but even so I get tired of them. What makes it worse is that you know you are confined, you are restricted, you are imprisoned, you can't get off or out. You are in jail. Yes, freedom is valuable! Each man needs freedom if he is to attain full meaning in his life. Even if it is just to take a walk where and when you want.

From the officers on down, there is no question we are all on the same team. Some of our boys have been shipmates with sailors from other ships, and when they get together and talk, it is fun just to listen to 'em. It seems each rated man seeks out a man of similar rate on the other ships. Yeomen look up yeomen, Emersin looks up the engineer, I go see the communications officer (boy, I sure have bummed a lot of knowledge the last few days), seamen stay with seamen, etc.

And always, sooner or later, the talk will turn to home. When were you there last? What was it like? I bet it's nice back in the States!

The messboy, Izzle, turned out to be a philanderer. He writes letters to at least six different girls and gives them all the same line. I wish you could read them. He starts out with "Time and opportunity premit [sic] me to write you," and later he asks, "Do you dig my jive, child?"

He sure is funny.

Please keep me up to date on our financial affairs. Since it costs me so little to live, I'm gonna buy you a few things here at the sub base. They have nice straw purses, carved wooden dishes, and other tropical items. I'll look around and any good bargains I can get I will purchase and put under my bunk. They don't have any electrical appliances at all at the sub base, but I'll look in town and maybe I can find some.

Ah, Gretchen. Let me thank you again for wanting the operation and wanting children, and loving me. I am rich to have you! When I think back on all the pleasant hours we've spent together I know I am lucky. And when I anticipate all the passionate hours and fun yet due us, I can hardly wait till I get home. I hope the war is over soon.

6/1/43

Dear Betty,

Last night I was getting a haircut from our ship's barber. He is not really a barber. He just "took it up" because we don't have a barber aboard and we seldom get a chance to go ashore for a haircut. The barber shop is a tall stool on the fantail. The "barber" is learning as he goes, with each head he cuts. The haircuts range from poor to passable. Some are weird!

Laundry service is so poor here that we are scrubbing our own underclothes. Emersin opened a laundry. He charges $5 for a suit of khakis. Of course the only business he gets is his own clothes!

Now about drinking. I am glad to say that your promise

is the easiest thing in the world to say yes to and comply with. You see, I have been analyzing my seasick feeling, and I came to the conclusion that when I am seasick, I have exactly the same feeling as when drinking too much whiskey. If you recall how you felt on our trip to Dallas, you will know what I mean. When you are seasick, those periodic spells of vomiting occur and the whole world has a horrid, nauseating outlook. I also get a headache and feel dizzy. Seasickness brings back all the memories of hangovers I used to have. I could no more enjoy whiskey or a highball than I could epsom salts and vinegar. Anyway, I can easily promise you no drinking for me. I do average two or three Cokes a day which comes out of our mess bill. I am amazed at myself for actually liking Cokes. Maybe it's because we get 'em so cheap.

6/3/43

Dearest wife,

It sure is a job to get any packages mailed from here. It cost us $1.48 to send the purses. Incidentally, the one with beads in it is yours and the other one belongs to Madeline. They cost $3.90 each so I don't know if we got a bargain or not.

I keep wondering how you would look in long black stockings with the quarter-inch mesh, and a garter belt and red shoes, high heels, and high ankle strap. Then a tight-fitting sheer skirt and a form-fitting blouse with long sleeves. Hair done up and puffed in front, Hollywood makeup, heavy earrings, a red hibiscus in your hair and a tiny black ribbon around your neck. Jesus, woman, you're a lovely creature, and much of the time before I go to sleep, I think up costumes for you to wear. Separations are terrible things, but think how joyous and ecstatic our reunions will be.

Dearest wife,

Today, we had oysters for dinner. Gee, they grow plump big ones here, the best I have ever eaten. This "tropical paradise" would be just that if you were here and I knew there was no danger of the Japs coming back!

Most of my hours the last few days have been spent waiting to hear that you came through the operation okay. Just what did the surgeon do? Cut the muscles and shorten them, or what? I am glad you are getting in shape for breeding. Such superior germ plasm as yours should be generated. (Ahem!)

Slowly I am becoming an officer. There are many duties and problems aboard ship, and I learn about as many as I can, when I can. For instance, one of the hardest parts of maneuvering a ship is bringing her into and taking her away from the dock. We go in and out from the dock sometimes twice a day, and almost every time we go in and out of the harbor, I go up on the bridge, close my mouth, open my eyes and ears, and take in everything. When the day comes for me to take her in, I'll be ready.

6/9/43

Dearest Gretchen,

Today I got the letter you wrote just before the operation. And Emersin got one from Madeline that she wrote just after seeing you when the operation was over. She said you were a little sick, but that you would be all right.

Your letter complete with illustrations was a honey!

Jeepers, creepers, I bet you look seductive in that hospital robe . . . I certainly hope the operation will do the trick, for I want children as much as you do. But it seems you are paying for them already. I'm thankful for you, Gretchen, and I hope your reward is in proportion to the effort you put in it.

It was fortunate that Madeline was there with you. She surely is a grand person.

It's surprising how much navigation I've forgotten. I took some sights last night and worked out our position. It was *only* about 60 miles from where I knew we actually were. This is lousy navigation, it will never do, but after all it was my first real try.

My mistakes were in use of the sextant. They are tricky to get onto, and you just can't pick one up and use it right off. You must become skillful. Once you can take accurate sights, working them out is just routine. It's interesting and I like it, and I bet you would just eat it up. In fact, there are many aspects of Navy work which would be duck soup for you, such as decoding messages, copying radio traffic, and anything involving mathematics.

Don't worry about me getting gypped out here. I'm not buying anything unless I am absolutely sure it is a bargain. I know this place is just a tourists' resort, but I'll be plenty cautious with my purchases.

6/12/43

Dear Gretchen,

One month ago we set sail, the same day of the month that Columbus discovered land. I don't suppose there is any connection between the two.

Emersin is treasurer for the officer's mess. Today he brought a whole batch of fresh vegetables aboard. Neely, the mess cook (steward) for the officers, made a wonderful salad and we had chicken. I ate a big meal, and it sure was good.

At present, Emersin is trying to get some empty shells or smoke bombs to make table lamps for us.

Well, today I breathed easier for the first time. I got a letter written from you "after the cut." I could tell you wrote it in bed, for some of the lines went up and down like waves. I certainly am glad you made it okay. Now for Pete's sake, take it easy a while and don't have any setbacks. Do not do any heavy lifting, don't get excited, reach too high, jump up and down, or anything like that—I mean it. Don't lift any heavy weights, either, like suitcases, packages or such.

I feel more confident now than I ever did that we can have children. Jeepers, when you wrote me all the stuff the surgeon took out, I wondered if you had anything left. I'm glad he did take out the appendix and tumor. It shows how efficient he was, and you should feel better all around. Maybe now you will feel better generally once you completely recover from all this.

You mean the cotton threads are gonna support the uterus? For many years? Seems rather fragile to me, but then I ain't qualified to judge.

6/11/13

My dear wife,

When the *Tern* was in the shipyard at Long Beach being overhauled, noise enveloped her. There were chains clanking, shouts, steam hissing, whistles, air hammering, thuds, pulleys creaking, bangs, water splashing, compressors, engines rumbling, whines, and wheels screeching. Racket everywhere assailed the ears and scraped the nerves.

I thought when we left the shipyard the ship would be quiet, but I have found out since that ship upkeep is continuous. As soon as we tie up at the dock, the crew starts to work. It seems they never finish scraping and chipping and banging and painting. When they finish one job, they start on another. The fight against salt water and rust and barnacles never ceases. It takes work to keep things shipshape. I guess it's like washing your face—it should be done every day.

Last night I censored letters and it sure was a funny job. They were the worst bunch I have gone through yet. Some (all) of the boys are getting sharp (i.e., hot, hard up, carnal urge, wicked, sinful, lustful, ornery, horny, mean, stiff-peckered, hard-on, studlike, bullish, in heat, you name it) and a few of them don't hesitate to tell their wives just how much they desire the warmth of their wife's body. But they say it so oddly. It's funny to see the working of a man's mind in writing.

I asked our executive officer (Sankin, my roommate) what to do about these "passionate" letters. He has been in the Navy at least 15 years. He gave me a scornful look as if to say, "How can you college fellas be so dumb?" Then he said, "Hell, if it ain't military information, let it pass!"

In *Gone with the Wind* I believe Rhett Butler used to whisper "vulgar endearments" to Scarlett O'Hara while they were *sitting in church*. Well, I say some nasty things to your picture, but you don't seem to mind. Also, people can write vulgar endearments. For instance, one man wrote his wife, "Honey, I want to suck your tit." Can you imagine? Now I would never say it that way. I might write, shyly, "I would like to kiss your breasts," but to come right out and slobber all over her . . . not for me. But I bet you he *has* "sucked her tit." And I bet he thinks about it almost every day now.

By this time, you should be well on the road to recovery. I hope you get over the operation without any complications. You will, too, if you take care of yourself.

Here again is the last half page, which I always save for Gretchen. I, too, miss you, miss you. My one thought is to return to you and never leave. It will be so rich and beautiful just to share your company (as well as your bed). I didn't know how peaceful, quiet and nice it is to live near a university till I got mixed up in this wartime bustle of noise, construction, action, responsibility and vague unease in a foreign land, apprehension, seasickness ad infinitum. But even when I'm seasick, I love you.

6/16/43

Dearest spouse,

I want to tell you about a little ceremony that takes place every evening at sunset. We are usually tied up at the same dock with several other ships (of our class). A few seconds before sundown, the ranking boatswain of this cluster of ships pipes "colors" on his pipe, and each man topside faces the flag on the main mast of his ship and stands at attention while the signalmen on each ship haul down the flags. Each sailor stops whatever he is doing and all stand quietly. Then after the flag is stowed away for the night, each man resumes what he was doing before. Somehow the whole ritual seems to be so much more real than any I witnessed back in the States. There is no band playing, and no crowds or fine clothes. Just a group of sailors in dungarees who stop a few minutes each day to pay homage to a symbol that is dear and terribly important to them all.

It always takes some minutes for conversations to get started again after evening colors for it seems to me each man's thoughts have crossed the sea to the States and home, and he has to bring them back again to the business at hand before he talks again. I know the ceremony affects the men, for several of them at various times have said casually to me afterwards, "Kinda gets ya, doesn't it?" Or, "I wonder how the garden is doing back home." "Gee, it's quiet this time of day back on the farm."

Being in the service has its little compensations. Few of these fellows can express themselves adequately, but their love of country is deep indeed. I can tell!

6/18/43

Dearest Gretchen,

This last week we have been busy. We were out every day, either towing targets or recovering torpedoes. The ocean was rough at times so I didn't feel good. But I do believe that I am becoming more used to the sea. However, instead of getting seasick, I am getting sick of the sea.

Did I tell you that floating around the ship are typewritten copies of pornographic (smutty) stories? Some of them are awful! Sailors really do get sharp. And it is entirely possible I am speaking for myself. I would be more so if my stomach wasn't turning somersaults all the time when I am seasick.

6/19/43

Dearest wife,

You know, we have a ship-service store on board. It is a wire cage below deck about four feet wide, with shelves and enough room for the storekeeper to stand inside. It is open for about a half hour after evening chow. It has candy bars, cigarettes, shaving gear and other odds and ends. Well, the profits from it are turned back to the ship's fund (whatever that means). We had so much money in the ship's fund that we (the Captain at crew's suggestion) decided to buy a car. And we did, a '34 touring Ford V-8—cost maybe $200; it has no top. It is for the use of the entire crew, and we have regular engineers to care for it and coxswains to drive it. We use it to pick up supplies, laundry, mail, and take men to town on liberty. Perhaps now it will be possible for me to see the rest of the island, for I'm sure the car will be available for sightseeing trips.

Don't worry, I won't drive it! There is too much traffic here for me.

Don't worry about me stinting. My wardroom bill for last month was less than $10 (including two, sometimes three Cokes a day, but not often because I don't like 'em very much). My laundry runs about $1 a week, so you can see how cheaply I am living.

I'm real anxious to get the debts paid off, church, Grange, Doc Harrison, and Russ. I won't be content till we don't owe anyone. We have a splendid chance now to erase our debts and I think we should make a good effort to pay them all by Christmas. If you can save $120–125 cash each month out of the $200, we can easily pay them off by January 1, 1944, and then we can start off right. The best Christmas (I figure I'll be here till Christmas) present I can think of is for you to write that we don't owe anybody. Then we can start saving for kids and a home.

And I do realize that the operation you underwent is a banner waving high, proclaiming your love for me. Now that we are so much in accord and understand each other, and mean so much to each other, we must keep it that way always. Let's try! We can make life so bountiful for each other and our children. It will be fun raising them, and teaching them, and loving them, and being proud of them. Being away like this makes me realize more than ever how fulfilling a happy home is and what a worthwhile institution it can be. Let's fill our house with good things, real things, and make it a sheltered place that friends will like to come to, and where you and I will be content. Oh, Gretchen, I'm dreaming, but we will make our dreams come true.

6/22/43

Dear spouse,

Emersin and I took the ship service car to go buy vegetables for the wardroom, draw spare parts for our machine shop and pick up the mail. He showed me where he and Madeline used to live. He also showed me some good stores to buy native curios in. It was fun to ride around the streets and not feel the ship rolling underneath me.

6/24/43

Dearest spouse,

As you know, I am new in the Navy. Therefore I am given those watches when the least is likely to happen, such as under way at night in safe water when proceeding here to there or from yay to yonder and back. But even so, to be officer of the deck at night scares me a little when I realize that down below in the ship are 60 to 70 men asleep who are trusting me that they won't wake up in the ocean.

Boy, the captain of a ship surely has responsibility and Captain (Lt.) Parry carries his well. He is 24, went to midshipman school at Abbott Hall and was at Pearl Harbor on December 7. He broke the lock off the ammunition locker with a hammer and set up a 50-caliber machine gun on the boat deck. Some of the crew swear he hit a Jap plane (at least it was smoking, and losing altitude, when it went out of sight over the palm trees at Hospital Point), but it was never confirmed.

I am learning to identify stars. Few seamen learn the stars and constellations as they appear in the heavens. Rather, they rely on star charts, from which they pick out the stars they will "shoot" with the sextant. But I just want to learn for the fun of it.

The Southern Cross is a pretty (what a trite adjective for a magnificent group of stars) constellation. Maybe you will see it someday on the deck of a ship with me.

We don't get enough exercise aboard ship, so I chin myself everyplace I can think of, and I do pushups and play catch on the deck with the crew. Just anything to keep my mind off the fact that I am here, and you are far away, and the days go by that I cannot be with you.

Jeepers, just to eat hot dogs on the levee by the Mississippi River of a Sunday evening with you and the crowd from the Plant Pathology Department at LSU sure would be fun.

6/26/43

Dearest Gretchen,

Last night I had the midwatch (2400–0400). We were out for searchlight practice. When I came on the bridge the practice was over and it was dark all around. About 2:00, a sickle moon came up out of the ocean and it sure was lovely. My thoughts were far away. The sailor boys on ship have a pretty tough time at sea. Watches for the deck hands are relieved every two hours, so nobody ever gets a full night's sleep when we are out. Sleeping below is not comfortable, for it is too warm. So the boys spread their mattresses on the deck. Sometimes they use their sweater or life jacket for a pillow and flop right on the deck. And, of course, the gun crews (in dangerous waters) sleep right around and near the guns. In walking about the ship one has to be careful not to step on the prone figures in the shadows. Some of these kids are not yet 20, and during the day they act grown up and mature. But at night, when they sleep, they often assume unconsciously the positions that children do in their sleep—one arm flung out, sleeping all curled up (like you do sometimes), or one leg bent. When you see fellows sleeping like that you realize how important it is to keep a "taut watch" and "keen lookout" so that nothing will go wrong. Of course in these waters it is relatively safe, but, just the same, on a dark sea anything can happen . . . Do I scare you? I don't want to, I just wanted to tell you a few of the things I think about.

6/28/43

Dearest Betty,

When I come home, you better be prepared to keep our house shipshape, 'cause being at sea certainly teaches one to keep things in their proper place. Every night (when we are out) before I turn in I always arrange my clothes just so. Thus, when I go on watch I can get up in the dark and get dressed with no fumbling about. On the hook at the head of my bunk, I hang my shorts over my shirt over my trousers, and just reach out and put them on. My shoes (usually I wear my moccasins on night watch 'cause I can just slip them on) I place as follows: the left one nearer the head of my bunk and the right one nearer the foot of my bunk. My socks I slip through the handle of one of the drawers. I keep the sweater you knit me in the middle drawer, left front corner, and my raincoat and jacket behind the door. My hat I hang over the light bulb, and I just reach up and put it on.

And you know there is always the "general quarters" alarm. We have never had one except in practice. My station is at the two after-guns on the boat deck. Well, in preparation for GQ I have my 45 automatic and my helmet (just like the soldiers wear) on a hook at the foot of my bunk, and my life jacket is in my locker at the head of my bunk. So you can see, I am all prepared to jump outa my sack into my jacket and overboard if necessary. All the officers carry automatics under battle conditions for numerous reasons—I am half scared of the goddamned thing, but I can use it if I have to.

One of our seamen is quite religious, and we have long talks in the night (he is a steersman) when I have the bridge. We talk frankly, in the night silence, with low voices. I question him about this and that and why he thinks in a certain way. I wish I had his faith. Death holds no fear for him, because in his mind he is all taken care of.

This old ship bounces and quivers and slaps and grunts and rolls and hisses and jumps and pitches and tosses. It's no wonder I get seasick. We had an overnight job and are just going back to port. I'm writing this at the breakfast table. I just came off watch and the others are asleep.

I certainly have learned what the phrase "walk like a drunken sailor" means. Only you don't have to be drunk. This old bitch of a ship sure gets me mad. To walk from bow to stern on just a moderately rough day, you must climb up and down about six hills. And not only that, the hills roll sideways so really you walk in a spiral or corkscrew.

The ship rolls one way and you lean forward to walk up the hill, then suddenly she rolls the other way and you find yourself running down the side of a house roof. So you reach out to grab something before you wind up with a bang against the splinter shield. Oh, I just love the seagoing life. It's so stimulating and heroic and romantic. Balls!

7/3/43

Dear wife,

I must tell you about censoring letters. Some of these guys are a scream. One sailor wrote to his buddy, "I met a WAC corporal back home on leave at a dance. After the dance I took her down by the river and bent her on three times. I stayed with her every night, and I coulda lived with her, only her folks got suspicious."

Get that nautical phrase "bent her on." Do you suppose he was lying?

One boy ended his letter to his girl like this: "I love you . . . 25 minutes . . . I love you again."

I am being educated in more ways than one.

The other day I went ashore and went swimming. There is an officers' club at the famous beach with bar, lounges, library, etc. I really enjoy going to the beach, especially to watch the surfboard artists. Wife, it is entrancing to watch them come riding in on the crest of a wave. The poetry of motion of the surfboard and rider, the water and surf, beach and palms, are pure delight.

7/5/43

My dear wife,

One of the married men on this ship wrote his wife that when he got out of the Navy, he was gonna stay home all the time, but he would take her to the movies once a month. Several of the enlisted men on the ship are married (some of the men are 35 or 40), and the letters they write home are touching indeed. Some of them are funny, too. One fellow (unmarried) wanted his girl to send him her picture in a bathing suit so he could see her physique. Only he called it "your marvelous phiseec."

When you come right down to it, that's the way it sounds.

I see by the *Time* magazine that cases of meat poisoning are becoming more prevalent. Be careful of the meat you buy, be sure it is government graded and not black market. Be careful, too, of cold meats like minced ham and bologna, and hot dogs, 'cause they put anything and everything in them nowadays.

Today I was coming back from swimming and two Australians rode with me. They were officers in the Royal Australian Air Force, and we struck up quite an acquaintance during our 30-minute ride. Their accents were charming and odd, and I deliberately got them to talk just to enjoy the accent. Taxi drivers here drive fast (they charge 25¢ per passenger from town to base), and I remarked I was always amazed to arrive safely. I didn't ask the Australians where they were from or where they were going (you don't do that here), but the short page they filled in my book of life was a pleasant one.

Yesterday I took the car and five of the crew on a tour of the island. I didn't drive but was chief navigator. Every time we passed a good-looking gal, native or otherwise, the crew would ask, "Shall we stop, Mr. Lucas?" And I would say, "Sail on, sail on!"

We saw some lovely homes. And the flora was magnificent. It was lush and luxuriant. As we got up in the mountains, the clouds closed in and it began to rain as a fine mist. The mountains are steep and we came to a famous waterfall. The water had not much volume, but it fell so far the wind caught it and tended to blow it back up in the air, so that the water sprayed out like a long, floating veil. Ah! it was nice. We had to look straight up to see it, and the waterfall came out of the clouds, so it seemed to be falling right from the sky.

When we got back to the big city, I took the boys to a café and treated them all to a beer (I had one myself, and it was lousy). I was the only officer there, but it was crowded with sailors and marines. My, you should have seen the other sailors look when I sat down with my five! I could tell the crew from the *Tern* enjoyed sitting there with me 'cause officers usually don't associate with the crew, especially socially, and you could just hear the other guys saying, "How come those guys are sittin' with an officer?" But no one there knew me, so it was worth it.

Gretchen, Gretchen, I want to be with you and live life normally again. I am no glory-seeking warrior. All I want is to finish up and come home. Sometimes I can hardly breathe when I think of your physical perfection and the adrenaline just pours into my stomach. That's why I want you to keep your figure. Be especially careful about your stomach and hips, 'cause when you start to lose your figure (10 to 15 years from now), your legs will get thinner and your hips bigger. I know it happens in men (skinny legs and a pot belly). And I've seen society women the same way—a beer barrel on match stems.

So, Bubbles, keep attractive, and when I return I promise to lead you into new gardens of joy and delight. And we can abandon ourselves completely because we know that in our delight, we will be creating a youngster to bring joy to us both.

7/9/43

Dearest wife,

Monotony prevails. Our life now is about as exciting as that of a lighthouse keeper in calm weather. When you are cooped up aboard a small ship, it becomes your whole world and your prison. You have to work hard to think and do constructive things; to remain occupied; to fill 24 hours each day with something else beside boredom and time-killing. I read a great deal. And one reason I am tiping [*sic*] this letter to you is to learn to type. Notic how quickly I pick it up and the lak of misteaks or omissions.

Sailors learn to pass the time in many different ways. Emersin makes lamps out of empty cartridge shells. The carpenter's mate builds outrigger canoe models. He gets koa wood (it's a mahogany color) and carves and polishes it till the smooth curves gleam. Makes you want to caress its warm smoothness.

Some fellows just "shoot the breeze," some argue, some play cards. One fellow weaves rugs. That interests me.

Probably I have been reading too much, for my eyes have been bothering me. So I am going up to the dispensary here and getting a complete examination for my eyes. Maybe if I get a new pair of glasses, I can get rid of these mean little headaches that have been my constant companion for the past two weeks. At first I thought they were part of seasickness, but I guess the glare of the sun on the sea is also a contributing factor. Now don't get alarmed about my condition. It is just one of those little things which are more exasperating than bothersome, and since the Navy is so well equipped, I might as well take advantage of any facilities they can offer. At least I will get a new pair of glasses out of it (I hope).

As you know, naval officers get one quart of liquor a week as their ration. I *give* mine to Emersin. I have heard some people pay $15 a quart for whiskey. Civilian workers out here make enormous wages. I guess some of them think $15 is cheap. Well, easy come, easy go!

As time goes on, it is interesting to observe how the sex appetite increases and grows—mine as much, if not more, than the other men, but I hide mine and I get a kick out of watching "the drive" express itself in the actions of others. Even Emersin, who is usually reticent, betrays himself now and then. The other night at the movies, when a nifty bit of sex walked on the screen, he leaned over to me and said, "How about that Luke?" And I said, "Why, Emersin, what are you thinking?" And he sorta laughed.

7/14/43

My dearest wife,

Do you realize I have been away two months already (it seems like two years)? The time will soon pass and you must not sit at home and feel miserable ('cause misery soon changes to self pity). I'm not scolding you, but since we are in this fix, let's look at it this way. Feel proud that I am doing duty outside the country. And when I come home and people ask me where I was during the war, I'll say, "The Pacific." Nobody will ever be able to say I slacked or shirked. And we do have a few advantages of being separated, although I would trade a dozen of them to be with you: 1) we can save some money, 2) you can finish school, 3) you can get in good health for some rough workouts and for motherhood (when I get back), 4) being apart makes us realize more than ever what we mean to each other, and 5) by getting my sea duty in now, there is a better chance of me coming back to the States later on and getting Stateside duty near the end of the war. Remember, ships go into drydock any time after twelve months, and by next July we should be all finished except the mopping up. Officers with sea duty go up fast, and it is not too farfetched to think that in one year I may become skilled enough to get a small ship of my own. So, wife, turn our misfortune into an asset.

I must close now, but write to me often. Letters from you serve as punctuation marks in the sentences of days which make up this chapter of my life and help speed it to an end.

7/17/43

Dearest wife,

One of our principal jobs is to remain on station, just outside the harbor entrance, in deep water, just in case some ship coming down the harbor channel gets in trouble. A neat trick for the enemy is to put a torpedo into one of our ships as she leaves port, hoping she will sink in the channel and block everything. Theoretically our duty is to put a towline on any disabled ship and haul her somewhere out of the way, but in no case permit the channel to be blocked. As soon as the gate crew opens the submarine nets that are stretched across the channel at the entrance gate, we proceed out (behind the minesweeper who is cleaning any possible mines laid the previous night) beyond the last channel buoy and cruise slowly back and forth until dark, when we are the last ship in before they close the net.

Let me tell you about the tropical moon. I do believe last night was the brightest moonlight I ever saw. I went to the movies at the officers' club. They hold the movies outside, and there are palm trees surrounding the building. Well this big, big moon climbed up over the rugged mountains and framed itself among the palms. There was a breeze from the hills, and the palm fronds moved just enough to make me realize it was not all just a picture. There were a few cottony white clouds in the sky and the moon steered in and out among them. The clouds were white, and I swear the sky was blue! Only a few stars could be seen because the moon was so bright. After the movie, as I walked back to the ship, I do believe I could have read a book solely "by the light of the silvery moon." My thoughts were of Gretchen and how nice it would be to *be* with her! How nice it would be to go on a beach party in such surrounds! How your body would glow in such light! Yes, wife, I will have to bring you to such a place when the war is over.

7/18/43

Dearest wife,

Today I went to church on a big ship. I must confess that I went more to see the ship than to listen to the sermon, but as it turned out the sermon was the best part by far. The service was held on the main deck and an awning was spread overhead. Signal flags were hung as decorations. They looked quite pretty with all their bright colors; William and Sail and Unit and Hypo. We had plain benches to sit on and the pulpit was just a stand with a mike nearby. The chaplain was a j.g. and was a guest speaker. He was young, wore glasses and had a good voice. Just before the sermon started, the bugler sounded church call and then a voice announced over the public address system, "Divine service, smoking lamp is out, knock off all card games, divine service." The choir consisted of three trumpets and a couple of other horns. They opened the service by playing "Oh, Come All Ye Faithful." They played it well. We sang familiar hymn and then the padre read the scripture. It was from the last chapter of Micah and exhorted man to believe in the Lord and walk humbly. Then we sang that hymn that says, "I would be true, for there are those who trust me, I would be brave, for there are those who care . . . " I believe this is the first time I ever read those words and was conscious of what they meant.

About this time a little old brindle dog wandered into the church. He must have belonged to one of the sailors, for he seemed perfectly at home and no one paid any attention to him. The pup wandered down the center aisle, sat down on his back legs and surveyed the scene leisurely with tongue out a little bit. Then he got up and walked over by the anchor chain and flopped down on his side, as if Sunday morning was such a bore.

The chaplain spoke on a "recipe for a successful life." He told us there was too much doubletalk in the world today, that men were not sincere, they did not keep their word, and that was why we were listening to him on the deck of a man-of-war. He likened our meeting to the meeting of ships on the trackless ocean, who salute each other and then pass on, perhaps never to meet again.

Every now and then the noises of the harbor would drown out his words, for work goes on on Sunday just the same as any other day. Indeed, all the men were in their blue dungarees. As the chaplain started to pray, a funny feeling crept over me and I began to realize that he was putting in words, or trying to, the answer to the old question, "What are we fighting for?"

Maybe I was sentimental and susceptible this morning, but that sermon was probably the best I ever heard, and I shall remember it always. When you come right down to it, I am fighting to keep the bombers away from Baton Rouge and Philipsburg and New York City, or any town where there are little people who must suffer and pay for the greed, lust, and hypocrisy of a few men in high places.

When the service was over the dog had disappeared, so I must have been swept away by the sermon, 'cause I had not seen him go. When I stood up I noticed that one link of the anchor chain was as long as my two shoes placed one in front of the other. It sure was a big ship. Later an ensign showed us around and good God! It sure did amaze and stupefy me and make me feel insignificant and small and silly. What a magnificent, terrible and complicated instrument of destruction. It is another good episode to tell you about some night in bed if we get the time.

When you read this, don't mention the big ship at all 'cause I don't want people to know that I tell you such things in letters.

7/22/43

Dear spouse,

Sometimes I am amazed at my wardroom companions. Either I am an unusually light-hearted fellow or else they are moody ones. Emersin is naturally quiet, especially since he feels at a disadvantage because most of the officers went to college and he didn't, and he feels not so well qualified to discuss the abstract. But at least he isn't grouchy. But Sankin and Glass, and sometimes the captain, really do get taciturn. They just sit quietly and eat their meals. Now I know the war is serious business, but heck, I think one should relax and expound a little at mealtime.

I am beginning to read *War and Peace* by Tolstoy. It is 1,400 pages long and is generally recognized as the best novel ever written, if there is such as thing as a "best" novel. All the critics say it is a "must" on any intelligent reader's list, so I might as well give it a try. I suppose it will take me about three months to wade through it.

Last night I censored letters again. It is strange how the various men express their longing to be home. One boy wanted to be sitting in the big chair by the window; another wanted a dish of homemade ice cream; one wanted a good home-cooked meal; one fellow offered to do all his wife's housework just to be home a week. And one boy wrote how the sound of choir music made him so homesick that he "felt like bawling, only he had no place private enough."

No matter how much I am aware of it, it still amazes me when I realize how every normal man in the Navy is tormented by the sex appetite. Every ship I visit, every barracks—be it officer or enlisted men—has its full quota of pinup girls and pictures of girls you don't see in magazines. Maybe Freud was right when he said all our actions can be traced directly to the sex urge. Emasculate man and he becomes like a capon, just content to sit around and get fat. I read somewhere that by sublimating the sex urge, Leonardo da Vinci was able to give the world so many beautiful paintings and statues. But I don't want to do any sublimating. I want to express myself completely and fully with you as my receptive vessel. Who was it that said "Joys are made greater when they are shared with others"?

I miss the way you laugh and the way you put on lipstick and the way you say, "Are my seams straight?" And the way we tussle, and that Dallas brassiere you had, and the daring girdle, and the way you say "Yippee," and even the way you cry, and, oh boy, the peasant blouse and red skirt. Make the war be over in a hurry so I can come home.

7/27/43

Dearest wife,

The other night Emersin was going to the head. Of course it was pitch dark for the ship was blacked out. He ran into a ventilator cowl, cut his forehead and gave himself a monstrous black eye. Everyone kids him about slipping around the beach and the lady's husband caught him!

Remember I wrote you about how grouchy the other officers get at times? I must retract the statement somewhat. It may be my imagination, but it seems to me the captain has aged just since I have been aboard. Gretchen, the captain of a ship, no matter how small, must be prophet, sage and wizard, and quick to make decisions. And if he judges wrong, there sure is hell to pay. No matter what your rank in the Navy, there is always somebody who can chew your ass out. Sometimes I wonder if it is worth it to have your own command.

I certainly am proud of the kids of this ship. Most of them are not 21 and yet they are eager, cheerful, willing and most of them quick on the uptake. I sure am glad to be shipmates with them. Very few of them give an outward appearance of being concerned with the "causes of this mortal conflict," yet I say that God help the man or men who deceive them and make them feel this is all a farce! These boys are willing to give up their lives for shipmates and country. When they come back home, few of them will take any horseshit from two-bit ward heelers and politicians full of pretty speeches and expensive whiskey.

7/28/43

Dearest wife,

The *Tern* must be a popular ship, for many of the men who have done duty on her in the past 25 years come back to pay us a visit when we tie up at night.

In the July 12, 1943, issue of *Life* there are some pictures of San Francisco Harbor. If you look close you will see that some of the sketches were made from a sister ship of the *Tern*.

One big topic that most everybody in the U.S. Navy still talks about and will for a long time is December 7, 1941. Many of the *Tern*'s crew were at Pearl Harbor that morning. Emersin told me about it. He and Madeline, you know, lived in an apartment between Pearl Harbor and Honolulu. After the planes came over and the radio told what happened he caught a ride back to Pearl. By that time there was noise, confusion, smoke, explosions, and general hell everywhere. Emersin was running down the dock and someone in the water called for help. Emersin picked up a piece of one-inch line lying nearby and threw the end to him. The guy grabbed it and Emersin pulled him out. The dock was about six feet above water but Emersin told me it was easy to lift the sailor up onto the dock. In thinking it over later, he wondered where he got the strength to pull that fellow, fully clothed and all covered with oil, out of the water.

Several tugs were in Pearl then. The *Tern* fought fire on the battleship *West Virginia* for three days. The carpenter's mate told me that many of the battlewagon's crew jumped overboard when it appeared the ship was doomed, leaving their shoes on the deck. He said, "When I came aboard her [the *West Virginia*] Monday to help fight the fire, I saw the rows of shoes. Then I noticed I didn't have any shoes on. So I asked a lieutenant nearby if I could put on a pair for myself." The lieutenant said, "Sure, help yourself, those other guys won't need them."

7/29/43

Dear old woman,

Remember how you used to run to the window when a plane came low over the house? Well, chicken, you ought to be on the bridge of this ship sometime. Jeepers, all kinds

of planes come by, and when we have certain kinds of exercises or practices, they really come close. Our fliers are
good and when I think most of the them are under 25, I
really marvel. One of the strongest, warmest feelings I
know comes over me when incidents like the following occur. Suppose, for example, the *Tern* bird has been out all
night and I have the 4-to-8 watch in the morning. Well, just
after sunrise the lookout reports a plane on the port quarter (left rear). It is just a speck, but soon it turns and starts
toward us. We know it is friendly (there are ways to tell—
they would and could raise hell with us if they were not
friendly), and it comes closer and closer. It roars by almost
close enough to hit with a potato. I can see both the occupants. The fella in the rear seat has his sleeves rolled up
and the plane's windows are open. He sure is takin' it easy,
but you know little escapes either him or the pilot. He
might even be whistling. As they turn to bank away, they
are broadside on and I lift my arm and wave. Lazily but
clearly and definitely, they return the greeting. They fly
away a short distance, then turn and come back to make
sure we are us (they look close at our number on the bow).
As they roar by, they wave and I answer back, then they
keep right on going to look for more. I don't even know
those two kids, but one thing I do know, they are on our
side and doing their job just as we are. It seems as if some
almost undefinable communication takes place between
us. When we wave it's as if each of us is saying "Everything
is under control, nice morning, take it easy, see you later,"
or, "If you see those bastards let us know and we will help
give them the business."

A person can speak volumes in just an exchange of
greetings between a plane and a ship by a wave of the arm.
I read somewhere of the "awkward tenderness" fighting
men have for each other. Maybe the feeling I get is some-

thing like that. It's a good, warm, honest, sorta choking feeling—like you say "all swollen up inside."

8/1/43

My beloved wife,

Every now and then we play penny ante in the wardroom when we get in too late to go to the movies or get somewhere where there ain't no movies. The stakes are real small. I've played about six times and my net losses are maybe $2.

Now, please don't worry about me gambling our fortune away. It's cheaper than going to the club where I would have to set 'em up for the fellas anyway, and I win back one night what I lost the night before. Once I won 50¢ and the next night I lost 40¢.

The other day I censored a boy's letter. He wrote, "Mom, when you get the new bedroom suite, get a big easy chair for me with something I can put my feet on—I guess you call them comforts. I don't know much about furniture. And tell the relatives not to visit us. They got a home of their own, so let them stay the hell away from us." It's too bad everyone is not as outspoken as he.

We have a third-class baker who came aboard just before we left the States. He is big and fat but young and subject to self pity. Well, we needed a cook instead of a baker so the captain made him a cook. The other day, he got ambitious and baked cherry pies for the crew. Creepers, they were good! The crust was the best I ever tasted (I better say next to yours). Well anyway, the crew really appreciated it and talked about it. Then two or three days later he made *chocolate* cake. And it turned out swell. I know 'cause I sampled generously both pie and cake. Well, when the crew found out his skill was no accident they really shined up to the guy. I believe he is the most popular fellow on the ship.

Emersin told me that a few days ago he got a letter from Madeline and she seemed upset. He said he had written her about us going to the dance at the warrant officers' club and she felt bad about it, or got the wrong idea, or something. So I wanted to write you this just in case she wrote you and mentioned the affair.* We went to the club but mostly because Claude Thornhill was playing the piano. There were probably 15 women there and 150 men. The orchestra itself is nothing special, but Claude himself is tops. He never uses any music, and his fingers are relaxed and skillful and competent. He, himself, is not much to look at. He is fat and red-faced and short, and he drinks a lot. He looks coarse until you notice his eyes, which are big and brown and bloodshot. They look sensitive and almost weak. He looks like a man who is trying to forget something.

Well, I started to tell you about the dance. There was a tall native girl there with a yellow flower in her hair. I mentioned to Emersin, "I'm gonna dance with her." About two numbers after that, when she was dancing with someone else, I noticed she had taken off her shoes. Her feet were big and long, and I never saw anyone's appearance change so, by just taking her shoes off!

8/6/43

My dear wife,

Well, here we are back in port. The sea really was rough the last two days. I was seasick. One of our signalmen used

---

*Betty had returned to LSU by this time.

to be on a destroyer, so I asked him if we rolled as bad as a tin can. He said, "Worse."

Let me tell you how much I miss you. I would be so happy just to have you by my side. It will be joy just to walk down the street again with my arm around your waist. And to hear your voice, and the way you laugh, and the way you look in the tub when you're bathing.

8/8/43

Dearest Gretchen,

One of the ships nearby has three dogs as mascots. One is just a brown roly-poly pup, one a slim white "puppy nuts," and the third is a black short-haired terrier. Ships aren't supposed to have mascots 'cause they get seasick, but these three don't. Today some mongrel dog got aboard our ship. He probably followed one of our men aboard. The kids made a fuss over him, and we put out to sea. If you ever saw an animal get seasick, you should have seen that dog! He belched and rifted and even *looked* sick. He got in the way of some of the men and they had a terrible time getting him to stagger somewhere else on deck and lie down.

Gretchen, it is strange to see dogs on a man-of-war. Especially is it odd to see how the fellas became so friendly toward them. To see a sailor on a blue painted warship fondling some nondescript dog creates a special tenderness all its own. Somehow there is an extra meaning in seeing some boy in dungarees being friendly with a dog, 'cause tomorrow the dog may be gone and the boy will be firing a gun. It seems to me that the sailors have so little chance to show their sentimental side that they take every rare and infrequent opportunity possible to lavish affection on a pet. These boys have practically no privacy. At any time, day or night, they may be routed out of their sacks for God knows what. And I tell you there is no more persistent, dreaded, mysterious, commanding, scaring, sound than the general-alarm klaxon. When that baby rings, you tumble out of sleep, grab your clothes, life jacket, and gun, and run out on deck as quickly as possible to see what is up. On board ship the enlisted men have no home life and few people, if anyone, to whom they can confide those things that every young man must confide to someone. So when a homeless stray dog or cat comes along, it seems there is a meeting of two kindred souls and they find comfort in each other. Anyway, that's the thought I conjure up when I see the friendship develop between the two.

Now for the good part. Quite often you tell me how much you miss me, need me, and love me. Well, I want you to know that I return it in triplicate. I will never tire of whispering to you that you mean all to me and that I love you "as long as we both shall live."

And just to keep us out of the ethereal heights, I lust after and for you. I torment myself with the remembrance of you.

8/10/43

Dearest Betty,

I have started weaving rugs. The ship's carpenter made me a frame, 24 × 40 inches, of 2-×-2-inch wood. I will weave some small rugs or bath mats out of sail twine, yarn or other suitable material. Since I can't read at sea without getting seasick, maybe working on rugs will enable me to pass my time profitably.

Stoneberger is asking for suggestions for names for his unborn first, in case it is a girl. He just showed me some pictures of his wife. She is pregnant, of course. I wish it were my wife who was pregnant instead of his.

I sure did think of you lustily during the picture *Coney Island*. And I think of your cinnamon rolls, and Johnny Bull pudding, and strawberry shortcake, and the voluptuousness of your hips and breasts, and your happy laugh, the way you toss your head. The thought of you is like a happy ache that can never be satisfied until once again we meet.

8/12/43

Dearest spouse,

You and I are helping to pay for this war. And so we should, in the years to come, agitate and lift up our voices for social reform and honest government. We should be quick to condemn hypocrisy. And above all, we should make others realize their duty to see that such a mess does not occur again. For if you and I, and all the others who are in it, get sick of the whole business and say, "Let's forget the whole thing now that we are together; let someone else solve the postwar problems," then sure as I write this, the whole thing will happen again. I surely wouldn't want to go back to the Navy at 55 maybe to help my son be trained to kill. We, the little people, the suckers, must take a more active part in guiding our destinies. No bunch of half-educated politicians should be allowed to get us into the same fix in the next 25 years.

8/14/43

My lovely Gretchen,

One of the experiences that comes sooner or later to every sailor is "missing ship." Several of our guys have had overnight liberty, and we shove off too early for them to get aboard. And one thing as sure as death and taxes is that when a ship is supposed to sail or shove off, she does—

and no waiting for nobody except maybe the captain (but in some cases even the captain gets left).

Well, today it happened to me. I missed ship. We came in and tied up alongside another ship. I went aboard her to check on some communication papers. While I was talking to the guy, I happened to glance out and I said, "Either your ship is moving, or mine is." So I tore off the boat deck down to the main deck. The old *Tern* bird was putting out and she was about five feet away and getting further every second. Emersin saw me coming (he was standing on our fantail) and he started laughing and yelling at me. I took one look at the distance, climbed up on the rail and gave a mighty jump. I made it okay, but the crew sure did get a kick out of me flying through the air. Emersin laughed and laughed. Boy I thought for sure I was gonna miss the ship that time.

And we have other adventures, too. I'll risk telling this one even though it may be half-censorable. We were coming in the other night from target practice. We were in a hurry to get in before dark. I had been in my bunk asleep and I noticed we had stopped (you learn to sleep half-awake, and by the sound of the engines and the decreased pitch and roll of the ship I knew we had slowed down). I came out on deck and asked Emersin, "What's the matter?"

He said, "We are now an aircraft carrier. We're gonna pick up a plane." Since he and I are always joking and I was still one-third asleep, I just grunted and walked away. But I noticed everyone up near the bow so I went up there, and sure enough about 100 yards away was a small amphibious plane, a scout plane from a battleship. Two men aboard. We came close by them, tossed a line, and after about 15 minutes of maneuvering and working and praying and cussin', we picked her up with the boom attached to the rear mast and sat the plane on the fantail. The ol' *Tern* bird groaned and muttered when we sat that plane down on our deck. The plane looked like a chicken sitting back there, the wings stuck out on each side, and our ship seemed to be saying, "Well, I suppose next they will have me hauling cattle." The two men were all right but the pilot was seasick. He was about 35 or 40. The radioman was not more than 22 and he sure was a good-looking kid. The sea wasn't very rough but still the plane bounced up and down and we banged it up a little. We got into port in fine shape, but it was way after dark. Emersin told me they had picked up planes before but I believe this was the first time most of the crew had seen it.

Well, there isn't much military information in the above, but just the same, be discreet and keep it to yourself.

8/18/43

My dearest wife,

I sent my brother, Russ, another $30 money order. Don't be alarmed at me running short 'cause I ain't. And don't buy any gifts for me, or clothes. I can get all the stuff I need at cost. Today I bought me one of those coat-pocket billfolds. I always wanted one. I got it at the sub base for $2. It's real nice. When I got it I said, "Now, Gretchen is buying this for me." I also am getting a nice leather jacket ($14.95), which will be a gift from you. Okay?

8/20/43

Dear wife,

Did I tell you the new bosun is aboard? His name is Edward Harmony Puregold. He is just a little fellow and much different from Glass. We also got a new ensign. His name is Joseph Songbird Karol. The ensign who was with us is now gone, so we have seven officers aboard.

One of our quartermasters was formerly on a battleship. As you know, in the Navy a quartermaster is one of the bridge force who aids the officers in navigation, steering the ship (their insignia is a wheel with the handle spokes), and taking care of charts. Well, this kid was on one of the ships sunk at Pearl Harbor, the *Arizona*. Only on December 7, he was home on leave. So he is alive today. The other day he told me his girl could never get over the idea that he used to steer a battleship but couldn't steer an automobile. I thought that was pretty good.

As you know, my duty is probably as safe as any Navy sea duty can be, but sometimes at night when we are out, I get awake and lie in my narrow bunk and listen to the sea. Many people have described the sea, and words like powerful, awful, deep and violent seem to have no meaning till one is actually on a little ship and can hear the water on the other side of the metal skin of the hull. Once Emersin and I were standing by the rail watching the ocean. The waves were big.

Emersin said, "Do you realize how strong those waves are?"

And then as I watched, I knew of their force and might. And I knew that Emersin and I and all of us were just tiny things, and I felt as if we were all caught in some evil, monstrous trap. What really angers me is that the young men of all nations are being forcibly and quickly erased, and few of them actually have the satisfaction of knowing that their death has helped purchase, by just a little bit, the good life of peace and equality and justice that each in his own heart wants. What a shame! How senseless! But mankind loves war. We have fought and killed each other for thousands of years.

8/22/43

Dear spouse,

Once a ship was at sea and the lookout shouted, "Sail, dead ahead." One of the men on the bridge was a little deaf so he passed the word, "Sailor, dead in the head." That is the current joke aboard the *Tern* this week.

8/24/43

Dearest Gretchen,

The other day I went swimming at the pool near the BOQ. It is nice there, landscaped tastefully with tropical plants, serene and quiet. There is also a small bar and clubhouse. The first day there I saw Commander Gene Tunney. He had just finished playing tennis and came in for a dip. I coulda reached out and touched him, but I didn't. I have always been a Dempsey fan myself!

In the clubhouse they have as curios a Jap officer's helmet, water canteen, and rifle with bayonet. All came from the island of Tulagi in the Solomons. Beneath the rifle the inscription reads, "A marine used this bayonet to kill its Jap owner."

I like those parts of your letters which indicate that you want me. One of the highest (ego-fortifiers) compliments that can be paid to a man is to have a good-looking woman let him know that she craves him. Anyway, I am glad that our separation is making us both realize how necessary and integral a part of happy life are satisfying sex relations.

As the man said, "In a happy marriage, sex counts only 5 percent; in an unhappy marriage, sex counts 95 percent."

8/26/43

Dearest wife,

Two letters from you today. One took four days to get here, the other, six. That is fast service! I can't understand why my letters to you don't keep rolling in. I write every other day. I guess they get slowed up because there is such an enormous volume of mail going toward the U.S. and some of my letters were put aboard a ship and not the clipper. They do that sometimes, especially if the load is too heavy.

Everyone seems to like the *Tern* bird. That's one reason I am making a new rug with the word "Tern" woven in it. The new rug is 40 × 22 inches.

Wife, look in the August 23 edition of *Time* under the medicine section. Be sure to read every part of that section. There is the story of a baby doctor working in Alabama and also some good accounts of epidemics. Under the "People" section, there is a notice about Errol Flynn, a yacht and a new girl 19 years old. Boy, I don't see how that guy gets away with it. He just gets out of court from one such case and, figuratively thumbing his nose at the law and the public, he turns in another. Well, I guess some people never change.

8/23/43

Dearest Betty,

Once again I refer you to *Time* magazine, this time to the issue of August 9. In the "Science" section is an article about a Dr. Lindegren and wife of Washington University in St. Louis who are *breeding different strains of yeast* for food use, flavors and other purposes. Immediately my heart leaped up, for I knew right away how closely related are the genetics of yeasts to the fungi I experiment with. They are similar in many ways. Most of all, any *laws governing the reproduction of one will probably apply to the other.* Jeepers, you can see why I was so glad, for it is not too improbable that a young Ph.D. trained in genetics might easily get a position as geneticist with some such concern. That article (please read it) made me homesick for the lab and anxious to get a degree and get to work somewhere. I don't want others to get ahead of me. Any good work I can do in genetics is bound to be a passport to a good position.

Goddamn, I wish I was out of this time-wasting, senseless war. I get so impatient when I realize that my life is going by and I am doing nothing constructive. Christ, I can't see why they don't knock off the Japs and Germans and stop fiddling around.

Another thing I have incorporated into my firmest of convictions: *Ignorance is one of the greatest evils.* Jeepers, you know many people have no idea at all of politics and government. No wonder we have so many such bastards in positions of responsibility. Ninety percent of the voting people don't know what is right and what is wrong. That's how we got into this mess. John Q. Public lets a few guys pull the wool over his eyes. So we must have more and better education. Don't hold up Thomas Jefferson or Henry Clay as saintly men, but point out how they handed out favors to whom and why, and the politicians they were. And Roosevelt is the same way. He purged his enemies the same as Stalin and Chiang Kai-shek, only he just took 'em out of office and the other two killed theirs. You must read *Our Foreign Policy* by Walter Lippman.

And all these things apply to you and me, wife. For if we close our eyes to the evils in government, and seclude ourselves in a cottage at the edge of some campus, sooner or later the harvest of such unstopped evils will bomb us and our children and the cottage into oblivion. I am firmly convinced that universities and colleges must be the leaders in reform, for it is there the thinking men congregate. We must make the uninformed, uneducated people conscious of what might happen and make each realize that he is his brother's keeper. And now I am written out on that subject, but I warn you, there will be speeches to type when I come home.

8/30/43

Dearest Gretchen,

Last night I caught two seamen in the radio shack typing an obscene story. I confiscated it and burned it, but not before I read it. Jeepers, I felt like taking a bath after I read it. And, to be frank, I felt guilty.

Once when I was a junior at Penn State and Russ was not married, he and I got in one of our few discussions on sex and man's general cussedness. We were talking about how powerful the appetite is, and he said to me, "Wait till you get to the point where you can't think of anything else." I should have expected it, for both Dad and Mother were lusty—11 kids is good evidence.

Won't it be fun to start a family? I don't know if naughty letters ease the pressure or make it worse. But one thing I do know, we are going to make our sex life a ritual, a ceremony and joy supreme. Here's what I want you to do, Bubbles. In secret and on the sly, practice swinging your shoulders (you know, the way you used to). Also practice doing the hip roll and bumps. Get to be proficient in all this. Practice daily before the mirror. And when you go to a movie, say a musical, watch the actresses' gestures, poses and how they walk. Especially learn the seductive poses and strutting.

I never knew I could miss you much in so many different ways. (By the way, these letters are a little daring, so be sure no one reads them but you.) Once this war is over I'm gonna hurry home as quickly as possible.

One young sailor said the day the war is over, he is gonna punch a commander right in the jaw, so they will send him home quick, even if it is to the brig.

9/1/43

My dearest wife,

As you know, youthful Americans are great for giving things nicknames. Sailors are no exception, especially when it comes to designating certain kinds of Navy chow. For instance, cream chipped beef on toast is known in the Navy as creamed foreskin on toast. Rather appropriate! Also, one of the Navy's staple cold meats is a coarse bologna about the diameter of a large coffee cup. They often fry it to make it more palatable. So the crew calls it fried, sliced, horse cock. Quite descriptive! Also they have small pieces of steak, irregularly shaped, about the size of a large marble. They cream this and serve it on toast. The crew calls it shit on a raft. They eat it and like it, but a squeamish person is soon quelled.

The rug should soon be finished. I figure it is pure profit because I work on it only during odd, stray moments that I would spend sitting around the wardroom gossiping. I am trying hard not to become lazy and kill time.

Wherever you go and whatever you do, remember I love you and want to be with you, for my greatest happiness is you.

9/3/43

Dearest spouse,

A few days ago we had an overnight trip, and I really enjoyed it. The sea was as flat as a table, and I didn't even approach seasickness. I had the deck watch in the afternoon. There was a gentle breeze, and the awning protected us from the hot sun. We had the radio on, so it was more or less like a pleasure cruise. The ocean was deep, deep blue.

The trip we made was around the island, so I saw parts of it I had never seen before. It was wild and rugged with steep mountains. In one place, as we chugged along on the flat ocean, we went right through a school of fish. Some of them were about two feet long. You can always tell where fish are, for the sea gulls hover directly over the spot. Everyone who could grabbed for a piece of fishing line and a hook (we always keep some handy), but nobody even got a bite.

I censored letters again today. Some of the crew utter unconscious truths. One boy was writing his girl about plans for the future. He wrote, "It's good to have someone plan your future, as long as it ain't the enemy." And one boy wrote his mother, "I never thought I would miss taking care of the lawn and flowers." Such things unexpectedly tug at the heartstrings. It is also touching to read the letters the men write to their wives. I know the men are all sharp as tacks, but each walks around sex as carefully as possible. Many letters are quite tender and I feel like an intruder when I read them. Many letters are dull and monotonous, for so many topics are forbidden.

9/5/43

Gorgeous Betty,

One of our principal chores nowadays is to tow targets for destroyers to shoot at, airplanes to dive-bomb or shore batteries to aim at and miss. The target is really a 15-foot sail on a toboggan-shaped raft or sled about 30 feet long. We pull the target with a three-quarter-inch (diameter) wire cable which is wound up on a large reel or spool on the fantail. The cable is more than 2,000 feet long, so that tar get is almost a half-mile behind us. But sometimes this is too close, the way some people shoot.

You know, one big thing I have noticed in the Navy is the discipline. Most men are good because it pays them to be. But every once in a while, one of them tries to buck the system. It doesn't pay, for in the Navy they have you cold. The regulations are specific and the captain of a ship is court, jury, judge and jailer. And the captain stands behind the officers. He has to. When I come home I can give you many instances and incidents. In the Navy for one person to strike another is a serious affair, and it is dealt with accordingly. Respect for rank is another prime requisite. Captain Parry doesn't run a tight ship, but he runs an efficient one. He handles the ship and the men well, he is a good navigator and does all quietly with no fuss.

9/7/43

Dearest spouse,

Every now and then when I sit down to write, I have absolutely no idea what I shall use to fill the pages. Now that we have been here almost four months and settled into a routine, the dull days follow tediously one after the other. We do the same uninteresting chores day after day. Even the weather changes little. There is lots of sunshine. Day temperatures for this time of year average about 81° and night temperatures about 74°.

In censoring the crew's mail, I have noticed the letters are much shorter. The sailors just can't write for there are so many restricted subjects, and we do the same things day in and day out.

I am enclosing Dad's last letter to me. Poor Dad, he is

so happy in his sadness. I wonder what would happen if all his sons and daughters gave him two-thirds of their wages and just let him run things, and each be submissive to him, and not argue with him, and not go out at night, and live in overalls, and eat fried potatoes and tomatoes? Then he would surely be unhappy, for he would have no complaints. I suppose he wouldn't be able to stand it. I guess he is unhappy because all his children are doing so well and he doesn't have to help them. *They don't need him.* Yes, I guess that is the secret—they don't need him, and he feels useless and old, and lonely and powerless, and life has passed him by.

Keerist, I sure am developing into a philosopher.

9/9/43

Dearest wife,

Occasionally after meals we have wardroom discussions of remote subjects. Sometimes I bring up my eugenics program for a better race. You know, start out by preventing the hopelessly insane, the idiots, those with lethal genetic traits, the hardened criminals from reproducing. But encourage or make it easier for the capable ones to have children. Isn't there some way we can breed a race of men who can satisfy their urge for power, not by killing with a weapon, not by waging war, or ruining an opponent in politics or business, or beating him up physically, but by exploring the universe, working and building constructive things, searching for the truth, practicing self-discipline and preaching truth in the dusty roads?

But you should hear the other officers criticize my eugenics program and jump me about every person's right to live, it's against God's will (how does anyone know God's will?), who will be the judge of who shall have children, and on and on. It's surprising how little genetics these men know, all but two of whom are college graduates.

Well, peaceful argument is exercise for the brain and mind and so long as it is friendly, nothing is lost.

And here is some interesting news for you, about your cousin Bob Mack. His ship is here. I am not absolutely sure, but I had the signalman send a visual message to a nearby ship that promised to relay the message. I asked Bob to come to our ship at his earliest convenience. However, if his division officer is as tough as you say, he may not let Bob off. Enlisted men rate liberty only one day out of four. And if this is not Bob's liberty day, they might not let him off. It's not easy for two ships to make contact even if they are in the same place, because they might anchor a couple of miles apart, boat schedules are restricted and some days they are in, and we are at sea, and vice-versa. However, I will do all in my power to see him.

9/10/43

Dear Miss,

The rug is finished. It turned out swell. But the red cord I used wasn't fast die, so the rug is sorta pink now that I washed it. I'll send it home to you anyway, but I sure am disappointed in it.

Today I went over to the officers' club to get a haircut. I noticed the admiral's car parked outside. It has three stars on the license plate and a third-class boatswain is chauffeur. I went into the shop and there I met an officer who was one of the teachers at Abbot Hall when I was there. We started talking. I noticed this rather old fellow in the barber chair. I looked at him and he looked at me. The j.g. and I talked some more, and again I happened to glance at the man in the chair, and again he was looking at me. Just then the barber unfastened the sheet from the fellow, and I saw three silver stars on his collar. M'Gawd! I could feel myself shrinking! I was standing right in his way.

I murmured hastily, "Excuse me . . . mumble, mumble."

But he didn't say anything. He didn't seem to react much either way. Maybe his thoughts were on something else. This particular admiral has quite a history, but I'll have to wait till after the war to tell you about him.

Later on, the same barber who cut the admiral's hair cut mine. Just imagine. You didn't know I was so famous, did you? But that's as close as I want to get to an admiral!

9/13/43

Dearest spouse,

This morning I watched the sun come up and the moon go down, with the *Tern* in between. My, how my thoughts leap and fly in those quiet hours when I am alone on the bridge. The wheel creaks as the helmsman keeps her steady and the wind hums in the rigging and the water flops with a swoosh-swish as it curls from the bow. And all the time the pitch and roll and toss, and wind in your face.

And the beauty. Quietly but persistently, the reality of it comes larger and larger and self grows smaller and smaller. I remember the smell of grass wet with dew, sidewalks in early summer, leaves turning all colors, the beauty of Indian summer, football games, house parties; going with my father as a small boy out of the mountain to get a load of sand. I remember the smell of trailing arbutus and sassafras and drinking from a cold spring; crawling into bed beside you, the svelteness of your body, your salt-sweet sea-wind breath; an old closet at home under the stairs, where we kept shoes and galoshes and gloves; Saturn and its rings, life on other planets. Verily my thoughts are interesting companions.

The 4-to-8 watch in the morning is a good one to have. When I came on watch, the moon was big and full as only a tropical moon can be. And our ship was a little world all of its own in the vast expanse of blue-black. Only the sea, the sky, the *Tern,* and the moon streak. There was just enough wind to make the rigging hum. It gives me a funny feeling to stand on the bridge and look back and down on the *Tern* as she wanders along. She sort of reminds me of a big, fat, good-natured horse. She isn't easily excited and she grunts peaceably to herself as she goes. She seems like some protective old body that takes care of her kids. Guess I'll never forget her.

It looks as if I missed Bob Mack. I looked over toward where his ship was anchored the other day and it was gone. They just slip out quietly and nobody knows the difference. Ships sure are peculiar!

Gretchen, don't buy me anything for Christmas. I have everything I need, and besides I can get things at the ship service much more reasonably than you could. You are the best medicine I know. Contained in an attractive package, wrapped smartly, shaped to fit the hand, cheap to me at ten times the price, easy to take, and beneficial no end.

9/16/43

Dearest gal,

We went swimming again today on the island in the harbor. It is peaceful in that little sanctuary. I never knew there were so many shades of green, and all so eye-filling. And I never knew grass and soil could smell so good. I guess my farmer blood will never be stilled by the vast ocean.

Today I sent off a large package which should reach you

in the next two to three weeks. The outrigger canoe is for show over the fireplace, and to get in the way generally. It has an interesting history. The bookends and little dish also came from faraway places. The shells were given to me, and I just threw them in to make the package heavier. However, they will make unusual paperweights.

I also saw in the paper where Mrs. F. D. Roosevelt got a mother-of-pearl pendant from a soldier in the South Seas on her recent visit there. Well, I have a nice one for you. I will send it with the Christmas stuff.

About the bicycle. When you got the job I said you could spend the money any way you saw fit. I'll stick to my promise, but at the same time here are some reasons why it wouldn't be too good. *First* off, you would have to pay about 150 percent of its value because of their scarcity, and it would be a rebuilt bike at that. *Second,* there is always a good chance that somebody would steal it, even though you locked it when parked on campus. *Third,* when you ride a bike you get all over grease—more than you think. And they make you sweat. *Fourth,* walking to the lab, though a tiresome job, is good for your figure and I guess that is the main reason. Of course, bicycling is good, too, but walking is better. So if I were you I wouldn't buy one, but if you think it best, it's okay by me.

There isn't much you can do about the withholding tax. They take it out right away. But don't pay an income tax next spring till you hear from me. You see, all men in the service get a $1,500 exemption right off. Also, you and I get our $1,200 exemption for being married. I have to pay tax only on my base pay of $165 a month. Also I don't have to pay my income tax till *after* I return to the States. So my base pay of $165 × 12 = $1,980. We are exempt until we earn over $2,700 ($1,500 + $1,200). So until you earn $720 we have no tax to pay.

Every so often I have no ambition whatsoever. I don't

read, don't study, or nothin'. All I do is go off by myself and think of you.

9/19/43

Dearest girl,

The other day I copied this about Socrates. He said it as he was being tried for treason: "A man who is good for anything ought not to calculate the chance of living or dying; he ought only to consider whether he is doing right or wrong." In my present circumstances, I think that fits my reasoning pretty well. I have an excellent chance of returning to you well and whole; this duty of mine, it is not hard. It is more boresome and monotonous than anything. But I am close enough to the scene and theater of war to realize that violent action and perhaps death might be on hand in the next act. It is the realization of a possible abrupt termination of my life on earth that makes me ponder and think on things so deeply.

I am contributing more than some to the war effort, and less than others, but the big job will be after the war. Then is the time when we (those who gave their youth, time, and in some cases, life) must raise our voices for progress, education, banishment of corruption and fair play for all. I'll bet there are Japanese and German soldiers who think of many of the things I do. All nations have corrupt men, not just the United States. And I know education will not make a man honest, but neither will ignorance.

I am convinced now that "all war is caused by love of money and money knows no country," as Professor Cloppet used to say. Put power in that sentence and I believe it is the meat of the whole affair. A few people want power and money so they maneuver millions of individuals, who have neither, into giving up their lives and freedom just to satisfy the vanity of the few on top.

9/21/43

Dearest wife,

Mr. Puregold, the new bosun, sure is a swell fellow. He is only about five feet four inches. He has the smallest hands and feet. He has a sort of dry humor that appeals to me. He likes Mrs. F. D. Roosevelt, and some of the other fellows here do not especially care for her. So he eggs them on to talk about "Eleanor." He used to be a chief quartermaster and he knows navigation cold. Aside from his kindness and general goodness, I would be wise to cultivate (parasitize) him for his navigational knowledge alone.

He has two girls—nine and six—and he is really proud of them. He was home this summer, when he made warrant officer, and took pictures of the girls. They both had on new shoes, and whenever I catch him looking at the picture he says, "I am just looking at two shoe-ration holders."

His brother was killed in a battle on a cruiser down south last year.

I must mark this bosun down in my book of memories as one of the more interesting people I have met along the way.

One thing about the Navy, when I come home I will have learned to size up a situation quickly, make up my mind, and act, or give orders accordingly; but sometimes when you are reprimanded for things you cannot help, and then cannot even reply to justify yourself, you just have to keep your mouth shut and take it!

Lovely girl, when I come home you won't get out of my sight, either. Stay young and attractive for me, for I am in great need of your tenderness and strength. How grand it will be to feel your arms about me and to hear your voice, eat your cookin' and to know the softness and joy of your body. Being apart has made us realize what a precious thing love is.

9/23/43

Lovely woman,

Our berth has been changed. The harbor masters have moved us to one of the side channels. It is a long way from everywhere although still at the same place technically. We are working every day. It is seldom now that we get ashore to civilization although we can get ashore. This place is so big that you have to go by boat (not ship) from one dock to another, and we are farthest of all. We are nowhere near houses or people. But so long as I am away from you, one place is just like another.

I've had enough ships to last me a long time. Now my sole interest is in sports events—wrassling! Now there is a sport for you. Umh! Umh! You know, when a person is thirsty and has been thirsty for along time, he does not shake his thirst with mighty gulps and swallows. If he is a wise man and one who has learned to live, he slakes his thirst by degrees, and slowly. He enjoys every second of satisfying his need.

Maybe my writings wander, but then I have been thirsty for a long time, with a deep and savage thirst, and I shall be glad to slake my thirst. It will take many days or ways, but I shall know the enjoyment of enjoyment again.

9/25/43

Dearest wife,

Yesterday the sea was the flattest I have ever seen the Pacific. It was just like a big sheet of plate glass or azure satin, and it was a perfect day. One thing about the mid-Pacific, there is no dearth of sunshine and fair weather.

In all the duress and boredom on board this vessel, the one shining highlight is thoughts of you. Sometimes I see you all dressed up in your best clothes, sometimes with not much on at all. I can never run out of thinking about you. I guess that is what makes this life bearable.

Today the officers had an argument about football games. So I came out with a drastic statement which said in effect, "Cut out all sports and movies until the war is over." Jeepers, did the fellows snow me under. I was only half-serious, but it sure is senseless to me that well-fed, carefree people should be having a good time back home when thousands of others are living in discomfort, anxiety and boredom, not to say fear of a sudden end. Why not put away all luxuries till the boys come home? Let everybody share, not just a favored group. By Gawd, in Japan, China, and Russia the war comes first, then the gallivantin' around, idleness, and good times. I suppose some people think we can win the war and have movies, horse races, and football games, too. But the war would be over a lot quicker if we cut out all the horseshit 'till we had won. Well, I am just one small voice, but I was always taught to share ice cream and my family. Also, we didn't get ice cream while the house was burning.

9/27/43

Dearest Gretchen,

Here's one for you. The other day in the wardroom, Emersin said to me in front of the other officers, "How does Betty like the new bike?" I said "Okay, I guess. She wrote and asked me if she should buy one, and I wrote back no. Then in the next letter she wrote she had bought one." Pause. "We always talk things over before we buy stuff."

Boy, the officers really did laugh at that one!

As for those folks who said this was soft duty, I'd like to wake them up some morning around 0300 to decode an urgent message to all ships, especially when one has just come off the 2000–2400 watch, and the deck is swinging under your feet like the trapeze the man flew on, and you have to break out a new sheet of paper because there was vomit on the last one, and the captain keeps calling on the voice tube from the bridge to the wardroom, "Haven't you translated it yet?"

So you sit down on the deck and put the code books between your spread-out legs and try to make sense of the blurred, dancing words as you transfer the code key from one book to the other. And the nausea seizes you and you lie over on your side till you feel a little better and then struggle to sit upright again and make sense out of the jumbled sentences. After you do figure it out, there is no exhilaration, you just don't care! You just laboriously, druggedly lock up the books again, then tortuously climb the waving ladders to the bridge to show the captain the message, which doesn't affect our ship anyway. All you want to do is lie down somewhere and die. It doesn't matter anyway. But something keeps you goin'!

Oh! for the easy life of an ensign in the U.S. Naval Reserve. But I am improving. I am writing this at sea and not seasick yet.

9/29/43

Dearest spouse,

Some of the radio programs we hear surely sound spurious, and half-ass, and over-emotional. I sure get sore at guys with oily voices sittin' at home "dedicating programs to our boys out there."

Today we had target practice for small arms. It was the first time I had fired my 45 automatic. At first I admit I was uneasy, awkward and afraid, but after the first clip of shells I liked it. It sure is a wicked gun. We had a little target astern of the ship. I believe I hit it once out of numerous shots.

Anything to change the monotony of everyday the same.

10/1/43

Lovely Gretchen,

The old *Tern* bird is showing the marks of her voyages. The moss and barnacles are beginning to show on her. She surely is a working ship. I guess I am attached to her in more ways than one—sentimentally and physically.

Last evening I had the 1800–2000 day watch. We were the only ship I could see on the empty sea. The sun was sinking in a sky of hammered gold, delicate pinks and silvers that merged into a sea of black purple. The bridge radio started playing island music. Some man with a rich bass voice chanted and the steel guitar strummed shivers up and down my back. The night wind was just beginning to rise and it moaned through the halyards and rigging. The helmsman said to me, "That sure is lonely music." And then I knew the key word to the whole scene. *Loneliness.* Lonely sea, flaming lonely sky, lonely ship, lonely wind, and me without you. It was all so piercing and haunting. I was homesick for you then, and my homesickness increased and accentuated the beauty of it all.

Today is payday and the crew is filing through the wardroom. They come in the port door and exit through the starboard. The paymaster, from the central pay office ashore, comes aboard with the money in a tan satchel chained to his wrist. He carries a gun and is accompanied by a lean marine who carries a gun. Both smile little. The paymaster puts the satchel on a chair alongside the one he sits in, unfastens the chain from his wrist, unlocks the satchel, opens it, and takes out several stacks of bills and a

list of our crew telling how much each is owed. As each
man is paid, he initials his name on the list and one of the
Tern's officers witnesses it. Farther down the table our
storekeeper has a list of what each man owes the ship's service. So before the sailors leave the wardroom they get paid
in one hand and give some of it back to the ship service
with the other.

Tonight there will be big card and crap games for the
fellows don't get much chance to spend their money nowadays, considering where we tie up. In a few days two or
three men will have all the loose money on the ship. And
usually it's the same two or three men who get the money.
We have a radioman first class aboard. He is about 30, with
red hair and freckles. He is cocksure, slick and almost inso-
lent. He always wins! And he makes no bones about the
fact he is gonna use his winnings to open a bar in San Diego
after the war. He sends $100 money orders home in
batches, according to our mailman. The card games are
"no limit," so the guy with plenty of money and lots of guts
can bluff out the weaker ones. I don't mind this radioman
winning from the older men, but I hate to see him take the
youngsters, who haven't been around. Still you can't stop
them from playing, it's their business. I have a sneakin' sus-
picion the radioman cheats, he wins too regularly and he is
a sly one, but there is nothing I can do about it.

The paymaster told me if anything happens to the
money he is responsible for it. I said, "Supposing that
money satchel came loose from your wrist and fell overboard, what would you do?" He said, "I would go after it!"

We have been to sea every day for more than three
weeks. I hadn't been ashore in some time. But I had to go
today on business for an hour or so. God, it was good to
be able to walk steady. Believe it or not, the ground rolled
a coupla times. At least I staggered. Now I know what it

means to "walk like a drunken sailor." The road was dusty and I just ate it up. A marine in a jeep picked me up, and it was wonderful to ride in a vehicle. After I got out, I ran about two blocks (in the sun) just for the relief of being able to go more than 185 feet in one direction without turning. And the grass smelled good, and I bought a milkshake, and I mumbled to myself 'cause it was good to get ashore and stretch my legs.

Karol was telling me the other day of a j.g. on another tug who sleeps with a pair of his wife's black-lace panties under his pillow. At least he says they belong to his wife.

10/3/43

Dearest spouse o'mine,

Although I shall never be sorry to say farewell to the sea, I am now becoming more adjusted to the ocean and the sky. The sea is fascinating, and I can stand for moments on end just watching the waves, the horizon, the clouds and an occasional gull. As for the stars, they now seem like old friends. I can identify 15 to 20 navigational ones with ease, to wit: Vega, Aldebaran, Arcturus, Polaris, Antares, Bellatrix, Sirius, Betelguese, Rigel, Caiph, Markab, and so on.

Our quartermaster calls Betelguese "beetle juice." And that's close enough for me!

Wife, you mustn't talk viciously to the civilians about me being out here. If you just make the statement, "My husband is in the Pacific somewhere, I haven't seen him in six months," then quietly change the subject, you will find it is much more powerful than to argue about it. Give it that Spencer Tracy touch of understatement. And don't be too peeved at others. Remember, I was called (shall we say forced) to go. I didn't step up and volunteer. I sidestepped the draft. So make the above statement, and if anybody wants to find out more, make them (seemingly) drag it out of you. Then the conversation will be under your control. You will be fighting an engagement at a scene under conditions of your choosing. One of the primary lessons of warfare, I have been told.

Another letter, and here I am on the last page and never once did I mention SEX. But don't think it isn't there. I'm deliberately suppressing it so that when I come home, the power will rise up and erupt with volcanic force. Be ready for combat the instant I glimpse you again.

10/5/43

Gorgeous Betty,

These few minutes before lunch I can utilize by starting a letter to you. No, I don't always have the 4-to-8 morning watch. Last night I had the 20 to 24. And tonight I have the good old mid-watch, 0000 to 0400. I don't mind the night watches. In fact, I like them because usually things are quiet and it gives me much time to think. Last night was new and interesting. The sea was seemingly flat as a pancake, but there were long, low easy swells about 500 yards apart which gave us an easy rocking motion. It was quiet and the silent, ghostly ship stole through the water plowing a furrow that soon became an unseen trail across the deep. No wind. The sea was the most phosphorescent I have ever seen it. As we slipped through the water, the sea curled away from the bow in long, flowing, frothy streamers of light liquid green. The color was like the hands on a radium wristwatch, only lighter. It seemed like the ship was wearing foamy petticoats. The sea itself was steel black but the curlers were fragile green racing flames of cold fire. Then as the water flopped over and splashed, each drop was like a sparkling little star as they splattered

about. The helmsman was a young kid who is learning to
be a quartermaster (we call him a striker for he is striking—
trying—for a quartermaster grade) said to me that the
phosphorescence was what he always imagined stardust to
be, and it was an apt description. If you can imagine shat-
tering a star into a billion flashing, sparkling, infinitesimally
small diamonds, you can imagine what the ghostly radiance
of liquid phosphorescence was like. Somewhere I read that
the phosphorescence emanates from colonies of protozoan
dinoflagellates of the genus *Noctiluca*. These microscopic
one-celled animals exist in great numbers in the ocean, and
at certain times of the year, say in the spring, the vernal
bloom of myriads of this organism causes a marked increase in the phosphorescence.

Today we were permitted to swim in the ocean. We had
a shark watch out just in case, and the rest of us jumped
in (we were at anchor off a remote island). The water
was warm, deep blue, and salty as hell. Jeepers, I sure enjoyed it.

10/7/43

Dear spouse,

Did I tell you about our seasick chair with the uneven legs?
I'm sitting in it now. It magnifies the roll and pitch by add-
ing a delayed little jerk at the end of each tilt of the deck.
Someday I'll get mad and toss the aggravating son of a
bitch over the side when nobody is lookin'.

You know, I don't understand why it is, but when I get
letters from you and begin to open them, my fingers shake
so that sometimes I can hardly tear the flap open. You must
be some woman to cast your spell over me when I am such

a far piece away. Sometimes the letters smell faintly of your perfume. At least, I think they do.

It tickles me every now and then you write something Madeline told you. You two must have become close friends. I often wonder what Navy wives talk about. I guess they talk about the same things men do, only in reverse. I asked Emersin about Mary Louise.* He seems to be worried about her. I hope she gets over lack of appetite. Emersin puts a lot of hope in Mary Louise.

I guess children are like octopi. They entwine their tentacles around your heart and squeeze. I wish we had some octopi!

When I told you about us going in swimming, I forgot to tell you that the sailor who was on shark watch had a tommy gun in his lap. He sat up on the boat deck like a shepherd watching his sheep. I'll never forget that swim in those warm waters. I swam beneath the surface and I could see the entire hull of the ship, real clear just like in the movies. The trip was good for crew morale.

Of course we had work to do, but that was incidental. One of the boys dug up some pink coral and brought it with him. It will make an excellent paperweight with its odd convolutions and curves. The working party ashore brought back some nice fish they caught (just for the crew, not for officers). One boy said if he walked down the streets of any of the island towns with those fish, he could get any girl he wanted. There is a shortage of fish here (no fishermen), and the people usually use fish as a big part of their diet. So it is not unusual for the "sporting" girls to buy fish (as a present) from sailors who have the fish, and let the sailors take it out in trade. They do the same thing

*Mary Louise was Emersin and Madeline's daughter.

for liquor. One boy told me that they use production-line methods in the houses here. The fellas have to line up ($3 per) and be quick like a rabbit. Some say the gals make more money than the best-paid defense workers.

10/10/43

Dearest Gretchen,

As you know, torpedoes are expensive. They cost about $15,000 each, I am told. Nonetheless, ships that use torpedoes as weapons need practice in using them. For target practice they use torpedoes that have the warhead filled with air instead of explosive. After these torpedoes have run out of propellant, they will float vertically and we retrieve them. This saves the Navy money. Sometimes the *Tern* acts as target for such torpedoes shot by submarines, destroyers or torpedo planes. In company with one of the aforementioned, we cruise out to the target area, about 15 miles offshore. After serving as target, we must go get the torpedo. The firing ships set the torpedoes to travel deep enough in the water to pass underneath our ship. Nonetheless it is a shaky feeling to see that torpedo wake coming straight at you. After the torpedo goes by, we chase after it till it runs out of "juice," then hoist it aboard with our boom and winch. We repeat this all day and by late afternoon we may have a dozen torpedoes lying on the stern. I don't trust them. But the crew is used to them. They perch all over the evil things waiting for the tin can or sub to make the next target run. Just before nightfall, we return to port and the torpedoes must be unloaded at the submarine base before we call it a day.

I guess the torpedo-plane pilots are the worst shots. Usually they are beginners and there is no telling where or how they drop their "fish." Everybody is on edge as the plane approaches low over the water, coming right at us. Finally the pilot drops the torpedo and pulls up and away. So far none of them has dropped the torpedo on us and no plane has crashed into the ship, but sometimes I thought they might. You hear our crew coach the pilot as he begins to make his run.

"Drop that goddamned thing, what are you waitin' for."

"You bastard, let it go."

"Jesus Christ, here comes a blind one."

Of course the pilot can't hear and the noise of the plane deafens us as he roars overhead. Oftentimes he waves to us and grins as if he is having great fun. Why not, these pilots are just kids in their early 20s.

When our ship visited that little island the other day, many of the crew were lying on the beach after lunch, resting. I heard one sailor say to another, "How would you like to be cast up here with Hedy Lamarr?"

The other one replied, "Anything would look good to me that didn't wear a cock, the way I feel right now!" Jeepers, I sure did laugh. The sailors are sharp, sharp!

I'm gonna make another all-white rug for you, same size. I can't make a bigger one, for it would take a bigger frame, which would be too big to store in my cabin. But I can make another one the same size. There are more than 4,000 knots in the rug. But I can tie each one quickly. I'll start another rug soon. Weaving soothes and pacifies me. I guess knitting, embroidery, needlework, weaving and quilting do the same for women. And it makes the time pass.

10/13/43

Dearest Gretchen,

We haven't been able to get the mail for three days, so I'm anxiously awaiting letters from you. It's good to get letters, but I'll be glad when the day comes that you and I never have to write them again. One thing about the Navy: when you are at sea, you have too much responsibility to spend much time pitying yourself.

But this is an unnatural existence. I can see why mothers, down through the centuries, have warned their daughters against sailors. Speaking for myself—and from all indications, 99.9 percent of the other men are like me—I can say I get sharp as a tack. The insistent, persistent, torment pervades one's being. The craving never ceases, and sex assumes enormous undue proportions. It affects your actions, your speech, your sleep, your gestures, your moods, your exercise, your nerves.

Our next honeymoon will be a humdinger, I promise you that.

Now and again my thoughts return to the little island, and the more I think of it (me and my vivid imagination), the more romantic it seems. You know it isn't often that I am away from the *Tern* and able to see her silhouette as she passes by. But once while on the beach I looked up and there she was at anchor. She seemed to be the only sign of civilization, and as I looked beyond her there was only sea and sky and horizon. There were a few whitecaps which made the scene all the more attractive. The beach was superb, and the only regret in my enjoyment was that you weren't there to run through the surf with me. The wind was cool, the air warm, the sand soft, and the sea spray invigorating. What a nifty place for you and me to be cast up alone and to swim raw in the surf. Jeepers, I sure would like to chase you down that crescent-shaped stretch of sand.

10/14/43

Faithful wife,

Bob Mack's ship came steaming by yesterday, but I might as well have been 2,000 miles away. Maybe I'll get to see him someday though.

10/15/43

My dearest sweetheart,

The bosun intrigues me more every day. He was telling us about the guy on a cruiser or battleship whose station was up in the foretop (top of the foremast). When the captain gave the order to abandon ship, this guy closed his eyes and jumped. "Yep, he jumped right down the smokestack." Boy, I did laugh. The bosun said, "I bet that guy was surprised before he burned up."

And the other day we saw a barge. On the back end was a Sears Roebuck library. It stuck out over the stern of the barge. It was a two-holer.* The bosun said, "That's pretty good, you can sit on one hole and fish through the other!"

Then the other day I got a splinter under my nail and the bosun said, "Oh, you've been scratching your head again!"

Bosun Puregold is one of those occasional and rare people you meet who does not have an evil bone in them. He is Dr. Truelove's type only with a 100 percent better sense of humor. He kids me a lot about plants. He said, "Pulantz! Why do you wanna study them? They aren't exciting."

The bosun is proud of the fact that he doesn't say "ain't"

---

*Frequently, toilet paper was Sears Roebuck catalogs. A two-holer is an outhouse that can accommodate two people.

very often. Except when he forgets, or gets excited, then one slips out now and then.

10/18/43

Dearest Gretchen,

The other day I went in town for the first time in weeks. It surely was good to smell flowers and grass and look in shop windows. But I soon got tired of it. There were so many people and the streets were dirty, and it was hot. I went into a place to buy a milkshake. It was terrible. They didn't shake it; I could taste cornstarch in it, and the strawberry flavor was just pink chalk. There was a piece of wrapper in the glass, and the glass was dirty. Just like every other store, here and back home, that sells anything. They do such a good business they don't care if the customer is satisfied or not. I ate at a table with a young sailor who had just gotten here. I never saw him before, but he seemed pleased that I sat with him. He asked me all about the place. I told him what I knew. Also I made the waitress bring him his milk-shake pronto, else they might have kept him waiting yet. Then when I got up to leave I said "I'll pay for yours, too," and took both checks. He gulped and said, "Thank you, sir." I could tell by the way he looked at me he had never seen an ensign like me before.

Another interesting experience is to be back at the dock when liberty expires and all the sailors are waiting for the boats to take 'em back to their ships. The dock is almost a quarter of a mile long and there is a loudspeaker there. The announcer announces each boat as it comes in, and in no time at all it is filled and races away over the choppy waters. Jeepers, you see all kinds of sailors by the dozen. Many of them are drunken, and it is not uncommon to see them taking care of each other just like sentimental kids. They sure stick together.

Recently I haven't written you any letters about my politics, but just the same I am thinking of it. Stoneburger's father sent him the book *Under Cover*. It deals with all the subversive societies and activities in the U.S. since 1938. This guy who wrote it actually joined societies to get his dope. It really is an eye-opener. It exposes Senator Wheeler, Senator Ham Fish, Clare Hoffman, Father Coughlin, and many others such as the Bund and Silver Shirts. Boy, it amazed me how much the Nazis had infiltrated the U.S., especially in New York, Chicago and Los Angeles. Anybody who wants to battle such elements must give his whole life to it. And there is no reward either, except maybe pain and death. By the way I saw *Watch on the Rhine* last week. It was good and showed just how the U.S. may become Nazified and what it costs to fight it. However, my main thesis remains unchanged. We must educate the people more. The universities must take the lead in this! It is only by appealing to the ignorant and uninformed that the Fascists can get anywhere. Do away with illiteracy and unemployment, and the organizers would have nothing to work with.

10/20/43

Dearest wife,

I really wish you could see the porpoises! They are friendly and appealing. They are sleek and streamlined, and love to frolic. Today it was calm and sunny. We were cruising along out at sea, and from somewhere a school of 8 or 10 of them started frolicking up near the bow of the ship. Most of the sailors off duty went up to watch them. I guess the fish knew they had an audience, for they really acted up. The porpoises would jump out of the water, and twist, and flop. They would swim madly away then suddenly turn and head toward the ship. Their antics made the crew laugh and shout. I don't know who had the most fun, the fish or the sailors.

Oh, yes, the other day we saw a whale. I got out on deck just in time to see where he had submerged. Some of the guys saw him spout, but I missed it. Also, we threw some garbage over the side while some albatrosses were following us. We weren't going fast, so I could watch the birds. They landed right on the water and sat like ducks. The waves were choppy and you should see how odd the birds looked riding up and down, picking at the garbage.

Remember I told you about the aviator whose plane we picked up once? Well, now whenever he comes by, he always give us a special salute. He comes by real close, guns his motor and waves his hand—and we wave back. It gives you a real funny feeling. I guess he appreciated what we did for him.

About the tug sunk out here, we heard about it just last week. One thing about being sunk, all survivors get 30 days' leave and then go to new construction. What a way for me to get to come home.

Yesterday I had a letter from Bob. We are going to try and make a liberty together tomorrow. That is if his ship is in port and mine is. I hope we can make it.

10/22/43

Dearest Gretchen,

Wife, if you could just see a battleship close up! A new battleship costs probably more than $50 million to build and has a crew of a couple of thousand men. And the whole outfit is built and dedicated and used for destruction. Now suppose all the warships in the war (the cost, I mean) were turned to the purpose of education, research, better medicine, free schools and highways. See how much better it would be? Hitlers and Tojos can only rise or grab their way into power by haranguing ignorant people and promising poor, destitute people something they don't have. I can't understand why people who can do something about it don't realize this and remedy the situation.

Well I got a day off to go ashore and meet Bosun Mack. I waited and waited but he never did show up. I'll just have to write him another note making a future date. I feel confident, however, that we will get to see each other.

Anyway, since I was ashore I ate a leisurely lunch at the officers' club, then went into town. I guess I told you before about the multitude of types (racial) one sees here. It really is an amalgamation. I read somewhere in a book about this place where a certain man-about-town boasted he could produce a prostitute of any nationality from a certain house in the city. So they asked him, "How about an Eskimo?" That floored him a minute, but I guess eventually he did find one. Anyway, the story illustrates the numberless hodgepodge of mixtures, crosses and hybrids.

Just to see your eyes sparkle, I would like to window-shop here with you. It is even more interesting than the Vieux Carré. Only here you want to look at the people, too. There are hundreds of curio shops, numerous jewelry stores, and odds and ends. It's typical of a place catering to tourists and travelers who have plenty to spend. You can tell money is free and easy by the number of jewelry and photography stores, because both jewelry and photos are luxuries for the common man. In some of the places you can find pictures of half-naked girls, obscene postcards and pictures, if you know how to ask for them.

I went into a very exclusive jewelry shop and priced a jade ring. The man, very friendly, said, "You don't want to buy that."

I said, "Why not?"

And he said, "It costs $7,500—yes, hundred."

I said, "I guess you're right. But how about those jade pendant earrings?"

"Well, they are only $445."

So I said, "Well, don't let me take up your time."

And he said, "Oh, that's all right, take a look around!" So I did, and boy-oh-boy, talk about quiet expensiveness. I have never been in Tiffany's jewelry store in New York, but I bet this place is just as nice.

10/24/43

Dearest spouse,

I wish I could somehow convey to you the feeling in me when the GQ alarm sounds. Gawd damn! It is the most insistent, irritating, uncomfortable, demanding, raucous klaxon I ever heard. Reminds me of a nervous cow, sick with the bellyache. Especially in the night, when everything is pitch dark. You know how small our cabin is (about 10 by 8 feet). Well, Sankin and I usually hit the deck about the same time. He thrashes around so much pulling on his pants that I grab mine and jump into the wardroom to put them on. Then I grab my shirt, helmet, gun and life jacket, and run. My station now is in the radio shack. When I get on deck, all I can see is dark forms rushing madly, shutting hatches (makes all compartments water-tight), pulling covers off guns, opening ammunition ready boxes and adjusting personal gear. Then after a few minutes, the word comes over the intercom system: "Attention all hands. This is the captain speaking. This was just a drill. This was just a drill. The gun crews took seven and one-half minutes before the guns were manned. This is too slow, too slow! We must do it faster. Our lives may depend on it. Secure from general quarters."

Enclosed you will find an income tax pamphlet. I think it shows quite definitely that you and I do not have to pay an income tax or victory tax for 1943. Here's the way I figure our income for January 1, 1943, to January 1, 1944. My salary: Two months as midshipman at $65 = $130. Two months at $150 = $300. Eight months at $165 = $1,320. Total, $1,750. I don't have to pay on my $100-a-month subsistence. Your salary for January, February, September, October, November, December will be about $500. So that gives us an income of $2,250.

Wife, why don't you send your sister $5–$10 a month? I know she can use it, and we can afford it. We might as well share some with her.

10/26/43

Dearest spouse,

You know the *Tern* isn't very big, but compared to a rowboat it is gigantic. The other day we were coming up the channel and a soldier was rowing across in a small boat. Well the rules of the road for vessels are just like autos. The vehicle approaching from the right has the right of way, and size makes no difference. But, anyway, the little rowboat stopped to let us go by. The captain hollered down from the bridge to the soldier: "You have the right of way, why didn't you take it?"

And meekly the soldier hollered back, "I ain't as big as you are."

It will be good to be intimate with you again, but equally as good will be the severe pleasure of just being near you, looking at you and talking to you. You are more warming

and life-giving to me than the best wool blankets. All the
pain of separation will vanish like snow in a furnace when
I'm kissing you again. Sometimes it feels as if it would be
too good to bear, but I know it won't. And when I come
home, if we want to bowl, we will bowl, and if we want a
Coke, we will drink two; and ice cream every damn night
till I get tired of it, and movies when we want 'em, then
come home and really put on an act that should shame
those in the leading role of the pictures.

10/30/43

Dearest Gretchen,

We have extra officers aboard so the bosun has to sleep on
a cot in the wardroom. But our cabins are so small, his cot
is not more than four feet from my bunk. Well, last night
just before we fell asleep, out of a dead silence the bosun
said, "If I ever saw a Wave gettin' tattooed I would kick
her right in the ass." Jeepers, that made me laugh. You see,
the bosun made the mistake of getting tattooed—all over
his body. He thinks it is wrong for a woman to be tattooed.
    In your last letter you told me about the nightmare
where you were having a baby, and I was running around
with a model or an actress, or someone. Who was she?
Hedy Lamarr or Ann Sheridan? If you don't quit having
such dreams, why I might as well get shore duty in Hollywood and make your dreams come true. So, enough of this
nonsense! When you go to bed at night, go to sleep, or else
dream and think of me. Or maybe I should tell you some
of my bad dreams. For instance, last night I dreamed we
were out and one of our fighters came over and strafed a
small ship near us. Immediately three men jumped overboard from this ship. They were escaped war prisoners.
Some friend of mine and I jumped in and tried to capture
them. Well, my buddy wanted all the credit, so he held me

under water awhile. Finally I got loose and got to two of the prisoners. One was just a kid, so I grabbed him and shoved him under water to persuade him to come along easy. Then I grabbed the other fellow's arm and we crawled up on the rocks. But our plane came back and started strafing us. I could see the bullets stepping closer and closer. Boy, when I woke up (I had been yelling at the plane) I had torn down my mosquito netting, and had the bed cover wrapped all around me. It's a wonder I didn't wake Sankin, but then he sleeps like a log anyway.

The Navy is passing out V-mail Christmas cards. So I took a bunch and have started sending them. I put the date 10/30/43 on all of them. I don't know how long it will take 'em to get there, but I want to be early.

10/31/43

Dearest spouse,

Our tug has been working hard lately. We haven't had a day off for a long time. The officers and crew seem to be going stale from lack of mail, new magazines, reading material and change of scenery. I, too, feel the strain for I am constantly thinking of you and home.

As I have written you before, my chief recreation is dreaming of you and our life when I come home from the sea. Yet I must admit that the sea is making its mark on me, even though it may be visible only as a few more lines at the corners of my eyes. I have often read of standing on the bridge of a ship with the wind in your face, but up until recently I was too seasick to appreciate it. But when you are on a ship day after day and see the ocean in all its moods and colors, to watch and scan the horizon for any sign of life, to see other ships of all kinds, to study the birds as they wheel and turn in endless flight, to laugh with the porpoises, to hear the rush of waves thrown out by the bow as our ship plows its furrow, to feel the deck quiver beneath your feet when a big wave hits you, to see land come up over the horizon, to see and hear and feel a plane approach, to smell the sea and smell the land, to realize the sea's age and vastness and depth and wonder, to look at the stars and watch them "wheel in silent circles in the sky"; no wonder sailors are philosophers.

The more I think of it, the more I realize the stupidity and foolishness and waste of war. No one I have met out here has ever spoken to me about how unnatural and silly it is to spend billions of dollars to destroy people and places. Everyone seems to take the war as a natural thing. Christ!

11/1/43

Dearest Gretchen,

I suppose I should lecture you for thinking, or even beginning to think, that I want you only as a "wrasslin" partner. I admit that as a result of our enforced separation, I may think of it more than usual, but I believe I have shown you (by actions, words and deeds) 100 times that you are more to me than a mere sex release. If I weren't attached to you by bonds a hundred-fold more powerful than the appeal of your lovely body, you and I would have broken up long ago. So don't you go gettin' any silly notion about wantin' you only for screwin'!

11/2/43

Dearest wife,

Two letters from you today and I devoured them both. First about the budget. You did a swell job on it. Your total was $1,158.61. Where did the 61¢ come in? I couldn't find any mention of it. Many of the things, like the bike, waffle iron, glasses, umbrella, lamp and blanket, are all good investments and things which we need that will last us a long time. And the ring and debts paid off can be considered as investments, too. I am glad you kept such an accurate account and it would be nice if you continue to keep an account "in the book," as you say.

As for the pictures, you said you gave that dress away, and it is a good thing you did. Are you sure you weigh only 136? That side picture of you on the bike sure made you look hefty. That thigh of yours had a certain ham-like appearance. Remember what you told me about Beulah and "gobs of quivering flesh." I warn you, spouse, if I come home and find you with spare tires on your tummy and fat on your broad beam, I will fling you on the deck and belay you with a stout piece of line till the fat is pounded away. Are you gonna welcome me looking like a barrel on pipe stems? I hereby order you to take those hip-reducing exercises, also cut down your weight to 132. That is the maximum I will allow, even though you are five foot nine. If, when I get home, you weigh over 132, I'll put you on bread and water for five days and break you to apprentice seaman. Now to be constructive. I wish I could see your long hair. And you don't look a day older than when I left. And I am glad you are wearing my watch. These things seem to make you "my possession" and I'm glad you want to be my property.

I showed Sankin the picture you sent of the rug you hooked and said, "It makes mine look sorta sick." He sure did laugh. The bosun told me I better get on the ball.

11/4/43

Dearest wife,

Sometimes we tow a target and sometimes we tow a real little target some distance behind a big target. The big target looks odd enough but the little ones really are comical.

They remind me of a small boy following his dad. The little target skips merrily over the waves just like a curious pup following a cat. They really strike me funny. The first time we towed one of them, a deck hand said to me, "What the hell is that—a sample?"

Captain Parry is planning to marry the girl he was with that night at the hotel in LA. He bought her a diamond out here. He got a seven-tenth carat and paid about $350 for it, tax included. He showed it to us the other night in the wardroom. We all congratulated him about it. In handling the ship the captain is self-assured. But when he told us about his girl he was shy.

Rumor has it the captain will be in the States by Christmas and get a new ship and get married. Don't tell Madge about this. She will find it out sooner or later from someone else. Let her tell you.

11/6/43

Dearest Gretchen,

Have you ever read any newspaper columns by the increasingly popular Ernie Pyle? He wrote many from North Africa and Sicily and is now home on sick leave. I enjoy his newspaper work. He writes in a vivid, homey style about many little things that other newspapermen would overlook entirely. Keep an eye out for his efforts in the Louisiana papers.

The other night I dreamed I was cutting the lawn in front of a nice house. I was in my bare feet, and I could feel the wet grass. Then you came out of the house and brought me a big glass of milk and some nutty cinnamon rolls. You were in shorts. After awhile you asked me, "Aren't you coming in the house?" I said, "Sure I am."

Just then the security watch woke me, and I sure did cuss to myself.

I really hope they can knock out Germany by spring. If they do, it will certainly shorten this war out here, but even so it is my private guess that it will be 1945 before the U.S. fleet steams into Tokyo Bay. By that time I should be long since qualified for a leave and a stay with you. And this time when I come home, if I have to leave again I am gonna leave part of me behind to keep you company, make you grow and ease your psychological cramps. *Et, ma femme, écoutez bien, parce que mon amour dure après la mort, aussi je t'adore, je t'adore et je t'aime* forever. Votre homme, Geoffrey

11/8/43

Dearest wife,

Before I get down to the serious side of this letter, I want to tell you more about the bosun. He asked me if I heard about the guy who drank eight Coca Colas and burped Seven Up. And tonight he showed me more pictures of his two little girls. He said, "One of them is a roughneck, she wrestles with dogs and everything," and I said, "You mean to tell me she would wrestle with Karol?" And Boats replied, "I said *dog*, not *wolf!*" Boy, that one brought down the house.

11/10/43

Dearest wife,

Two letters from you yesterday. You aren't the only one who needs letters for a lift. We now call our mailman Santa Claus because almost every mail trip he brings a few Christmas packages to the boys.

Once when we were out 40–50 miles we saw a big sting-ray. It was triangular and about four feet long at the widest part. It was a dingy shade of brown and looked weird and mean. Sometimes we see little ones close to shore, but this was the biggest I've seen.

And flying fish are always with us. They never cease to thrill me. Sometimes whole schools of them shoot out of the water and sail silently, swiftly and serenely across the sea. They glide along so effortlessly just a few feet above the waves for a distance of 30 yards or more.

Also in the harbor we see thousands of jellyfish. They look like parachutes with legs. These "parachutes" range from the diameter of a pin to a basketball, and are odd and graceful-looking in the water, but when you flip one with an oar up on the dock it looks like half-solid, colorless jello. Ugh!

11/12/43

Dearest Gretchen,

This is a good night to write to you. It is just chilly enough outside to appreciate my cabin, and a big silver moon is hanging in a blue sky with black-gray clouds as a background. Wife, I miss you. In fact I am stumped when I try to describe my longing for you.

The bosun was telling us that in Acapulco, Mexico, the girls rub you behind the ears instead of kissing you. You and I must try that.

11/14/43

Dearest spouse,

Boy, I certainly get fed up with the boundaries of this small ship. I'd sure like to go on a good long hike, or plow all day, or chop wood—anything to expend a lot of physical energy and soothe my nerves. I am too active a guy to be penned up on a ship all the time.

Because we have five officers to stand deck watches (captain doesn't stand watches, but he is on the bridge most of the time anyway), we now stand two-hour watches instead of four. This eases the monotony a great deal. Well, last night I had the 10–12. There was a full moon, and I tell you it was grand. Perhaps I have become more sensitive to beauty, but last night sure affected me. There was just enough cool breeze to make me appreciate my leather jacket. The sky was a pale blue, sparsely bedecked with fluffy white clouds. The precipitous mountains on our port hand were a black-green—the sea was black and silver, and the light was bright enough to read a newspaper. And there was the *Tern* silently chucking along with the water whispering at her bow and the wake streaming behind like a frothy, lazy streamer. It was good. And there was island music on the bridge radio.

Last night when I came off watch, I couldn't sleep so I went up to the bow of the ship and sat right behind the jack staff (flagpole). The sea wasn't very rough. I sat there and soaked up the silence and moonlight and the sound of the waves against the bow. The ship had a sort of hammock-like soothing motion. Most ships make little noise under way. I was surprised because I thought the engines would make much more noise. Emersin keeps our engines in fine shape. I guess the propeller makes quite a racket in the water. But on a dark night, a ship could pass within 100 yards and you wouldn't hear it, unless you had a "sound" watch* on lookout, or if the wind made any noise at all.

*The "sound" watch would have sonar equipment.

When I write letters at sea, I brace my head against my bunk and secure the chair against Sankin's bunk. That way I am part of the ship, and no matter which way she rolls my relative position is unchanged.

It's strange how men become attached to a ship. The other day we had to transfer five seamen for reassignment to other ships out here. Not one of them wanted to leave. I guess the one boy (18) would have a cried a little if the other sailors hadn't laughed him out of it. I like this ship and the duty, but I would quickly sever my relations to get back home to you.

11/16/43

Dearest wife,

Recently in the papers and magazines there have been several articles on penicillin. Just to show you far behind the public is: when I came to LSU in 1940, one of the first seminars I heard was given by Professor Christover (bacteriology) on some antibacterial agent secreted by *Penicillium*. From all recent accounts I guess it is even better than sulfa drugs.

Today I received a present from your folks. It was a New Testament with a gold-plated cover. It is designed to be worn in the shirt pocket over the heart. On the cover these words are inscribed: "May this keep you safe from harm." Somehow I felt proud of that gift.

11/19/43

Dearest wife,

I sent your dad a box of cigars, your mother a tablecloth, and your sister a pen-and-pencil set and perfume. To Philipsburg I sent seven purses. Altogether I spent about $100 (whew!), but I had it saved up and I got a kick out of spending it. As fast as I get any money saved, I am going to invest it in things to send home. Incidentally, Emersin reduced our officer's mess bill to $15 a month, so we really are living cheap. How does he do it? Well we eat much of the same chow as the crew, for which we reimburse the U.S. Navy at cost, but if Emersin buys any special food ashore, like papayas or green onions or fresh pineapple or radishes, we have to pay for it. Once he brought back two pounds of Limburger cheese because *he* likes it. He charged it to the officers' mess but he and the cook ate it all themselves. None of the rest of us could stand the stuff. Jesus, it stinks!

Today I went swimming in the freshwater pool near the aviators' quarters. It was not crowded; it was peaceful and quiet. I was sitting in a chair sunning myself when a New Zealander (at least I think he is, for he had an accent and I believe I had seen him there before) came and sat near me. He had a portable radio so I mentioned, "You have all the comforts of home." He shared the radio with me and we sat in the warm sun and chatted and talked. He told me of some of his adventures but I didn't quiz him too much. John Charles Thomas was singing on the radio (a rebroadcast) and he was excellent. The whole scene and atmosphere all blended into a sort of half-awake unreality, for the sun was soothing me in its warmth, and the music was soothing and the Anzac had just finished telling me of Tarawa, and I realized I was far from home and so was he, and there we were sitting in a quiet, peaceful, beautiful spot, secluded for a short period from the reality of steel decks and the monotony of a stagnant war, where inactivity and routine depress the spirit and rob one of initiative. He is luckier than I, for he can take a training flight to get the kinks out of his system, but he told me, too, that long flights become deadly tiresome and wearying when one flies hour after hour over nothing but ocean.

11/21/43

Dearest wife,

I suppose you heard the news about the new landing the Marines have made in the Gilbert Islands. It looks as if we are taking a big step forward. When Admiral Nimitz and Secretary Knox announced that "Vast naval forces were prowling the Pacific," they were not lying, for I saw most of it.

If it were not for the fact that I look forward to, long for and anticipate coming home, this life would be as uninteresting as sweeping the floor of an unused empty room seven days a week every week. It is beyond me how fellows can stay in the Navy year after year.

I never thought it would come to pass that I would have to warn you against the evils of drink, but don't you let Sally get you into bad habits of drinking cocktails every time you go out. If you do, I shall tell your mother and you know how that would affect her. I don't mind you sampling them, but I am afraid you will find one you like especially well and then you will overwork your desire for it like you do black olives. Besides, I never could see paying 35–50¢ for 5¢ worth of gin or whiskey and 2¢ worth of Ginger Ale or Coke.

11/24/43

Dearest wife,

Last night, about 2:00 A. M., I listened to Radio Tokyo. Jeepers, it was funny to listen to that announcer and the absolutely preposterous claims he made. I don't see how the

Japanese public can fall for such hooey. If they believe that announcer, it's just another glaring instance of the ignorant masses being hoodwinked by an unscrupulous few.

When I think of the billions spent for war, and how graduate students (who in their own small way try to produce something useful) must struggle along on $30 to $60 a month, I have to laugh at the ridiculous irony of it all. Billions of dollars to destroy men, and pennies to better his lot.

11/26/43

Dearest wife,

Yesterday was Thanksgiving and we had turkey with all the trimmings, including black olives. The bosun is crazy about them. I told him that you and he were the only two people I ever knew who liked ripe olives excessively. He said, "You should meet my family, and you would find three more." He told me once he and his wife ate a quart of ripe olives in one hour. It will be a treat for you to meet the bosun, for I believe he has a tender affection for his wife and family, and I know he is honest and kind. He has taught me a lot about navigation and the Navy.

11/28/43

Dearest wife,

Every so often, it is necessary for our motor launch to make a trip in to the beach or else make a trip out to the ship as she lies a couple miles offshore. The other day I had to make the trip out in the motor launch to the ship. As we left the port, the water got deeper and deeper and changed color from gray to green to deep, deep blue with whitecaps. The green is about the shade of green apples. The sea wasn't real rough but it was choppy. And the ocean looks big enough from the *Tern,* but from a little boat it is immense. The boat bounced around like an acorn in a whirlpool. Everybody (there were four or five guys) sat in the stern to keep the bow high up out of the water. The worst times occurred when we got right on top of a wave, and then suddenly the front end would fall out from under us and we would go scooting down the other side. Sometimes the wave would drop us hard enough so that the boat slapped the water and made enough spray to sprinkle us good. Aside from the big waves, there were a lot of little ones, and since we were heading across the waves with the current on our port bow, we had a corkscrew, or rolling, motion. Strangely enough, I didn't get seasick. Maybe 'cause it was so much fun, for the shining sun glanced off the waves, and a good wind was blowing, and the spray was salty. It was exhilarating, but just the same I was glad when we came alongside the old *Tern* on her lee side like a pup nuzzling up to his ma for some chow.

Once again I must gossip about my shipmates. Recently we have been fortunate to get ice cream issued by the Navy. It's the first time in three or four months this was possible. Of course I like ice cream, and at the table I remarked about it. Now I guess I am the only officer aboard who doesn't drink, and I don't criticize or pass judgment on those who do. We had been talking about prohibition and liquor, and I said I could do without whiskey and that I would much rather have ice cream. Immediately they all swooped on me in a chorus of denials and scoffing. Well, it's just another case of intolerance of the tastes of others. I think we are lucky to have such a bunch of good officers and I wouldn't change this ship for any other.

Dear spouse,

Did I tell you I am studying radio? Since I am communications or radio officer, I figured I ought to know a little about our equipment. Also, as we are a training ship, I have all the books, pamphlets and directions which our radiomen must study to advance in rate. Anyway, in my spare time I am studying about receivers, amplifiers, transmitters and other stuff. Maybe it will do me some good some day. At least it will make me a better-qualified officer.

You spoke of me singing "You Are My Sunshine." I regret to say I haven't raised my voice in song since I came aboard. Sometimes at night on watch I hum to myself when the wind will drown the sound, but it doesn't do for an officer to go about singing. It seems the moment I relax the least little bit why something comes up to sober me in an instant. And the minute you try to become a good guy or fraternize with the crew, why right off someone tries to take advantage of your good nature. Occasionally after the evening meal Karol, Puregold and I, and sometimes the other officers off watch, gather up on the fo'c'sle to watch the sun go down. We joke and laugh a little, but even so one is constantly aware that the seamen are always watching. Also, sometimes in the wardroom we relax a little and laugh, but it is not often. But don't be afraid I am growing grouchy, for in the solitude of my bunk I talk to you and chuckle over things we have done, jokes shared, and fun we have had. And I contemplate our joys to come and how much fun it will be to take up with you again and reteach you all the things a proper spouse and wife should know.

Last night I was reading a sea story about a young sea captain. And I realized that if the war is prolonged two years yet (I believe it will be), that probably I will have command of a vessel. Jeepers, I was suddenly conscious of the responsibility involved and the decisions to be made. Do you realize that a new tug just a little bigger than the *Tern* costs $1 million, and the captain of such a tug (usually a guy in his 20s) is responsible for her well-being 24 hours a day, through one emergency after another? And no matter who fouls up or dopes off and runs the ship into trouble, why the captain is responsible.

For instance, once a destroyer rammed an aircraft carrier while both were on maneuvers. Someone remarked, "Well, I guess he will get a court-martial for that." And someone else said, "Yep, he will either get a court-martial for ramming, or else a Navy Cross because he got his destroyer back to port without sinking!"

And one time a ship went aground. One of the young officers said to the captain, "Don't worry, Captain, *we* will get her off the reef." And the captain replied sadly, "Yes, *we* always get her off, but only *I* ran her aground."

12/1/43

My lovely girl,

On board here we have a ship's carpenter, first class. He is a great big husky fella, weighs over 220 and has been in the Navy 8 or 10 years. We call him Bull. He doesn't go much for women but he surely likes to drink. And when he goes ashore he gets drunk, and fights, and fights! His body is all covered with scars; there is one across his chest which is fully a foot long. He got it from a knife fight. But when sober, he is a good sailor and a competent ship's carpenter. He made the rug looms for me.

He is master-at-arms of the crew's mess and is in charge of general cleanliness of the mess hall and keeps order. I tell you, he really keeps the place clean and keeps our boys on K P (only we call them mess cooks) on their toes. Bull likes to drink, but he has been to sea so much he rolls and staggers without drinking. Well, anyway, sometime ago he went ashore and got drunk. The shore patrol picked him up for "staggering." Bull brought the SP report back to the ship and he had to be restricted to the ship for awhile. Later I heard him remark to one of the crew, "Huh, they pick me up for staggering. Christ! I walk like that all the time!" It sure was funny the way he said it. Bull is one of those fellas who seem to be insensitive to physical pain. (He is the one who got drunk in Long Beach, a car ran over his feet, and Bull didn't know it!) He's the type of fellow who is the backbone of the Navy and who would really clean up the Japs.

Bob Mack is back—at least his home is. If we can arrange it, I am surely going to try to see him this time. At the first opportunity, I am going over to his ship and *ask* to see him rather than write a note. I'll have three chances out of four of finding him aboard, so I'm going to risk it.

Yesterday your Christmas package to me came and I felt funny inside. I knew right away what your gift to me was, for I sorta had a hunch anyway ('cause you wrote me once you hoped "they," or "it," fits) and I knew from the way you wrote before that it cost more than a couple dollars. So today I opened the package and there, sure enough, was the wedding ring. The engraving was a swell idea and I would rather have a plain gold band than anything fancy. When I put the ring on, I didn't know whether to cry or what, but I tell you I felt all stuffed up inside. When I read the inscription inside the band, and realized it was through your efforts and wishes that the ring was bought and prepared and sent to me, why I realized very deeply that I was your man and that marriage implied a definite *belonging.* I don't know just how to describe my feelings, but if I had ahold of you now I sure would kiss you good and proper.

12/4/43

Dearest wife,

Remember in the last letter I told you I was going over to see Bob? Well, that afternoon I did so, and sure enough I found him. The sailor who was directing me took me down to Bob's division office, and from there a chief took me to a fuse box at which a figure in blue dungarees was working. It was Bob. We shook hands and did a lot of talking in the next hour and a half. We stood and crouched right there in the passageway. He told me some of his adventures (I tell you that he and his ship have really been around—I feel second-rate compared to him), and I told a few of mine. We talked of you and home and relatives and everything! Maybe I am biased, since I know your mother and his mother are sisters, but I believe I could detect a resemblance to you in his features. He is a nice-looking guy!

Next day was Bob's liberty day, so I got the day off and we made a liberty together. We went in town, rode up to the university, out to the famous beach, had lunch at a nice hotel there, then sat under the palms and watched the ocean. We also went to the aquarium. But mostly we talked, and I am afraid I did most of it. Indeed, I was quite loquacious, but Bob talked, too. In fact we got along swell. I showed him the little store where I bought the purses and things for you. You told me he was a tall fellow. Why, I am taller than he is, only he is huskier than I am. It was a well spent day, and it did both of us good, at least I felt good to see someone from home (well, almost home, anyway).

The next time Bob gets liberty I am going to get off, too, and we are going swimming. Maybe before we separate we can make a couple of liberties together. I told Bob about the V-12 program for which he is eligible. He could go to college while in the Navy and take up engineering (electrical) like he wants to do. Also, he would be ashore in the States, which is a good way to fight the war. But Bob has seen enough action that he would have shore duty with a free conscience. Very few men in the Army and Navy can wear three campaign ribbons for this war, but Bob is entitled to them—also some stars on them for major engagements.

12/6/43

Dearest Gretchen,

Tomorrow is December 7, 1943. Two years ago it happened, and I am in the middle of it. I hope in two more years the war will be a memory. Tonight I am depressed and serious. I just came back from seeing *This Is the Army.* The color and music and movement were pleasant and enjoyable, but as most of the entertainment is now, it was a tearjerker appealing to the superficial emotions and glossing over the pertinent things.

One incident I can't forget was the other day when I watched a hospital ship unload casualties from the Tarawa campaign. When they started to unload, the dark green ambulances, each with a large red cross on a white circular background painted on either side, were lined up for almost a quarter of a mile. It took the ambulance crews all day before they finished. An ambulance would pull up to the gangway and the corpsmen would carry the wounded on stretchers down the gangway and slide them in the back of the ambulance. One or two walking wounded would sit up front with the driver. The loaded ambulance would start out, carefully, drive through the Navy yard, then up to the hospital on the hill. After the ambulance was unloaded it would return to the end of the line of parked ambulances and wait its turn for another load.

Some of the men were seriously hurt. You could tell by the feeble way they waved to the few onlookers who were watching. Some of the wounded reminded me of boxers who have been severely beaten and punched. You know, they are groggy and weak. But they pretend there is nothing seriously wrong. They try to get up, but can't. But they keep on trying. They won't give up. And that's the way it should be. Never give up!

One pale young kid I noticed tried to raise his head from the stretcher, but he couldn't make it. He did wave a little bit, but it was just too much of an effort. He didn't even have any clothes, just a hospital shirt and a small kit for toilet articles someone had placed beside him. I thought to myself, How ignominious and degrading! He has no personal belongings, no clothes. Where is his wallet? Probably in the sand back on Tarawa where they cut away his pants to dress the abdominal wound. I suppose most (all) of his youth was lost on Tarawa, too.

It was quiet around the hospital ship. You could hear the waste water splashing from the ship's discharge pipes into the still water by the dock. The whole area near the ship smelled like a doctor's office. You know, that vague faint mixture of iodine, alcohol, ether, bandages, iodoform and disinfectants in general. And the white hospital ship and nurse's white uniforms contrasted to the blue dungarees of the sailors and the dull gray and blue of the warships and the green grass and foliage.

I guess I shouldn't write letters like this to you. But if I write an occasional letter like this, you can perhaps understand better the man you married. Sometimes I feel so frustrated. My, oh my, oh my! I surely wish I was home tonight.

I am still convinced that man is an animal and the only

way to avoid war is to breed a race where the genes for love
of power, greed, lust and double-crossing are nonexistent.
The more I see of people, the more I am convinced that
the more money you make, the more crooked you become
and the meaner things you will do to keep what you have.
At least children are honest animals because they haven't
yet learned the tricks that grownups acquire.

People are not stern enough with themselves. They
don't know when to stop or say no. They give in too easily
to temptation and are too prone to take the easiest path. A
girl once told me, "Weakness is a sin." It didn't make sense
to me then, but I guess she was right. And the football
coach told us, "Don't get too close or rely too much on
weak people. They will fail you."

We should not let our emotions run away with us, but
always strive to let reason prevail.

A man needs something to put his faith in, Gretchen,
some quiet, well-protected anchorage where he can find
succor ere he goes out onto the life-ocean again. Since I
haven't yet found my God or faith in the Supreme Being, I
must of necessity rely on you. Oh! Wife of mine, be a good
anchorage to me and be my faith, for I need you and love
you, and love you.

12/10/43

Dearest Gretchen,

Yesterday I was swimming in the pool at the officers' club
for aviators when some guy walks up to me grinning and
says, "Hello, Luke." It was Henry George, an old friend
who was in my class at Penn State. I think you remember
him. He is good-looking, average height. He majored in
poultry. Well, Henry is a j.g. now, and wonder of wonders,

he is a pilot of a torpedo plane on an aircraft carrier. We sat and talked for a while, and then I got dressed and he introduced me to a bunch of guys from his group. We sat in the club and they drank beer (they had acquired a thirst for they were out a long time), and I had my Coke. I really felt odd because through my spectator's eyes, I could picture these fellows as a bunch of college guys just sitting around joshing each other and having a good time. Yet here they were in khakis, all with wings, and most of them (including Henry) with their name in the papers. Golly, how we talked.

If anybody is fighting this war, the carrier pilots are! When I get a chance to whisper in your ear and the information will no longer be of military value, I will surely relate to you some truly amazing things. I can say that George has crossed the equator six times in the last year. He also has some Jap money and calling cards. But I gotta stop, or else my enthusiasm will make me write what I shouldn't.

Henry seems to have the feeling that his job is not particularly dangerous and that he will get home safely. You should hear him relate some of his meetings with Jap Zeros. Tonight he came to our ship for supper, and Sunday (if possible) I am to visit his. Isn't it strange that he, a poultry farmer (more or less), is now thousands of miles from home dealing daily with weapons of death so that others may stay home and live in peace and raise chickens without fear that bombers will fly over them.

12/13/43

Dear wife,

On board ship, we must use air pressure in the sewage drainage system instead of gravity as they do in houses.

And, as fresh water is valuable, sea water is used as a flushing agent. Well, sometimes Emersin's engineers get too much pressure in the lines and when you bend over to flush the john you are liable to get well sprayed. It happens at the most unexpected times, and between the noise and spray and disgust it is quite aggravating. Also the pipeline runs through the boiler room and occasionally the water gets hot. Then if you happen to flush the throne while sitting on it you get an unexpected combination of hot shower, douche and saline enema all at once!

I happened to see Karol flush it the other day. He sneaks up on it from an angle and kicks the lever with a cautious toe. Somebody goosed him just as he kicked the lever. The following all happened simultaneously. He yelled and jumped; the commode erupted like Old Faithful; the ship rolled; the noise scared the messboy nearby, who dropped a pot of coffee on himself; and Karol and the other officer lost their footing and fell with arms and legs entangled into the shower stall.

Yesterday I met those young men who make history— those kids who are our first line of defense. Name any big important military step in the Pacific in the last nine months and these men were in it! I must confess I was (am) a little envious of them, and at the same time I am proud that in a distant way I am one of them. I, who dwell on the fringes of war, was greatly impressed by these gallant young cavaliers who are correcting by skill, courage, ingenuity, and daring, the mercenary mistakes of some few old men.

Gretchen, most of them are younger than I am, and the lieutenant commander in charge of the torpedo planes is just 28. He most of all impresses me, for he was quiet, soft-spoken and was the epitome of capability. We sat around and talked and laughed and joked awhile, and they drank prodigious quantities of beer. I suspect much of their hilar-

ity was release of nervous tension, but just the same, they
seemed to be a carefree bunch of fellows. Yet they spoke
of narrow escapes and hair-raising episodes in every other
breath. Every one of them feels sure he will get back, but I
know some of them won't.

12/15/43

Dearest Gretchen,

Did I tell you that Bosun and Karol have declared war on
the cockroaches? Every night they get the flit gun and stalk
them down. Karol sprays them and then the bosun pulls
their teeth so they will starve to death. The bosun swears
they may be crossed with flying bats, for he saw a big one
the other day—like the big ones we found occasionally
when we first moved into our apartment in Louisiana.

Our ship is not so bad off as some, for they have rats
which are bold and run all around the ship at night. We
must fight vermin constantly, else it will contaminate and
harm us. And there are all kinds of vermin; ignorance is
vermin.

12/17/43

Dearest Gretchen,

The other day I was on a bus and a woman of about 30 got
on. She was carrying a little baby about two years of age.
He was a cute little rascal with eyes like shoe buttons. She
sat down beside me. I had on my sunglasses and they fascinated that baby. He kept picking at my sleeve, and finally
pulled himself over to me till he got ahold of them. I finally
worked them loose from him. He chuckled and mumbled
and had a great time. There were some sailors on the bus,
and the baby was a great favorite with them.

English sailors look funny (peculiar) in their tropical uniforms of shorts and socks that end just below the knees. I wish we wore such a cool (literally) kind of uniform, but I suppose you would laugh to see me in such.

Sailors are odd people! The other day I saw a young kid coming back from liberty. He was carrying a cat. It was about half-grown, but he was taking it aboard to keep. And he did. Sailors have the strangest assortment of dogs, too. It seems the more mongrel the dogs are, the more sailors like them.

12/19/43

Dearest Gretchen,

We have just had "swim call," and after such a refreshing dip in the blue, blue Pacific I feel like writing to you. This is Sunday and everyone sat around to listen to Command Performance on the radio with Bob Hope, Jack Benny, Fred Allen and Dinah Shore. It was a swell program with good jokes and excellent Christmas carols. Of course as I listened to the songs, my thoughts were far away. Last year this time, you and I were spending our holiday honeymoon in Chicago. The Allerton and Sherman hotels, movies, dinner at the Drake, but most of all you and me, just you and me, alone together for many hours, free to love, and to talk as we pleased. How many times did I tell you I love you then?

Now the radio is playing "White Christmas." Yes, wife, some holiday we will spend among snow and pine trees and sleigh bells. Maybe next Christmas you will be plural and then we can plan Christmases for our begotten offspring.

Sometimes I wish you could stand a night watch with me. All is completely dark, and the helmsman is a dark shadow, and the signalmen are dark silhouettes. Now and then a lookout reports a light or ship, but usually it is quiet. At such times when it is dark and the sea is all around and the stars peep through the clouds, then it is that I could tell you how deeply, completely and profoundly I love you. I am fighting this war so I can come home to you in peace and know we have security and safety and need never know the terrible actuality of bombs and gunfire and discomfort, disease and hunger.

12/22/43

Dearest wife,

I want to tell you about the ritual of coffee-making in the Navy. Now Navy-issue coffee isn't so good, so each group of sailors goes ashore and buys their own brand. The engineers, firemen, electricians, yeomen and bridge force all have their own coffee pot, and it is always working. But to make a pot of coffee is no simple matter. First of all, three or four guys must get together and argue who shall make the coffee and who made the last pot. Well, whose coffee is it anyway? So finally they decide who must make the coffee. Then they argue who will wash the cups. This takes time, too. Finally they argue how strong they want it (it is mostly drip coffee; they get the boiling water from the urn in the mess hall). Well anyway, the coffee is fixed and the water drips and cups are washed (more or less) and finally it is ready for drinking. And you don't just drink the coffee. You have to sip it a little, then talk about women on your last liberty, then you go over to the side of the ship and spit in the ocean. Finally the coffee is drunk and everybody sez, "Christ, what lousy coffee," and they go work for 15 minutes. Then they congregate again and it starts all over. Whose turn is it to make the coffee? In the wardroom as soon as we get a visitor, the first words are, "How about a cup of coffee?" and it is never refused. Our Navy is the coffeeist drinking Navy in the world.

Dearest dear Gretchen,

Christmas Eve and what better way is there to spend it than by writing to you? When I write you letters, it seems, sometimes, as if you are in the next room and I'm just talking a monologue to you. The only thing is, I can't go into the next room and grab onto you. I truly believe that if I had to die, my only regret would be that I didn't have the chance to spend as much time with you as I have wanted to.

If I had to, I could handle this old *Tern* bird in a pinch. If I had to. I am learning enough about the ocean to respect and circumvent it. My favorite occupation, on watch, outside of thinking of you, is to imagine certain incidents pertaining to shiphandling and what I would do if they came up. For instance, what would I do some dark night if a Jap sub surfaced 200 yards away from us? It's a good way to learn, and it helps a lot.

Today we got our booster shots for tetanus and typhoid. You get them one year after the original shots. My left arm feels heavy, but I have no other ill effects. Boisee, pharmacist's mate, fixed up his gear (mostly needles) in the mess hall and marched us through. One guy said he "would rather get hit in the ass with a truck than take shots." That got a big laugh from the crew.

Wife, we must have a pretty good ship, or else we serve good food, because almost every day some of the crew from the other tugs sneak over to the *Tern* to have chow with our crew. About 15 minutes before meal time, the crew starts congregating at the port and starboard entrance to the mess hall, which extends from one side of the ship to the

other. Then when the mess cook (who doesn't cook at all—
he is combination waiter, scullery maid and KP agent)
shouts, "Chow down" at the top of his lungs, the crew
swarms into the mess hall. What noise! They eat fast, too.
Bull can eat a roast beef dinner, with second helpings, in
less than seven minutes.

Usually unrated seamen are the mess hands. These un-
trained kids are the lowest echelon on the ship and get all
the KP duty and other unwelcome jobs, like keeping the
head clean. Our pharmacist's mate is in charge of cleanliness, both galley and head, and keeps after the men. Periodically the captain has inspection and I tell you the men
use plenty of soap and water and do much scrubbing.

The skipper was all set to go home and get married, but
now they won't or can't relieve him. He is a capable man
and I think one reason they won't let him go is because
they have no adequate replacement for him. The captain
felt bad for a while, but it is one of the discomforts of war.
He has toughened a lot since Stateside days.

12/26/43

Dearest Gretchen,

We had a wonderful Christmas dinner. Turkey, cranberry
sauce, vegetables, fruit cake, pie and candy. Since we had
worked hard lately they gave us Christmas off. Christmas
Eve most of the crew got feeling good from a nearby Army
canteen and various sources. Songbird Karol drank too
much and slept on the deck all night in his cabin. He didn't
eat anything all Christmas day. This morning he got up and
said, "Boy, those typhoid shots really hit me!" Of course,
we all laughed.

Even though I don't have dangerous duty, I can see the
war is affecting me. I read as much on politics as I can, and

sometimes I get cynical and bitter. It just occurred to me. Probably some of the men who are fighting this war will come home and develop into half-assed politicians. We are always breeding a new generation of half-assed politicians. The question is, How can we stop? One way might be to require all citizens to take an active part in politics, or in government.

Do half-assed politicians realize they are half-assed politicians? Do they think they are good guys? Or don't they really give a damn about the rest of us?

12/28/43

Lovely Gretchen,

As you know, we have a ship's service aboard. This tiny store is about as big as an oversize clothes closet and is located in the forward hold just aft of the paint locker. But we sell much candy, chewing gum, cigarettes (two packs for 15¢), toothpaste, and other odds and ends. All the profits remain in the ship service fund. Well, we accumulated so much reserve, the captain decided to give each man (including officers) a $10 present for Christmas. As I write this, the crew is slowly filing through the wardroom, each man gratefully accepting a $10 bill. Of course they are just getting back some of the money they spent, but they think it is a nice present. So do I.

Today I was proud of myself. The sea was rough, really rough, and many of the crew aboard the *Tern* got seasick, but not Salty Dog Luke. I was agreeably surprised. We rolled and pitched and tossed. The wind was "real fierce" (as my mother used to say), and there were whitecaps and rain squalls, and sunshine. I stood up on the bridge in good health and had a pleasant time watching the ocean fume and foam and spray as I listened to the sweeping wind.

But, just the same I was glad to get back to the tranquillity of port again.

1/2/44

Dearest spouse,

Did I tell you there used to be a chief signalman on the *Tern* who was skillful with the sewing machine? All signalmen must know how to sew, repair flags, make flags, patch awnings, etc.

Well, our present-day signalman was telling me how the chief signalman used to "build" dresses for his girl. I thought that was real funny 'cause I could just see the chief getting out a hammer and saw to build a dress. Odd choice of words, wasn't it?

Like most of the ships of the Navy, our crew is a cross section of the U.S.A. but the *Tern* also includes one man from a certain outlying island. He is Portuguese and part native, I guess. He is a good-looking guy, very tanned, well built, white teeth, and curly hair. He is likable and has an intriguing accent. I like to hear him tell stories. One of the boys asked him if he liked corn better than peas and he said, "The difference makes no matter."

We also have Swedes and Dutch and English, and all kinds.

I wish I could take some pictures of the crew and send them to you. What a wild-looking bunch at times! When we are working at sea, they take off all their clothes but their dungaree trousers and roll the pant legs up to their knees or just below. They go around with no shoes on, for the deck is usually wet. Most of the boys are deeply tanned and care not too much if their hair is not combed, or they remain unshaven. Of course when we get in port, they get all cleaned up, but out at sea everyone is natural. Often I go back on the fantail just to watch them work. It is almost like a movie, for often the wind is blowing briskly and the white-capped waves toss us up and down. The men shout directions to each other and laugh and balance themselves on the swaying deck and splash around in the water which comes on board. Always there is the background of the sea and wind against which the men on ship pit their strength.

More and more the strain of being away from home is becoming evident in the actions of the men. They talk of home endlessly and what they will do and how good it will be. I don't talk about it much anymore 'cause it just aggravates me more. All I know is that I will be one big bundle of glee when we head the bow of the *Tern* northeast again.

1/4/44

Dearest Gretchen,

Tonight, two ships nearby were showing movies. One was *The Spoilers* (Dietrich, Wayne, and Scott); the other was *The Bride Came C.O.D.* (Davis and Cagney). Since neither one appealed to me, I sat and watched them both. The screens were only about 40 feet apart so I watched the best parts of both of them.

Today it was bad weather out on the ocean and I was seasick all day. I thought I had seasickness licked, but today showed me different. I don't know how or why it is, but sometimes I get sick and sometimes I don't. I stood my watch and spent the rest of the day in my bunk. Drank two cups of good hot soup. I didn't vomit any today, but my stomach was like a churn, and I had a bad headache. It is misery to lie in a heaving bunk and pass the time in enforced idleness just waiting for the rocking to cease and the stomach to subside. Thoughts are unregulated and you view yourself with detached apathy and wonder how you got in this place and where are you going?

Tonight, the auto ride over to the fleet post office was especially enjoyable. It was just sundown and the dust and herbage and gasoline all smelled good to me, after the rolling and pitching of the ship and the roaring of the wind. Later on, a slight breeze came up and it was cool and I could smell flowers and grass and damp earth. Then the half-moon came out in the night, blue sky, and I sat there in the auto and thought of you.

1/6/44

Lovely Gretchen,

Just came back from the movie *Scattergood Baines*. It was fair. Mostly I get a kick out of watching the audience. The sailors sit on the rail, on the deck, on gun mounts, in the rigging, on barrels, anywhere. Some of them lie right on the deck at the base of the screen. I asked one guy if it didn't hurt his eyes to watch from that position. He said, "No, but the girls look tall and thin."

It's fun to hear their expressions; hate of villain, love of hero, lust for pretty girls, and the way they coach the participants in a love scene. Everybody in their work clothes forgetting the day's toil. And while the reels are being changed I can look over the bay, see other ships, watch the searchlights, look at the mountains, and think of you. Tonight there was a moon, scattered clouds, and blue sky.

I am becoming more and more addicted to *Time* magazine. No kiddin', I think it is the most "aware" publication of any. It certainly has its fingers on the world's pulse and presents problems fairly and accurately. At least as far as I can tell.

1/8/44

Dearest Gretchen,

This letter is written late at night, when honest sailors should be asleep. But if I stay up late tonight, I can sleep tomorrow during the day when I am not on watch while we are at sea. When I sleep, I am not seasick, and the problem is solved!

Wife, I wish you could see the kids on this ship at mail call. As soon as the mail boy (he has a big leather pouch just like regular mailmen, only he wears a blue sailor hat and dungarees) comes up the gangplank, he is surrounded. The sailors follow him with hungry looks. Then they stand around patiently while the mail is sorted. As their names are called, they grab each letter greedily and each goes off to some corner of the ship to read in solitude. And those who get no letters try to hide their disappointment as best they can. They turn away and talk of something else. Also the kids wear the letters like badges. They put them in their shirt pocket or hip pocket, being very careful that parts of the envelope stick out and everyone can see that "I got a letter today." I tell you, mail is the best morale builder I know.

The more I see and associate with the U.S. fighting men (men! why many of them are just kids, but they are *men*) the more respectful and admiring I become. Truly, I am thankful I come from a country that produces such fine people. If you could see the cases of utter unselfishness in their relations to each other. And the tougher the going is, the more they stick together and help each other. The Marines are especially this way. I could tell you stories of heroism and sacrifice that would make you cry. That is what makes me so mad when I read about the dissention, strikes, stealing and cheating at home. I see guys who willingly give up their lives for their buddies or their ship, and back home they want 12¢ an hour extra. Jesus, what a laugh!

I don't know how this last half page will turn out since I have to ride the typewriter* and think up the "sugar" words, too. Besides if I said what I really wanted to, probably the keys would melt and run together.

1/10/44

Dearest girl,

Last night the moon was full, a pale yellow. It floated over the flat, calm sea in the warm night air. A few fluffy white clouds sailed high in the pale blue sky admist the bright tropical stars. The moon streak twinkled and danced on the black flat sea. I went up on the fo'c'sle and lay down right at the prow. I could hear and see the black water hissing and foaming as the ol' *Tern* plowed on her way, muttering and chuckling to herself. We were going as fast as she could go, almost (which is all of 10 knots, military secret), and she quivered and trembled. It gave me an odd feeling to lie there on my back and watch the ship following me. I could see our lookouts on the gun deck plain as day and the silhouette of the mainmast against the blue sky. The bosun (who was OOD) hollered down to me a couple of times from the bridge. But most of the time I just lay there soaking up the beauty around me and let my mind wander where it would. The vagrant night breeze can play havoc with the imagination. I talked to you and told you strange stories. Some true—some that happened to me—some not true, but they happened to me just the same. I can see why

---

*In rough weather, the author explains, the typewriter bounced around so much it was difficult to hit the proper keys, let alone spell correctly.

the sea and ships have fascinated men since time began. The romance and loneliness must appeal strongly to many adventurous souls.

Dear wife,

Today I am gonna tell you about the skipper of a neighboring tug. The tug is a new one about 30 feet shorter than the *Tern* and much more maneuverable. The *Tern* is bad enough when it comes to pitching and rolling out at sea, but I bet that tug is like a cork in a bathtub full of kids. Well, this skipper is, I'd say, about 30, and I believe a former officer in the Merchant Marine who joined the Naval Reserve, and when the war broke out he came in the regular Navy. He is about an inch taller than I am, but large-boned—a big frame, but lean, and he has big hands which one can tell are just aching to grab onto an oar, line, hammer, wheel, anything, and make it work! He has rough features, big teeth, wild hair and a rugged chin. His English is atrocious but he "gits sed what he aims to say." Well, this skipper (he is a lieutenant) has more get up and go, actual push, than most anybody. Professor Sloan's tenacity of purpose is one of the mind—a mental push—but this guy's nervousness is one of physical impact. He is always on the go and just aching for some problem where physical inge niousness is required. For instance, once he needed some steel cable spliced. His men who were doing it were too slow, so he pushed 'em aside and did it himself. And he gets mad and runs his own winch, etc. It's a pleasure to watch him. He reminds me of some of the raw-boned type of farmer-woodsmen one meets in the hills back home. A typical pioneer type who loves to do battle with the wind, rain, ocean or any form of nature. You have the feeling he would go out in the woods with an axe and build a wagon or most anything. Or he could build his own ship, or improvise repairs of most any type.

I have seen him wrestling (a thing unheard of in the regular dignified Navy) on the fantail with his executive officer. The captain always gets pinned cause the exec is a real big fellow, but they just tussle to get rid of animal energy. This skipper can handle his tug well. The way he gets in and out of corners reminds me of some mechanic driving in a crowded garage with a jeep—he turns and backs and pivots and swings with ease and confidence. This tug works both in the harbor and out. Formerly he traveled all over the Pacific, but he is doing such a good job around here they want to keep him, but he is just aching to get at the Japs. He was in the African campaign last year. I don't know on what kind of a ship, but I can imagine him being right where they needed a tug most. Out here they use him to get big ships under way. Formerly they would use a whole mess of little harbor tugs, but this guy tells the little tugs to lay clear and then he snuggles up to a big ship, gets lines aboard her, and first thing you know, his little tug is snorting and chugging and kicking up a tremendous wake and the big ship will be headin' right where he wants her to. Yes, and the skipper of the tug and the pilot on the big ship will be hollering and cussing at each other like men do when they've got a tough job licked between them. The draft of his tug is not much, so he can go in close to any beach and pull off larger ships, or he takes barges to various places.

I have to laugh at him trying to say the polysyllabic, multi-vowel names of some of the islands. He makes up his own name and then hangs on a "goddamn it" afterward. For instance if he said "Atchafalaya," it would be something like this. "I was goin' up this Atchafalaya-goddamn-it-river when the towline parted."

He is a good friend of Captain Parry and he always comes over to our wardroom at night when we are in port together to play poker or shoot the breeze. Only when he talks, it is not just idleness but stories of the sea, of the African campaign, of down South, or how to make up a multiple barge tow, or how to get work done better. He is always thinking up new ideas, and how to get around red tape. A conversation that he is in never lags. And he doesn't brag, he just tells the story of the day's problems and how he solved 'em. His laugh is almost noiseless, and when he laughs his eyes twinkle and myriads of wrinkles radiate from the corners of his eyes.

I believe he would die in six months if he didn't have some outside job to do that required physical combat. Probably if he could read this letter he would say, "Where do you get that horseshit?" But just the same he is as I have written of him to you. Somebody must have told him that Stoneburger was a lawyer and that I "taught" in a university, for he seems a little in awe of the tremendous amount of books we must have read and the things we know, but Stoneburger and I are as children compared to him when it comes to transferring barges from our tow to another ship at sea with a high wind kicking up the waves.

And that is the story of Lt. Reuben Roy Gupton—a real interesting guy. Just like the aviators I told you about, as long as we have guys like him on our side, the Japs will never bomb San Francisco and get away with it!

1/16/44

Dearest wife,

One afternoon in early January, Emersin went up to the warrant officers' club, the one near the submarine base, to drink some beer, shoot the breeze and generally pass the

time away. When he came back to the ship he had a little
pup with him, and the dog was drunk! He wasn't much
bigger than a one-pound package of raw hamburger. It
seems that they spilled beer on the table at the club, so they
put the little brown dog on the table. Whereupon the dog
proceeded to lap up the beer with gusto. He cleaned it up
so they gave him some more. Nobody knows there the dog
came from in the first place, but Emersin brought him back
on the *Tern.*

Emersin said when he and the dog started out, the dog
would walk two or three steps and fall down. Then he
would get up and walk right into the bulkhead. So Emersin
had to carry him. He brought the dog into the wardroom
and the pup started to walk in circles. He sure was funny.
He walked with a starboard list and he couldn't close his
mouth unless his tongue was hanging out. So he wandered
around sideways with his little pink tongue hanging like a
flag at half mast. Sankin picked him up to pet and cuddle
him, but the dog's breath was too strong.

Well, the dog was sober by the next morning and the
crew adopted him. Nobody knows what kind of dog he is
except he has short brown hair and his tail has just been
cut off. He is a dog that doesn't get seasick (at least he
hasn't yet), and he has proceeded to take over the ship. He
seems to be paralyzed or has nerve trouble for his neck is
twisted to one side and even now his tongue hangs out a
little when his mouth is closed. But he is a cheerful little
rascal. The crew named him Schlitz after the famous beer.
I hope nothing will happen to him, but probably his fate
will be the same as most ship pets. Everybody will feed him
and pet him and soon he will have digestive and nervous
disorders. And he will get sick and have to be destroyed.
Everybody will want to be nice to him, and too much attention will be the death of him.

The other night the captain congratulated me for the first time. In fact, come to think of it, I have never heard him come out and give a "well done" to any of us, but then that is to be expected for the captain is one who doesn't say much. As long as he doesn't say anything, you know you are doing right. But the other night, things were happening pretty fast on the bridge (I had the watch) and I heard the captain say, half to himself, "Atta boy, Luke." It is not often he calls me by my nickname. I think he is a little shy with all of us, for he is several years younger than all the officers but me. Usually he addresses us by our last name. In front of the men, it is always "Mister"

Every so often, someone in the Navy who has to do with morale—and I don't know who "they" are, those mysterious people somewhere who decide how things are to be done, what size toilet paper to issue, when to attack, width of bell-bottom trousers, and all those millions of orders and decisions necessary to run a Navy—sends us a box of paperback editions of books. The crew immediately grabs up the westerns and mysteries and sexy ones. Usually by the next day, all that is left are autobiographies, philosophy, economic analyses and *How to Succeed in Business.* Last week we got a shipment. One of the books was *Square Knot, Tatting, Fringe, and Needlework.* No one else wanted it. In fact the mess cook was gonna use it to set hot kettles on. So I rescued it. It is a nifty instructional book and maybe now I can learn to make purses, belts, cigarette cases and fancy underwear. At least I can pretend I will. I can hardly wait.

While on watch one moonless night I was looking at the glittering stars in the vaulted blue-black dome over the flat ocean. To the right and left the dome soared over me with height and distance after distance. Out yonder, way out, out there, up there, to the twinkling pinpoints of silence.

A voice at my elbow said, "Mr. Lucas, do you want a cup of coffee?" I turned my head and struggled back to look at the shape next to me. I could feel my brain laboring to return from those endless millions upon millions of miles where the stars swam, to understand what this sound meant. To come from out there, empty and free, weightless and speeding, to comprehend the shape of a cup and taste of coffee. Here, now on the steel deck, with physical sensations of heat and touch and smell and sight. Out there, only sight, and the impact of space, and dark and reaching, reaching, speeding, speeding, seeking, seeking, going, going.

I could see Aldebaran and Venus close together up above, yet in space they are 100 million actual miles apart. In one glance I saw 100 million miles with no time interval—at the same instant I recorded it somewhere in a brain cell in my head, and it registered, I knew it. I was here, but I saw it out there. I was aware of space and night and seeking, seeking.

God, I felt insignificant! Infinity has no bounds!

1/19/44

Dearest wife,

Gretchen, one thing we must not forget nor lose track of: $5 saved now, when it is plentiful, will be equal to $8 or $10 five or six years after the war. So don't be afraid to save. Rather than buy something not too special, let's bank our dough. Of course some nice thing which we have always wanted we will buy. But let's not spend recklessly. I figure that all the money I spent out here on things for you and Christmas presents were a bargain, and nice things we always wanted, and things I might not get the chance to buy again. But I've seen sailors go into town and spend $80 for a wristwatch they could buy at ship service for $50. Every town I have been in, people spend money like water, especially sailors. And five years after this is all over, many of them will be on relief.

Now for some news to make you envious. The captain finally got his orders to return to the United States. He really is happy for he had just about given up hope. I'm glad he got to go back—he deserves it.

1/21/44

Dearest wife,

The other day we were out at sea and there were large lazy ground swells. There must have been a big storm way off somewhere, for these ponderous rollers came regularly. I have been told that it requires the force of a constant gale wind blowing from a given direction without obstruction to build up the largest waves. Oceanographers call the distance that the waves have run unobstructed "the fetch," and when the "length of fetch" is 1,000 miles or more over the open ocean, these large swells appear.

The waves or swells were anywhere from 15 to 20 feet high and from the crest to the hollow maybe a little higher, but anyway it seemed the waves were standing still and the *Tern* was climbing up and down hills.

In the eight months I have been aboard this ship, we have never messed up on a job or got in trouble once. We have a pretty good record, and I just hope we can keep it up. As to that, only time can tell.

We bought Captain Parry a wristwatch. We had to buy it in town and pay tax and all, so it wasn't a real nice watch but the ex-captain was glad to receive it. Sankin called the crew to quarters on the fantail to make the presentation. It sure looked odd to see the men standing in two double rows facing each other with the officers between. As usual the wind was blowing across the clean, empty blue water, and it was hard to hear the words. You could feel the screw turning beneath us, and the slight vibration of the ship. I thought of all the different places those boys came from, to live and argue and be with each other a few months, and then perhaps never to see each other again.

When the captain left this morning, we put him ashore in the motor launch. His last salute to the colors was a snappy one and as the boat pulled away he stood facing the *Tern* until the boat was just a little speck, and I could no longer distinguish the occupants.

The new skipper took over at 1800 the other day. This is his first command. There wasn't any ceremony at all, and the old *Tern* never even stopped working. The new skipper, as I told you, is a former bosun and is now a j.g. He isn't 40 yet, at least he doesn't look it, but he has more than 20 years of service in the Navy and has been all over the various oceans.

He started off by stomping down hard on everyone. He is much stricter than Parry and much more demanding. About these things I have no objections, but about his personality, I do have. Of course you realize all this is forbidden talk, but I must let you know my analysis of him. First off he is a big guy. He has a big, broad nose with coarse nostrils, and overactive skin pores which make his nose glisten with oil and sweat. And he played football for the battleship *Pennsylvania* (I wonder what he would say if I told him I played football at Penn State.)

He is not a genteel person. He shouts at you one minute and then expects you to be chummy with him the next. I do not mind showing respect to a person but I at least want to be regarded as someone worthy of consideration, too. Fortunately the captain doesn't know anything about communications so I can run my department as I please so long as nothing goes wrong. I sure hope things work out okay. But the turnover of personnel on tugs is so rapid that this will last only a few months. Maybe you can head west in the summer after all, for when I make j.g. most anything can happen, and after a year or so out here, they sometimes give us new construction back in the States.

1/23/44

My dearest Gretchen,

The new captain is rigorous, I must admit. He keeps everyone working and on his toes—no slack. He writes the officers little notes on pink slips telling us how he wants things done. One thing I can say, each of us will get our ass chewed out regularly, just to let us know who is boss. For sure I am not letting him catch me with my pants down! As long as I do my job, he can't bother me much.

1/25/44

Dearest Gretchen,

Gretchen, one thing I have noticed out here: it is comparatively easy to tell the men who have been to sea long, especially if they don't wear sunglasses. They squint their eyes so much that creases or lines form like crow's feet at the corners of their eyes. Even when such men don't squint, the creases are white whereas the temple is tanned. I guess this comes from squinting the eyes at the sun and scanning the horizon and watching the sky for things that shouldn't be there. I wear sunglasses most of the time, but even so I notice little wrinkles are beginning to appear.

1/27/44

Dearest Gretchen,

Today I think I will tell you about the small boats and craft which are a necessary part and nuisance in any big port or harbor. Most any day one can look across the water and see dinghies, motor whaleboats, big motor launches, little motor launches, admirals' barges and captains' gigs. It always puzzled me why the admiral rides in a "barge" and the captain in a "gig" when both boats are the same, except the admiral has two, three, or four stars on the bow of his barge and the captain has nothing on his gig's bow.

Then there are landing craft of all sorts and sizes. There are fast picket boats which skim gracefully over the water, but probably the fastest and loveliest are the airplane-crash boats, which go very, very fast. Indeed, they must if they have to get to the spot where a plane might have fouled up in the harbor waters, if they want to aid the pilot before the plane sinks. These crash boats seem almost to fly. They make an enormous bow wave which curls beautifully out and upward as the boat skims along with only the stern in the water, and the boat seems to have white-green wings. Then there are little tugs which puff! puff! puff! But they get there just the same.

There are also Japanese sampans, which were appropriated for naval use. And there are pilot boats, which carry the harbor pilots back and forth. Besides these, there are all sorts of patrol craft which guard the shores. Throw in a few ferry boats, and you see what a job it is keeping harbor traffic straight. I have seen one outrigger canoe here. And there are little rowboats and punts (square-end boats with no bow or stern distinguishable each from the other). Then there are big tugs (harbor) and scows and most any damn thing. Once I saw some amphibious tracked vehicles, too. Time and again I have wished you could ride this tug with me to see some of the activity.

You can always tell a ship which hasn't been in before, because everybody is standing at the rail and they often have winter clothes on. It is interesting, too, to watch a big ship come in for she moves so stately and majestically. In the quieter waters of the harbor there are still fish. Several times I have seen a native workman standing in the bow of his little tug or dinghy ready to spear any stray fish he may see.

In any harbor the waters are often covered with debris of all sorts. Bottles, bits of wood, paper, oil, planks, anything that floats accumulates. So they have boats which go around collecting floating waste. They even have a launch they call Juicy Lucy. Lucy goes about the harbor skimming up waste oil which collects in corners. She is dirty and oily and really sloppy. The kids that run her get all messy with oil. But they don't seem to mind. They holler, "Make way for Juicy Lucy . . . make way for the slickest, smoothest gal around." And whenever she goes around the harbor everybody says, "Here comes Juicy Lucy." Everybody seems to like to say those words.

Oh, yes! I forgot to mention dredges and pile drivers and floating cranes. Now remember, these are just the miscellaneous stuff. I haven't even mentioned the big ships and little ships, for which the harbor was built in the first place.

So, there you have some idea of what the place is like and how busy it is.

1/29/44

Dearest Gretchen,

Our pup is getting ugly now and awkward. After much investigation, research and study, I am forced to the conclusion that the dog is not very keen. In the first place, he doesn't know his own name. In the second place, he uses the wardroom deck for a head. Also he has succeeded in getting fleas. A minor mystery is where did he get the fleas? Did we have them on the ship all the time? The dog hasn't been off the ship since we got him. Did he bring them aboard? The crew argues about the fleas. One kid said, "All dogs have fleas, always did, and always will." It was no mystery to him.

One of the fleas got on the dog's testicles, or where his testicles should be. Of course, he couldn't scratch said flea or fleas, so he bit at them. Unfortunately his balls got in the way and he nipped them thoroughly. Man, you should have heard him yelp!

I guess, too, the collar with a jingle bell isn't such a good idea for every morning about 4:00 he comes in the wardroom to scratch, defecate, urinate and do other necessary functions which are part of a dog's life.

After 4:00 A. M., when going to the head, especially in the dark, it is best to proceed with caution to avoid fording any ill-smelling rivulets that may be coursing across the wardroom deck, and to avoid running afoul of small, sticky, smelly heaps of dog manure. In the night-order book, we now have the notation: "Security watch remove dog from wardroom at 2315 and place aforementioned animal in box on boat deck; said animal not to be allowed access to main deck till 0715. Be sure dog has visited head before he enters wardroom in morning. Handle said dog with tenderness."

And every night a seaman from the security watch comes in the wardroom at 2315 and asks, "May I get the dog, please?" And he picks up the dog and leaves. Of course the dog looks at us reproachfully, but we cannot have the officers washing their right foot every morning because they stepped in something.

Everybody in the crew likes the little dog, I guess because he is so dumb and helpless. He visits different people according to the time of day. Early in the morning, when it is chilly, he seeks out our chief machinist mate, Shoal. The chief is an old Navy man and in the morning he is usually sipping coffee out of a thick white mug while sitting on his haunches against the engine-room bulkhead. (Rumor has it the black coffee is one-third whiskey, but where would an old Navy man find a steady supply of whiskey aboard a small U.S. vessel?) So the little dog goes back there and jumps in Shoal's lap to keep warm. When the mess cooks call out "Chow down," the little fella trots to the galley where the cook gives him a bowl of bread and warm milk.

Whenever we go near other ships, sailors bark like dogs to attract our dog's attention. Of course he gets all excited and ferocious and brave, but as far as I know, our dog has never been within 100 feet of another dog in his life (at least since we've had him). I must admit that he is a better sailor than I am for he hasn't gotten seasick yet. Maybe it is because his tongue is at half mast all the time.

1/31/44

My dearest wife,

The end of another month and still no sign of coming home. One thing I am thankful for is that the days go by so fast. Maybe they go by fast because we are so busy. Anyway the faster they go, the quicker I can get home and since this is what I live for, I'll be glad when the day comes.

Bosun Puregold (now Ensign) is also navigator and assistant communications officer now. So Karol is in charge of the deck hands. Of course, he knows comparatively little about the care of a ship, and since our new skipper was a former deck hand (bosun), he really tells Karol how to do things and keeps after him all the time. Poor Karol—he was walking around in a daze the first three or four days.

2/2/44

Dearest spouse,

Today I had the afternoon watch. The good, clean sea wind was moderate, the sun hot, clouds white and fluffy, sky and ocean a blue, deep blue. There were a few whitecaps and as we steamed along, we suddenly flushed a big school of flying fish. They rose out of the water like a flock of quail and went skimming along a few feet above the waves. They are slate blue in color and very graceful. The biggest was about 18 inches long and the smallest about 4 inches. We chased them quite a ways. In one place they sailed over a floating coconut hull and the whole scene suddenly struck me with loneliness and unreality. Here I am, guiding a ship in south seas off a tropical island with flying fish, blue ocean, whitecaps, and floating remnants of coconut palms. Jeepers, it was like something out of Kipling—me thousands of miles from home—I was suddenly aware how little we know what is in store for us and how unreal and unpredictable life is. Now I know why people turn to religion; it comforts them and gives them something to rely on against the unknown, the unreality, the fear and dread of what is to come.

You probably have heard on the radio about the Marshall Islands being attacked by "the strongest naval force of fighting ships ever assembled." The *Tern* helped them get ready. I saw them go and knew lots of them wouldn't come back. Yet I wanted to go, too.

Don't worry about any adventures I have. Our only worries are "perils of the sea," with now and then a report of a Jap sub in the vicinity. But so far, I have not even seen an enemy ship or sub. No, things are quiet with us. Ours is the drudgery of preparing gear for other ships and helping them get squared away, but we are too slow to keep up with fast-moving attack forces. Of course, if the Navy should have a serious setback with many ships injured, the *Tern* would probably get some excitement, but so far we have a routine and peaceable outlook.

Every time I see a baby picture I feel desolate. Our prime objective now is for me to pluralize you, so you have someone to keep you company, and be wise, and big and brave, and modest and skillful, and good lookin' and rich, like me. (If some censor should get ahold of this letter and read it, I can just hear him say, "Why that conceited bastard, how does she stand him?")

You asked about my weight. I'm glad to tell you I have gained. I now weigh about 148, as much as I ever did, and I am lean and hungry at 5 feet 10 inches. In fact I am sharp as a razor and as belligerent as a torpedo cruiser. Boy, would I love to torpedo you right below the belly button.

2/4/44

Dearest spouse,

Tonight we saw *So Proudly We Hail* with Colbert, Goddard, and Lake. It was all about Bataan. The bosun has been there and he told me much about the place. Several tugs of ours were there—the *Tanager, Bittern, Quail,* and others. They were all sunk or scuttled. I guess some of them put up quite a battle before they succumbed.

Gretchen, don't worry about me kicking over the traces against authority. I keep quiet and I get along fine. Only in my letters to you do I say such things. This duty isn't so bad, and I can learn to live with anyone. Before you know it I will be home.

2/6/44

Dear spouse,

I am typing this in the radio shack. I would like to write daringly, but the radioman is sitting right beside me copying traffic from the wavelength we guard. So I must be proper. Besides, I would rather express myself by actions than words.

I'm curious about your red hair. I hope it turns out all right. Only don't overdo it. In staid college circles, I like you to be proper and demure-looking, but when you get out to Frisco or LA or Hollywood, where no one knows you and you want to look chic, sexy, soignée, and whorish, well I can look at you and enjoy you myself for a while before we decide it's time for you to change clothes and become an ordinary housewife again.

Sankin and our new captain made j.g. at the same time, so they will be promoted at the same time. Sankin may be the only one who likes Himmel (our new captain), but even if he didn't like the captain, Sankin has been in the Navy long enough to know the smart thing to do is not admit it. As for me, I will do my job and keep my mouth shut.

The other day one of Emersin's old friends came aboard. They knew each other when they were machinists before the war, now they are both warrant officers. Anyway he went ashore in Chile and bought one dozen pair of silk stockings (two-thread) for some ridiculous price like 36¢ a pair. He took them home to his wife who blessed him adequately! Olsen says nothing down there is rationed and prices are low, low! I surely itched to go there and buy you lots of stuff.

One of the things that troubles me most is that during all this time in the Navy, I am not improving myself in any noticeable way, so far as genetics is concerned. Just think, if it were not for the war I would now have my Ph.D. But I must not complain. You bet your boots that after the war, I will get one!

And despite all cynicism and skepticism I am maturing mentally and molding a philosophy to guide me in years to come. I am developing self-confidence and the push that I need. I also look inward a great deal to discover what kind of a guy G. B. Lucas is—his motives, impulses, desires, and general conformation. I am aware of my shortcomings. At least more so, say, than in 1940, and I know my assets and liabilities. This sounds a little like anthropology or psychology or conceit, but you would be surprised how much thinking one can do aboard a ship that is mostly at sea.

2/8/44

Dearest Gretchen,

A hard part of ship handling is tying them up or making a landing. Yesterday we were coming in and I was officer of the deck. As we started up the channel the captain said, "Mr. Lucas, you take the ship in and tie her up." I had never done it before, but I took her in all right and tied her up to the dock, and I must say, I did fine. In another year I ought to be capable of being skipper of a ship like the *Tern*.

2/10/44

Dearest girl,

Every so often the ship service out here gets a shipment of
Bulova wristwatches for women. The last ones I saw were
nifty, dainty and feminine. They were 21-jewel and cost
only $39. They also had some 17-jewel ones for $28, I believe. That delicate Bulova sure would look nice on your
wrist. Then when I asked you the time, you could look at
that wristwatch and say, "We have 30 minutes before we
must get up and get dressed."

2/12/44

Dear wife,

Gretchen, I wish you could see rain squalls at sea. They
surely are odd. At sea we are in the center of a huge circle
with a radius of approximately 12 miles. When there are
scattered rain clouds, each will have under it fine vertical
streamers of rain. It seems as if the cloud is supported by a
pillar of rain. And just outside from directly beneath the
cloud, there will be no rain at all. Thus, if the rain clouds
are not too close together, one could almost steer the ship
in and out among the pillars of rain almost like winding in
and among irregularly planted hills of corn. You would be
in sunshine all the time, but if you miscalculated it would
be like walking underneath a bathroom shower. At other
times when there is wind, the rain will move toward you
with a solid front. Just like projecting a cylinder through
space.

The bosun told me of a ship that had to be towed
through the Strait of Magellan while a storm was raging.
So the skipper of the tug sent this message to the ship's
captain: "If wind and sea do not abate, I cannot tow

you through the Strait." And the skipper of the ship sent back: "So long as you have wood or coal, you'll tow me through, goddamn your soul!" Just another sea tale, but I liked it.

The food they serve us is good, especially when we are near refrigerator ships. Often we have quick-frozen vegetables from our freeze locker. But somehow foods aboard ship, especially if the sea is rough, do not have the "extra goodness" of home cooking, no matter how well prepared they are. I am surprised how finicky the appetite becomes. For instance, canned pineapple juice or sweet orange-ade can send me running for the head or rail (whichever is nearest), and I used to like them. Tomato soup, oyster soup, and shrimp have lost their appeal. Fried eggs and sausage are bad, too. But I just crave prunes, I eat some most every day. And I can drink great quantities of fresh lemonade. Even the smell of lemons seems an antidote. Sweet foods leave a vomiting feeling in my throat, but salty peanuts seem to settle my stomach. So I always have a can of peanuts open on my desk.

If I run out of peanuts, I sprinkle salt on the back of my hand near the base of my thumb and lick it like tequila drinkers do. This will pacify my stomach for a short time. I can eat anything in port, but out at sea I guard my diet as an aging movie queen would guard hers. It all boils down to the fact that when we are at sea I avoid certain foods.

Certain odors are bad. In a closed room, cigar or cigarette smoke is particularly obnoxious and nauseating. It causes my temples to throb and my eyes to burn; the acrid, penetrating smell gives me a headache right now. I can even *smell* the blue color of smoke. At least I think I can. Paint smell is another thing, or the musty smell of stored provisions. In fact, I don't go below decks at all during rough weather unless I have to.

Something else I must tell you about are the albatrosses. They are a dirty brown with a wing spread of three to six feet. In flight they are a beauty to watch, especially while soaring, which they do effortlessly. In rough weather I never see them but on other days they are numerous. They skim over the waves turning and wheeling. Never yet have I seen their wing tip touch the water, although they soar for 100 yards or more, circling and wheeling, and never more than a foot above the waves.

2/14/44

Dearest Gretchen,

Wife, please make me a pair of pajama bottoms. Just the bottoms, not the tops. The tops are practically new, but my three pairs of bottoms are showing signs of wear. Another thing, try to get a drawstring that is at least one-half-inch wide. Drawstrings the width of shoelaces are too narrow.

I can sympathize with you, wife, about our separation for I know well how you feel. You and I are caught in a trap and all we can do is wait till we get loose. We belong to the middle class, and the middle class is always the sucker when it comes to war. They are the folks who pay the taxes, whose sons get killed, and whose homes are ruined.

My release is to go off by myself every chance I get and just do as I please. I never make a liberty with anybody from the ship because, Christ, I see 'em 24 hours every day, and that's enough. I don't know what you can do to rebel. I hope you don't get drunk (I know you don't), and I wouldn't like you to date anyone. There is only one word of caution I would like to give you. Don't rebel so violently that you will do something drastic which you will regret later on. God knows I am tempted often enough, but I am proud to say you are the only one, and I mean that. Since I have been out here I have heard many stories of infidelity and unfaithfulness, and I have seen the results of some of it. I hear all sorts of stories of fellows here moving in with other men's wives as soon as the husband's ship leaves.

Gretchen, I want you to know that I have complete confidence in you, and I know how you miss me, and how dull life is, and how exasperating it can become, but my sincerest advice is to hang on—sweat it out, our day will come.

2/16/44

My dear wife,

When the moon is full out here, the nights are unusually beautiful. I have written you before about their spell and how my thoughts leap across thousands of lonely ocean miles to the couch which you keep warm for me. Many, many times I have thought how entrancing it would be to sneak into your room some night, quietly undress and crawl in beside you. To put my arms around you, feel your nakedness against mine, your breath on my face and to stifle your cries of surprise and delight with ardent kisses would be recompense enough for our long separation.

I must raise my opinion of the dog. He isn't as dense as I first thought. He is developing into a compact terrier type with short brown hair. He is agile, never gets seasick, is always cheerful, has dark, alert eyes, and is absolutely the most friendly critter I have known for a long time. He is the most popular man aboard.

2/20/44

Dearest girl,

Your letters come through regularly now. They take five to seven days to get here. They really hit the spot, and I read them again and again. I enjoyed the curly lock of hair. I looked at it in the sun and the only time it looked red was when the sun glinted on it.

Jeepers, we ought to be able to save $1,000 in 1944, especially since our combined earnings are more than $300 per month. But to get to the budget. Just for criticism, I will pick one item: underwear $32.30. Sweetheart, if you spent that much, you must have some sexy, slinky skivvies to show me. I guess I haven't realized how clothes prices have risen in the States.

2/22/44

Dearest Betty,

You spoke of vapor trails. I have seen them often out here. I never tire of watching the antics of planes and aviators. One favorite relaxation of these young aviators who are full of piss and vinegar is they buzz airports, ships, people, towers, anything. Out at the famous beach, I have watched four-engine bombers, two-engine bombers, fighter planes, in fact most every kind come zooming along barely 100 feet above the water. One guy kept diving on a place for over an hour. He would get way off from the place, come screeching in and down, and then pull up on one wing. From where we watched he was lower than the trees. He buzzed the place seven times while I watched. Often, too, when we are out, various kinds of planes will take a dry run on our ship. Torpedo planes will come sneakin' up on us just above the water. Man, they bear right down on us and finally veer off or pull up to clear the mast. They make a terrible racket as they go by, and the pilot will be sitting in the cockpit grinning to beat hell. And often I have watched seaplanes take off. They come quite close. And I see practice dogfights often, or a bunch of pilots, say six or eight planes, will play follow the leader. Jeepers, they go way, way up and make S curves and circles and all sorts of figures. I'm sure you would be enthralled at all the diverse, multitudinous variety of air activity which is a part of every day. They get so common I hardly bother to look up unless it is particularly interesting. But I'll remember to tell you all about it before we go to sleep at night. I sure got lots to tell you, wife.

Our dog has a new collar. The nameplate reads "U.S.S. *Tern.*" Some guy offered Emersin $5 for that dog, but Emersin wouldn't take it.

On one of our sister tugs there is a bosun's mate who gambles, drinks, and chases women. He is a rough one, a typical sailor who goes ashore, gets drunk and carouses in general. The other evening just before the movies I overheard him talking to some other sailors. He had just come back that morning from a liberty of debauchery and drunkenness, and he had a terrific hangover. He said, "There is nothing in the world uglier than a completely naked woman. Now, if they have on just a pair of shoes they don't look so bad, but a completely naked woman is the ugliest thing I ever saw."

What do you suppose he did and saw on liberty that made him utter such a philosophical deduction? I don't agree with him.

2/23/44

Dear spouse,

Things in the Pacific are beginning to pep up, and I don't believe they will slacken off any. However, our ship continues in the same old way, doing our job by working for these and them, and going here and going there.

We have a boy who was just rated quartermaster third class from seaman first. This kid is young, and you can tell by just looking at him that he comes from a nice family, for he is clean and fresh and innocent-looking. He is only about 18, and hasn't been around too much. I can tell the old sex appetite is beginning to assert itself in him, for whenever the more blasé and rough guys start to tell of their sex experiences in various parts of the world, or dirty jokes, why this kid will listen furtively and sort of ashamedly, but eagerly just the same, although he hates anyone to catch him listening. Well, as you know, a quartermaster wears a helm, or steering wheel, on his sleeve to designate his rate, and if you don't know his name you call him Wheels, just as a carpenter's mate is Chips, and a gunner's mate is Gunner, and a signalman is Flags, and a radioman is Sparks, and a boatswain is Boats. Anyway, this kid got promoted so the fellas started to call him Wheels. Boy, does he like that! When we call him Wheels, he sticks out his chest and ass like a rooster.

Tonight we saw an education movie about Russia in the war. It was absorbing and thrilling and moving to watch. There were many battle scenes actually taken under battle conditions. I was particularly pleased that the enlisted men in the audience paid such close attention to the picture. It is good for these men to realize what the present conflict is all about and how other people are fighting with and for us. Like I always said we must, "Educate the people, all the people." But Plato and Abe Lincoln said the same thing long before I did. Now, how in the world did they get the same ideas I do?

I think of you constantly and our post-war plans. You know we put $1,000 in the bank this year. That will make a nice down payment on a house. We don't want too big a house at first, but we will build it so we can make additions to it as we make additions to our family. I don't know why, Gretchen, but for some healthy reason I get recurrent visions of you. I look at your picture and remember the warmth of you, your gayness, and vivacity, your pealing laugh. Sometimes at night, my hunger for you is so intense I cannot sit still, so I go out and pace the deck and let the sea wind cool my cheeks. Surely you must feel how often and intensely I think of you, for I do it as regularly as I breathe.

2/27/44

Dearest wife,

Perhaps you have read about it in the papers. Anyway, a custom has sprung up among U.S. sailors in the Pacific. It is becoming quite popular. Some sailors are now wearing *one* earring. They have the ear (usually the left) pierced and put a gold or some odd-shaped earring in it. Vasconcellis has one. On bushy bearded sailors they look fierce and exotic. But usually the type of guy who wears the earring is the same guy who likes long sideburns, a moustache and tattoos. At first I was surprised, but as I've said before, no telling what a U.S. sailor will do once he sets a mind to.

My night watch is from 2:00 to 4:00 A.M., a very inconvenient time, for it really breaks up a night's sleep. Before dark I check my leather jacket and see that my pencil flashlight is in the left-hand pocket. Then I hang it inside the locker where I can easily get it. Next I get out my blue sweater that girl from Pennsylvania knit me, and lay it on my desk where I can get it easily, for it may be cool tonight. And I get out my overshoes just in case it rains. Just before dark, I take a turn around deck. Low scudding clouds portend a black night. I go to the radio shack to see how things are running. As I open the door to the shack, all the lights go out; I shut the door, lights go on, and the operator on duty looks around. I hear the shrill dots and dashes coming from the earphones; coming out of the gray dark ether of the blanket of night. It is a comforting sound, for I know it is our contact with safety, aid and succor (if need be). It is cozy in the shack, with all the dials and receivers and noise and different lights over gauges. Nothing much is coming over so I go outside. Below me I can feel the engines pulsing and beating and hear the ventilators blowing and the noise of the waves against the hull. I go down on the main deck and talk awhile in the darkness to some of the men who are batting the breeze and waiting to go on watch. About 2030 I turn in, not because I am sleepy but because there isn't anything else to do. I undress in the dark. I put my clothes where I can get in them in the dark. The ship is rolling normal, which is bad. I lie in the bunk in the darkness rolling back and forth. Finally I wedge one leg in behind the mattress and the bulkhead and that stops me from rolling pretty well. I think of my wife and how nice it would be to be home and I remember how she laughed, and how tall and well built, and I think of kissing the twins, and I long for her body. Finally, I drop off to sleep; I am awakened by a voice in the darkness.

The black silhouette of the security watch who has awakened me goes out of the wardroom to call someone else. I pick up my wristwatch from where it is hanging on the bulkhead. The luminescent figures are dim, 0148. Out on deck again it is pitch black, and chunks of phosphorous seem to be floating in the water. On the bridge, the wind is howling. Sparks and bits of phosphorous glow and gleam in the water as it slaps against the hull of the ship. It is dark, and no stars can be seen. The sky is just a lighter shade of black than the sea. I hunch my shoulders against the wind and rain, and I am glad I bundled up good. Now and then I hear the helm creak as the steersman fights the wind and sea to keep the old bird steady. It is real chilly up there in the wind. I remember how warm you are and how I would enjoy crawling in beside you.

The time wears on slowly. Finally, the security watchman goes below and calls the new men to relieve the watch. I crawl into my bunk in the dark. It is 0355. I lie down and soon, despite the roll, I sink into a slight slumber. When I next awake, the mess boy is setting the breakfast table, and a gray white dawn is breaking.

That's something of how it is, wife. Nothing much happens usually (for which I am thankful). When I think of all those fellas sleeping down below relying on us (and me, especially) on watch to make sure they don't wake up in the water, why then I get scared a little bit. But this is safe duty we have.

2/28/44

Dearest wife,

Still the dreary days of sameness. Still the same dull, dreary days—flat and unexciting.

Before I became a member of the *Tern,* she spent some months on a tour of duty about 1800 miles south of here, near a well-known romantic island. Some of the crew came to know some of the maidens ashore and occasionally receive letters written in French from their amours of yesterday. On one such occasion, a young sailor diffidently approached me making sure no one else was near, and asked me to translate his letter. As I slowly read the letter, the sailor bowed his head and softly scraped the toe of his right foot back and forth across a rivet head in the steel deck.

Spouse, it is grand that you can build your own clothes so economically and use a sewing machine so well. By golly, when Jack Vinson and you and me collaborated in the purchase of that instrument, we saved more than I knew. Like the blouse you made for much less than the purchase price of $20, and pajamas for me, and skirts and slips. I guess you are mechanically inclined.

And I would like to incline you across a bed right now.

About sending your sister a Pullman ticket, do so, by all means. Hell, we can afford it, and now that we have the chance to do things for others, let's do it. I don't like to think of her riding in a day coach, which in Europe is third class, so send her a Pullman ticket. And considering how hard it is to get meals on trains, why don't you suggest she bring along a lunch or two just in case?

I'm glad you like the "go-aheads." They call them go-aheads because if you walk backward in them, they will slip off your feet. They cost $1.50. Not bad for a pair of Japanese bedroom slippers.

3/3/44

Dearest wife,

During bad weather we live mostly on sandwiches, coffee and soup, which we eat out of cups. There is an iron rail around the top of the galley stove. The cook ties the pots to this rail, when the ship is rolling badly, and thus the pots will not slide off. But if they are too full the contents splash out, hit the hot stove surface and fill the galley with steam and burnt food odors. Usually the cooks don't serve anything fancy in rough weather, and there aren't many who have big appetites, anyway. The cooks must be careful, too. Oftentimes they get thrown against a hot stove or pot and get burned.

Sometimes, during rough weather, in the wardroom the drawers slide out of the cupboards and spill their contents all over the deck. As you come in the wardroom, the table and chairs are in a heap in one corner.

Once I saw a signalman slip and fall on the port side of the bridge. He lay on his side and slid, as the ship rolled, over to the starboard side ending up with a bang against the windshield. Boy was he surprised!

When the wind speed is 10 to 12 knots, whitecaps appear. I have seen that. When the wind speed is 20 to 25 knots, the wind begins to blow streamers of water across the tops of the desolate lead-colored waves. I have seen that. And when the *Tern* gets in the trough of waves created by strong continuous crosswinds of gale force, she will roll 42 degrees from the vertical. I have seen that. And when she rolls like that she dips her rail. In such weather we forbid the men to vomit over the side, for there is great danger of them falling overboard. So they must stay inside and vomit in a bucket which is emptied at the first opportunity. Only don't throw the contents *into* the wind!

3/5/44

Dear wife,

Well, one year ago today I was commissioned ensign in the U.S. Naval Reserve. And immediately afterward I was on my way home to you and an enjoyable ten days. It seems such a long time ago, and I am so anxious to see you again.

The other day the captain called an officer's conference, ostensibly to discuss crew morale. He told us to talk frankly, and boy we did! We snowed him under with bold facts concerning his methods, demands and treatment of the crew. But he asked for it, and he got it. So now things are much nicer, and I hope they stay that way.

Recently for several days we had to assist a disabled aircraft carrier that could not steer properly. To add to the trouble, the weather was stormy.

Now life on a small ship is inconvenient, to say the least, during protracted heavy weather. When it gets rough we close all hatches and doors. As a result it becomes moist, damp, smelly, and sticky. The men come in out of the storm in damp or wet clothes and track all over the deck in their wet feet and soon the wardroom and cabins are a mess. After three or four days of such living one is anxious for a change and when the sun finally emerges and the waves flatten out, life assumes normal proportions once again. But during the storm when one man out of three is sick (even Emersin went light on the food), and only the essential work is done, there is much time for thought. Geez, I had a headache for three days and my stomach seemed to run to an evil shade of green. I could eat, but it was all tasteless and I forced everything down. Then too, besides fighting the sea, we had a tough and important job and were under tension. All in all it was the most miserable six days I have put in yet for the Navy. It will be an excellent story to recount to you in future years. I stood watches, ate, and hit my sack.

Of course, I couldn't sleep all the time with the rolling (bad rolls, too) and pitching. Jeepers, the bow would raise way up in the air, then drop out from under to thud into the trough with a quivering shudder. Then when the fantail raised up, the screw would come out of the water and speed up and groan and quiver. Foam everywhere, and spray and waves and wetness and salt. Well, to take my mind off the predicament, I would lie in my bunk and think of you and sex. I laugh now to think of it. For the primary reason I thought of sex was not essentially to recall or anticipate the joy and ecstacy but to remove my mind from present surroundings. Can you imagine me relegating sex to a secondary position and using the imagined scenes not for sex pleasure, but as a device to avoid thinking of being seasick and big waves and howling wind. Then too, I thought of autumn at home, and picnics and green grass, and apple blossoms, the scent of plowed earth, haying, dances at Penn State, football games, picking apples, planting cabbage, anything with good old terra firma as a basis. What a time!

And the wind! Jeepers, it was a living, tearing, insistent thing which roared in your ears and yanked at your coat and slapped your face. It blew and blew and I felt like shouting and beating at it to make it subside. It really was a coincidence, our biggest job yet, and the worst weather yet to do it in. Mr. Puregold was taking headache pills. Stoneburger was a pasty white color. Karol was generally disheveled. And a seaman suggested we name the dog Shitalot, for obvious reasons.

To show you the difference between a big ship and a little ship, one morning when we were taking waves over the bow and rolling and pitching and most everyone sea sick, I looked over at the big carrier near us. To my surprise, there was group of men—a hundred or more—lined up on the flight deck doing calisthenics!

3/7/44

Dearest Gretchen,

The seasick, storm-swept days are over and things are back to normal again. But I won't forget those six days in a hurry. The baker couldn't bake any bread. It was too rough! We ran out of eggs and fresh fruit, and started living off canned food. Things came up too unexpectedly, we had no chance to stock up properly. We left in such a hurry we had to get along as best we knew how.

With Emersin gone, I am the new mess treasurer. I buy all the fresh stores for the wardroom. Today I went to the Navy commissary and shopped. I was buying with wardroom money, so I didn't skimp, I bought the best.

Today the Bosun told me a real funny story about China duty. It seems there was a U.S. gunboat stationed in China for a long time. When the captain anchored the ship, he always used the port anchor. Well the crew got hard up for beer, and since the captain always used the port anchor, why they traded the starboard anchor off for beer. And they had a Chinese carpenter make a *wooden* anchor exactly like the steel starboard anchor. The carpenter did a good job, and the crew put the wooden anchor in place and painted it good as new and no one knew the difference. Well the old skipper got relieved and a new one came aboard (just like our ship). The first time they had to anchor, the new skipper said, "Prepare the starboard anchor for use." The crew said, "Oh, Captain, why we never use the starboard anchor—we always use the port anchor." "I don't give a God damn what you use, I'm using the starboard anchor," said the captain.

The crew sighed and carried out the preparations. Then the captain said, "Let go the starboard anchor" (the wooden one). They let go. The captain said, "How does she tend?" Whereupon the man on the fo'c'sle said, "Anchor is slowly *floating* aft, sir."

At this point I laughed so loud, the bosun never did get to tell me about the look of surprised puzzlement and bewilderment on the captain's face as he rushed to the side and watched the anchor go drifting by.

Dearest gal,

Time magazine for March 6 reported on the ancient, B-class movies the Navy often shows its men. It's true, for I have seen lots of them. In this same article it says that Pearl Harbor, Kodiak and Noumea are "country club" duty. That may be true for men based ashore at these bases but not so true for ships that work out of those bases.

Karol is going to be our new executive officer, a tough job to fill on this vessel now. Sankin has received orders to leave. He may not get back to the States, for they may re-assign him out here to another ship. Jeepers, I hope they don't do that to me when I make j.g.

Dear Betty,

Our dog has signs of mange, so one of the sailors bought some mange medicine (with a tar base). Every day Chips, our chief carpenter, and one of the men put the dog on a bench and rub the "dope" on the dog. They rub it in good to be sure to get it next to the skin. During all these ministrations the dog stands with his head up, posing for all he is worth. Usually a crowd hangs around to watch, and you can just see that dog feel important. He stands there pretending to ignore the rubdown and just a trifle impatient as if to say he is a busy dog, but he will put up with it. All the time they rub him he pretends to be keeping a careful eye on something off in the distance. He surely is developing an ego.

Just recently I saw magazine previews of *Lady in the Dark*. Boy, if you had costumes like that! You and I shall be completely uninhibited on our honeymoon. Our sole object should be to rediscover our love for each other; to find new depths of experience in each other, to probe ever deeper into the bliss of each other, and to melt and fuse into creating a third, who shall carry in him the best of both of us. I want a baby now as much as you do, spouse. We need kids so I can tell 'em lies about how I won the war, but I won't be lying when I tell them I love you.

3/17/44

Dearest Gretchen,

Here it is St. Patrick's Day, but it isn't much different from any other day. The four-leaf clovers you sent came in handy. I gave one to Emersin and one to Mr. Puregold. They were glad to get them. I kept the five-leaf clover for myself.

Occasionally when sailors go ashore, they get tanked up. Out here the bars sell mostly imitation or synthetic liquor and it is pretty hard on the guys. It knocks 'em out quick and cold. But what gets me is the way the fellows take care of each other. Men come off liberty and one guy will be crapped out solid, but his buddies will be carrying him back to the boat landing. They lay him down, wait for the boat, then place him therein and take him back aboard ship. They take care of each other to keep out of the hands of the shore patrol. The SP's are pretty decent, but if they pick you up drunk they must make a report, which results in the man going to mast to be punished. So whenever possible, they look the other way and give the sailors all the breaks.

Saw two good movies recently: *A Guy Named Joe* and *Thousands Cheer.* The Navy must be getting on the ball, showing us movies less than 18 months old. I like Spencer Tracy but the plot was pretty farfetched. *Thousands Cheer* was more my type. It was in technicolor and Lena Horne, Eleanor Powell, Lucille Ball and Anne Sothern showed up well. I suppose you have seen it already. I get as much kick out of the sailor audience as I do the movie!

Dearest girl,

Before Emersin left, he and I performed a strange contract. He had Stoneburger draw up a legal paper complete with carbon copies, ship's seal, witnesses, and legal phraseology and mumbo-jumbo, whereas and to wit. It goes on and on, but finally I end up as owner of "one mongrel dog named PLUTO."

Now the ice is broken. This is the first time in my life I have ever legally owned a dog. God knows I never realized I would have to join the Navy to buy a dog (price: unpaid Coca-Cola debt of E. H. Atkynsen to be assumed by G. B. Lucas). And such a dog as I got! My! My! To make matters worse, Emersin *stole* the dog in the first place, so I am receiving stolen goods. But Stoneburger promised to act as both defense council and prosecutor in case anyone ever accuses me of accepting stolen goods. To wit, "one drunken, lopsided puppy brought aboard the U.S.S. *Tern* in mid-January 1944."

You asked if I have changed, and have you changed? We must wait and see each other before we can be sure. War is really meaningful to both of us now. We both know what anguish means, and good-byes, and loneliness, and exasperation, and frustration. We must never forget these meanings we have been forced to learn.

3/21/44

Dearest spouse,

Every ten days or so, I take the ship service car (a '34 Ford touring with no top) and go ashore to buy fresh stores. I enjoy it, for it is a half-day off, the drive is pretty, and it is a relief to be away from Navy reality. I wish you could see the Navy commissary. It is bigger than any supermarket I ever saw and has everything except fresh milk: quick-frozen vegetables, and butter by the gross, and beautiful, beautiful steaks. I'd like to watch your eyes bulge at the meat counter: no rationing and everything's cheap. Many different and exotic cheeses, a variety of fruits from tropical to temperate, loads and loads and loads of canned goods (just take all you want, spouse, and only the best 'cause we have to spend $50 a week on groceries), good candy, all sorts of drug and toilet articles, all kinds of bread and cookies, and all this without one ration stamp.

Once again you came through. You wrote words which sounded like a song to me.

3/23/44

Lovely Gretchen,

Probably the cruelest photography ever performed takes place in the piano-box stands which line the streets of any town crowded with servicemen. I knew you wanted a picture. I was walking down the street when I saw Polynesian Studios—while-u-wait. I walked in, and 12½ minutes later I walked out with the enclosed photo and poorer by 75¢. If ever I become conceited or swell-headed about my looks, I shall have another "study" made of me in a sidewalk studio. I can see, wife, that you didn't marry me for my good looks or the impeccable way I look in my natty uniform. Jesus, what a picture: tie hanging crooked, shirttail almost out, belt not neat, trousers wrinkled (only the second day I wore 'em, too), and my mouth awry. I tried to look humorous, but I guess he snapped it too quickly. Well, I'll send the picture, but I think I should have torn it up. Anyway my eyes look honest.

The other day I saw a girl who was part Chinese who had fingernails at least three inches long and painted a deep red. They weren't revolting, but I couldn't classify them as chic either. Also I saw race amalgamation "in vivo." An attractive Chinese gal got on the bus, and right behind her was an Army sergeant, light complexion and typical American. He carried a child wrapped in pink blankets. They sat down together, and I could tell the way they talked to each other that they were married. The girl was refined-looking. I wanted to see their baby but it was all covered up. As I sat there covertly watching them, I just imagined to myself how similar marriages were, and will, take place all over the world. I believe that with such speedy transportation as we have now and the migration of millions of young men (with big appetites) to far places, that there will be many such matings, lawful and unlawful, and that this global war will be a big step in the scattering of new seed, new genotypes and the creation of many new hybrids. But so far as I personally am concerned, I am content to hybridize you alone and I sure wish that day would soon arrive.

3/27/44

Dear Gretchen,

I see Emersin now and then. He is still nearby and likely will be for some time, so far as I know, unless his ship or mine is ordered to follow the westward thrust. This could happen, for they need tugs now, both old and new.

The other night I dreamed I was wrasslin' you. Boy I really had you where I wanted you and you couldn't get away (I guess you didn't try very hard). Anyhow, it all seemed so real I could almost feel you, and it was good, good, good!

I guess you are thinking that all I think about is sex. Well, it is mostly, but sex to me is you, and, since you are the biggest part of me, it all reduces to the concentrate that I think of you all the time.

3/29/44

Dearest spouse,

I am not kidding when I say that I probably will get to go home for a while when I make j.g. Assume I make j.g. on June 1 (perhaps even May 1), well I will have been out here 13 months and no leave since March '43. When Stoneburger and I make j.g. we will have four aboard (Stoneburger, me, Himmel, and Karol). This is too many for our complement. And if any of us get transferred, it will be I, for Stoneburger is now navigator. (I would have been, only they had no one to take communications.) Baxter is now assistant communicator and he would take over communications, but no one could take over navigation except Karol, and he is exec. Besides all this, the captain will probably be glad to transfer me and Stoneburger.

3/31/44

Dearest wife,

Sometimes when we are in at night, we tie up alongside other tugs. We put bumpers made of thick rope (called fenders) between the ships to keep them from rubbing, but sometimes when other ships pass by, we rub anyway and bump, due to waves. Well, the other night we were tied up alongside another tug. They have a dog, too, a female mongrel with some collie in her makeup. She tried to jump from her ship to ours but fell in between. It was evening and several guys were sitting along the decks of both ships. They saw the dog fall and they hollered for help. She fell in the water (I guess there were eight or nine inches of space between the ships), but any second the ships might bump and crush her. Well everyone came a running, from ensigns to mess cooks. And what did we do? We all pushed and pushed—there must have been 20 or 30 of us—and we held the ships apart enough till one sailor (it must have been his dog) slid down between the ships and grabbed the dog and handed her up to us on deck (a distance of six or eight feet). The guy would have been crushed, too, but without stopping to consider the consequences, he went after his dog and everything turned out safely. The collie dog sure had a guilty, shamed look on her face. The incident goes to show how attached the men become to pets. I guess the same is true concerning affection between shipmates or members of the same outfit.

Yesterday a new j.g. came aboard for duty. His name is Skogenlager, he is of Dutch extraction and seems to be a nice fellow. I was glad to see him, for we are short-handed. But strangely enough, Stoneburger got orders to leave. He is going to the officers' pool, which is maintained out here to fit out ships and replace officers. I don't know if he will get to go Stateside or not. The circumstances of the whole deal are strange.

4/2/44

Dearest girl,

Yesterday I received two letters from you and was glad to get them both. Your letters sorta sound as if you were actually talking to me, and make me feel close to you, even though we may be separated by thousands of miles. I know how attractive you are to other men, and I know how lonely you must get at times, and I know how much you would like to go out. So I am grateful when you refuse all dates and wait for me to come back. It gives me a safe, strong feeling to realize that you are mine alone, stalwart and faithful, and yearning.

4/4/44

Dear wife,

I must tell you more about Pluto. The other morning we went out and couldn't find him. So it was necessarily assumed that he had "jumped ship." Everyone was sore at him for going on liberty and not even reporting to anyone. When we came in that night, there he was, sitting on the dock as big as you please, and he didn't even have his liberty card. I guess the night before, he scrambled out on the dock and met up with some of those no-account "beach" dogs, and he ran around all night and didn't get back in time. So he was charged with being AWOL for 23 hours and 15 minutes. He is now confined to the ship and at present is sleeping on the wardroom deck. He is growing up fast, but so far as I can tell his hormones ain't working yet, for he still squats to urinate.

The other day I met a young ensign who went to Abbott Hall with me. He had been over in England and now they sent him here. He hadn't seen me since we had gotten our commissions. First thing he said was, "You've changed a lot. I wouldn't have known you if it hadn't been for the scar on your temple." So that night I looked in the mirror and I couldn't see where I had changed any. Of course, I am brown, but I have no beard and I still look young. You will have to wait till I come home before you can determine if I have changed.

Now for something that will surprise you. There is a boy on here who is enthusiastically religious and a member of the Salvation Army. He passes around little pamphlets on "How to Be Pure," "How to Conquer Sin," etc. I happened to read one about impure thoughts and how to avoid them. I decided to see if I could prevent myself thinking of wrasslin' you and poses, and sex. So I tried, and for the last three or four days, whenever I catch myself pondering on your "sensual seductiveness" I switch to memorizing semaphores or navigation, or I try to think of the binomial for potato (*Solanum tuberosum*). And I must admit I have succeeded somewhat, although not completely, for your letters throw me for a loss and you know how belligerent and lusty Luke is, but anyway I am glad to know that my brain is still dominant over natural appetites. But even so I catch myself remembering the silky smoothness of your bare skin and I recall how satisfying it is to feel your body cuddled up against mine in the security and warmth of a bed on a cold winter night. How good it will be to come to you again.

4/6/44

Dear Gretchen,

A couple of months ago we acquired a new messboy. His name is Johnny Lee Stolbur and he is about 17 or 18 years old. Whenever he has to work, he has only two speeds, slow or stop, and it takes him an awful long time to get to the end of a sentence when he talks. When he walks, he shuffles along just like an old man. But when it is time to go to the movies or go on liberty, he can skin over the side of the ship like a scared cat climbing a tree.

I like to hear Stolbur talk to Pluto. Stolbur talks to him just as he would to a friend. Half the time I expect Pluto to answer him, but he never will I guess. We have about 70 men on our ship and Pluto knows them all. But he can pick out a stranger right off, and he barks and growls at them.

Speaking of the number-one dog in my kennel—yesterday I gave him a bath. I expected him to kick and squeal and squirm, but he really surprised me. I took him in the crew's head and put him in the wash trough, which is big enough and deep enough for him to stand in. Then I soaked him good with water, and one of the firemen first class helped me soap him down. Ol' Pluto stood right there as if he enjoyed it. We washed his ears and face and from nose tip to tail tip. Then we "wrenched" him good, put him on the deck where he shook himself thoroughly, and the bath was over. I took off all my clothes but my shorts to wash him, and even so I got soaked. Can you imagine me bathing a dog?

4/8/44

Dearest wife,

Since we have only six officers aboard now, we stand regular four-hour watches. They seem more than twice as long as a two-hour watch. But last night there was a brilliant full moon, so I didn't mind too much. It was quiet. Only the creak of the wheel, the beat of the engines and the hum of the ventilators broke the silence. Sometimes while on the bridge like that with our dark ship, the only sign of life on the ghostly, lonely ocean makes one's imagination begin to work overtime. I get the odd feeling that time is standing still and all the cosmos seems to be centered on one tiny point. Sort of as if one is suspended (from nothing) in a vast black emptiness or void with no boundaries. Maybe the sea and the night have me hypnotized. I can't explain it exactly or even approximately, but I do know it is full of mystery, and the unknown, and unreality, and nothingness, and everything. How strange it all seems, and unreal and eternal, yet ephemeral.

Part of the time, we had the radio on tuned in to Radio Tokyo. It was quite amusing. First a man with an American accent spoke, then a man with an English accent spoke. They made foolish claims of our ship losses and told how well the campaign was going in India. But they made no mention of Japanese losses in the Pacific. Several times we have listened to Radio Tokyo, but usually the reception is bad.

It is time to eat chow, and we are beginning to roll anyway, and besides the end of the page approaches, and I have to go on watch, and I will write again soon.

The preceding are some of the excuses the men use to end their letters.

4/12/44

Dearest wife,

The last few days or so we have been busy. We never go far out, but we work from dawn till late. It's something like doing farm chores day after day. Only in this case we are "toilers of the sea," for the sea is our biggest opponent, and against him we are always pitting our strength and arranging our work so as to circumvent him best.

The ink smears on this page are the result of the salt spray which blew in the porthole. I forgot to close the port, and a few big drops of salt spray came in.

The other day we were coming home in late afternoon. We were heading north and the wind and sea were from the NE. It was rough, and occasionally a big wave would hit the starboard bow and the spray would go way up in the air. I had the deck watch. I saw a big wave coming. The quartermaster heard me holler and tried to cover the charts, but he got soaked, and so did the charts. The signalman tried to duck but hit his head on the gun mount. That knocked him down 'cause the ship rolled and he also cut his head open (but not badly). He fell on the deck and really got wet. Down on the main deck, there was about 18 inches of water flowing aft, and Pluto's doghouse was floating on it with the roof knocked off. The bridge of our ship is at least 25 feet above the water, so you can deduce that the spray bounced high in the air and it was a *big* wave.

4/16/44

Dearest wife,

When I was little, if anyone had told me that someday my wife would pay almost $20 for a pair of shoes, and I didn't even care, why I would say that I must have grown up to be a rich man.

As for getting me back in one piece after the war, we must be philosophical about that. Sometimes one must go out and meet fate or else cower forever in timidity and shame. I know I sound highfalutin and all that, but there is little actual danger for personnel of the Service Force except for certain infrequent moments. I know this letter sounds cryptic and mysterious, but try to understand anyway. And if my number is up, it is up, but I sincerely believe my chances of living through the war are 20 to 1 in my favor. So don't worry too much, spouse, everything is gonna come out fine.

4/18/44

Dear woman,

I surely wish you could see a battleship at close hand. You know how scared a dirigible makes you feel. I betcha a battlewagon would make you feel the same. Someday I will tell you the stories of Tarawa, Kwajalein, Eniwetok, Palau, Ulithi, Saipan that I heard. Here is one: A heavily constructed pillbox was literally blown to bits by a battleship salvo. That is, the top deck of the pillbox was blown to bits, but the below-deck underground was covered over with debris and sand as a result. Some Japs were down there but all the openings were buried in sand, so they couldn't get out. Well, our men left the Japs in there three or four days, or more. Then one marine wanted some souvenirs, so he got a pick and uncovered the pillbox. They dug through the concrete roof. When he finally got a hole through, the odor almost knocked him over, but two Japs in the box were still alive. They were crawling around on their hands and knees over the decomposed and rotting bodies of their dead companions. Awful, isn't it?

4/21/44

Dearest Gretchen,

Of late I have grown increasingly aware what an implacable opponent the ocean is. It is pitiless, relentless, never-ceasing, unconquerable, and restless. Yes, and even treacherous. Notice how I sometimes refer to the ocean as "it" and other times as "he" or "she." I see the ocean in many moods; it impresses me in different ways. Therefore, I use different genders for the pronouns.

As you know, we are a working ship and more concerned with sea labor than sea battle. Frequently the wind increases our worries (yet they call this the Pacific). Golly, the wind roars and roars and picks at you with insistent fingers, and it doesn't take long for the wind to get on your nerves. Then, too, in such weather the old *Tern* staggers and rolls like a drunken man walking across a ploughed field. And the spray dashes high in the air, the wind howls in the halyards and I must yell orders to the helmsman to make him hear. Truly the sea wearies a man, for she is never licked. Man gets tired, but the wind and unceasing waves scream out of the past, rant in the present, and tear into the future. Up and down, down and up, back and forth, blow and blow—wipe the salt spray off my glasses, hang on to the rail as she rolls and pitches. My! My!

My respect for fishermen has increased immensely. They who do battle year in and year out with such an eternal, implacable foe surely must learn early in life what strife really is.

I got the letter with your financial statement. I can't find a thing wrong with it. Food has increased in price, which is to be expected, but otherwise you are doing swell.

4/26/44

Dearest Gretchen,

For some time I have debated whether to tell you now that your birthday gift is a dress, but I guess I will. And just to remind you again, what is your bust and hip size? Don't alter the log but give me the actual soundings, because they are what I need. I'm reluctant to confess that I believe the dress is a bit daring. It has no midriff in the front and is called a hostess or cocktail gown. Of course the motif is tropicana. It is floor length, handblocked and launders well. Of course I want you to bring the dress with you, but if you have a chance to wear it to good advantage at some party, why do so. Only it sure gripes me that other men can see you in nice clothes, but not me!

Gretchen, now I must scold you a little. In several of your letters you have written you have no pep, ambition, life, etc. Now the worst thing you can do is to let this become chronic. I know life is pointless while you sit and wait, but you must exert yourself to spend the time profit-ably. Read up on all the latest dope on child care, experi-ment with new dishes and foods. I warn you, I have great expectations in your culinary ability and how you will feed me post-war. Read all you can find on how to build and plan a house, and look at plans for gardens. In fact, if I was strict, I would demand that you plan and furnish a house and send me the sketches. Read up on dogs and hobbies; join a sculpturing class. Ah, woman, I could keep you busy day and night. The main thing is, don't get in a rut of boredom.

Most of all I want you to learn self-discipline. Emotions are necessary to a loving, vibrant person, but the mind should be the captain. And no matter how much I lecture you wife, I love you 1,000 times more.

4/28/44

My dearest gal,

Why is it that sexy movie actresses soon acquire that hard, brassy look? Grable has it, Goddard has it, Rogers has it. I guess it is a lot of things, like living too fast, using too much makeup, not enough sleep, drinking too much, and seeing too many blasé, coarse things, or putting too much empha-sis on the body and not on the mind.

Just like I promised, I am gonna take up most of the space in this letter to tell you about taking Pluto ashore. I had to go to the Navy yard on business, and since the dog had been ashore so seldom, I decided to take him, espe-cially since he is a liberty hound. All Pluto has to do is see me put on my tie and, boy, he won't let me out of his sight till he sees me leave the ship, or until he knows definitely that he can or cannot accompany me. So one fine morning I called Pluto and said, "Let's go, boy."

I believe it is the first time he had ridden in the boat, so he got a kick out of that and looked about eagerly at everything. When we got ashore amid all the hustle and bustle, he certainly was taken aback and stayed close aboard the protection of my legs. In fact, he stuck so close to me that I kept stumbling over him.

Trucks, bicycles and scooters really puzzled him. And at one place a railroad switch engine was emitting steam in great gasps. Boy, old Pluto was scared and amazed at that one, and he sure was glad when we got safely by. When we got to the building where I had to do business, Pluto saw the first woman (a thin, unattractive stenographer) he had ever seen. I really laughed at him. First he would bark at her, then he would sniff from a safe distance (probably her perfume), then bark some more.

Later on, we came to a grassy place where some pigeons and starlings were. Pluto growled softly, then began to stalk them. Of course he couldn't get within 15 feet of them, because birds out here know all about dogs, and anyway Pluto didn't know what they were. And of course there were lots of posts and trees to be investigated where other dogs had left their calling cards. These really stumped Pluto, for even now he doesn't raise his leg. Well, we got back to the ship okay and Pluto trotted up the deck very satisfied with himself and his liberty.

4/30/44

Dearest spouse,

Recently I happened to be present when a group of natives entertained nearby. They were all women. The vocalists and instrumentalists were all big, tall and fat, but they could really sing. The dancers were younger and some were pretty. They had two little girl dancers, about 8 or 10 years old, who were really good. I can see how, at one time, these people must have had a pleasant, beautiful life with their customs and songs, all of which are coarsened and cheapened now by war and money.

It made me pensive and sad, for I began to feel that all things are transient and fleeting, and is anything secure? Life to me is a puzzle full of ill-fitting pieces. But knowing you and loving you has taught me to understand some of the pattern.

5/2/44

Dearest Gretchen,

I saw Mr. Puregold after an absence of several weeks. He is now navigator on a refrigerator ship. He says it is splendid duty. He expects to see his family, back in the States, more often now. He told me the boys out there were glad to see his ship pull in, for fresh fruit and refrigerated stores are more precious than gold, and almost as gratifying (in a sense) as the love of a good woman.

Wife, I don't (or won't) see why you should be so horrified at some of the things I say. They happen every day, multiplied 100 times all over the world. Personally I think each newspaper should have a big picture daily of some rotting body (Jap or U.S.) and a story of how so many men each day meet death. Then, if or when all the people become disgustingly, detestably aware of the stinking, miserable filth of both mind and body which are a necessary part of war, then soon war would be no more.

My life out here is comparatively a decent one, for we have good food and quarters, but I have seen a few men die sudden death (plane crashes) and I have come on the scene just a few hours after ship collisions, and I have been part of a few narrow escapes, and that is when I begin to realize that war is an evil, real, demeaning, unfair thing. And sometimes I wonder if the men in the world today between the ages of 18 and 40 aren't taking a terrible, terrible screwing, especially if they must die to help clean up a mess left by a few selfish, uninformed old men who were too busy filling their own pockets to care about what might happen later.

5/6/44

Dearest Gretchen,

Periodically all ships must go into drydock to scrape the barnacles off the hull and make needed repairs. In the Pacific there aren't many drydocks, so the Navy is building floating drydocks (they look like large rectangular boxes) to be used in Pacific anchorages. Usually a commercial tug tows them from the U.S. to the mid-Pacific, where we assist them into port. This takes careful handling and good seamanship, for the drydocks are awkward and difficult to move. Let me tell you, when three or four tugs take hold of one of these monsters to bring her into port, there is no foolishness. Usually a harbor pilot is in charge and he will chew out a tug captain the same as he would a seaman. And everyone around can see and hear. It wouldn't surprise me if later on the *Tern* were given the job of towing one of these babies to a forward area.

The other day I talked to a tugboat officer who has been out here 67 months. He surely wants to go home. I guess he will soon, for he certainly deserves it.

Because I am a censor I read 10–20 love letters every day. Most of them seem to be manufactured by the same machine, but how inadequate words become when one person endeavors to convey the longing and desire he has for someone with whom he has eaten, slept, kissed, argued and made love. To me, you are what I am fighting for (only we work, not fight) and my next big aim is to come home to you. Until then, all I can do is write you faithfully and say the same words over again and again.

5/10/44

Lovely Gretchen,

Pluto and I have just come back from a movie, and he is sprawled out on the deck on my feet as I write. We have been to sea a good deal lately, so after chow tonight I took Pluto for a walk (since we got tied up early). Neither of us had been off the ship for a few days, so it did us both good.

He does seem to be developing into a one-man dog, for no matter what he is doing when I whistle, he comes a'running. The past four to six weeks, whenever anyone teased or tormented him, why I always gave him shelter between my feet and I petted him (I never teased him), and I always took him ashore with me whenever possible and gave him water when thirsty. Pluto, as a result, now trusts me and whenever he wants respite from someone teasing him, he always comes to me. Of course he and I frolic a great deal, but I am always careful to let him win, especially in a tug of war with a rag, or squeezing out of a hold when I get him down. And after we are finished, I always give him some morsel. Three things he likes best are apples, peanuts and chewing gum. I hold an apple for him and he nibbles the whole thing until it is gone, and looks so solemn while he eats. And I hold a fresh stick of gum between my fingers so he can get only little bites, and he eats that, and I give him a peanut now and then. Also, I never laugh at him as the crew and officers do.

Pluto knows when they are laughing at him—you can tell by the way he holds his ears back and looks out of the corner of his eyes. So my general plan of attack is to shelter him, feed him and never abuse him. Consequently he is my dog now, and I can do most anything with him.

When Pluto is eating something and anyone comes near, he will growl fiercely and he means it, too. And if they persist, he snaps at them with bad intent. But so far he has never snapped at me, and he will eat from my hand. Whenever I drink a Coke, I pour a few drops in my hand from time to time, and Pluto solemnly laps it up. I believe he is almost full grown now. He is only about 15 inches high and 24 inches long, about the size of a Boston bull. He is quick and agile. I am really glad that Pluto came into my life. I'd like to bring him home with me, but like most shipmates, we live awhile together, then we must part.

It seems Emersin is going on a trip. Not a particularly dangerous one, so don't get alarmed. Also don't tell Madeline, for it will make her feel worse. Emersin's trip is nothing but a freight job, but it may be a long one. I had a bottle of brandy saved, which I was gonna bring home with me. But I suddenly realized Emersin would get a lot more kick out of it (and less headaches) than you or I, so I gave it to him as a going-away present.

I watched him as he walked away down the long wooden wharf, with the bottle wrapped in newspapers, tenderly cradled in his left arm. His right arm swung in stride as he walked. He was thin, had on faded khaki pants and shirt and a black visored cap.

5/12/44

Dearest wife,

Since I last wrote you, the new AlNav [a notice to all Navy personnel] came out. All ensigns who hold rank as of 4/1/43 are promoted to Lieutenant (j.g.) effective 5/1/44.

So my days as an ensign are over, provided I can pass the physical. The captain approved me with no fuss at all (which surprised me), and tomorrow I am going over to be examined. I can't lose either way. If I can't pass the physical, I must be given shore duty, and if I do pass, I get the promotion. So after the exam, which is not too rigorous, my eyes are the only thing to hold me back if anything does. I will sign my acceptance, get my silver bars and then be a j.g. Hurray! Hurray! Seriously, I don't feel any different.

5/16/44

Dearest wife,

Starting May 15 we are called ATO 142 (auxiliary tug old).

Yesterday on my way to go swimming I bought a *Time* magazine for the week of May 15. On the cover was a picture of Dr. Alex Fleming, who discovered penicillin. The caption read, "His drug will save more lives than war can spend." Right away I knew it would be a good write-up about him in the feature article, and little chills of pleasure pursued each other up and down my spine for I knew he was working on "antibiosis," which is one of Dr. Flintstone's pet seminar subjects and one which has been the source of many arguments on Wednesday afternoons at seminar. I also got a thrill because he was working with a fungus the same as I am, and probably with similar genetic laws. Now, Dr. Fleming also indicated that it would be strange if the first substance found were the best one. It is improbable that I will ever find any great healing drug, but there are infinite possibilities to investigate. For instance, why couldn't some strains produce more antibiotic substances than others, and why couldn't it be a genetic trait, and why couldn't heavy producing strains be bred, and why couldn't my wife do some of the chemistry of it in the lab with me in between nursing the kids? Probably the chemists will soon be synthesizing penicillin in great quantities, but just the same, many fungi produce substances, and since I intend to specialize in the genetics of fungi, why shouldn't I give the matter some heavy thought?

I urge you to read the article. The medicine editor of *Time* (or the guy who writes the medicine columns) seems to think Fleming will be accorded a high place in the ranks of famous men of the 20th century, and compares him to such men as Galileo and Newton.

5/26/44

Dearest Gretchen,

Now that I am lieutenant junior grade, do you realize I am earning $3,600 a year? *Jesus Christ!!*

Enclosed you will find two bonds—a $50 and a $25—I had enough extra money to buy both this month. Put them in the safe-deposit box with the rest of our valuables. I'll buy bonds every payday, if we are close enough to a headquarters ship to buy one, and send them home to you. It seems unreal to me to go aboard a big gray ship in these far-away, godforsaken anchorages and have some yeoman type out my name, rank and address. Then I give him $50 in green paper and he gives me back a piece of green and white paper, and I put it in an envelope to you. Ten days later and 5,000 miles away, you put it in a metal box in a bank I haven't seen.

Does all this have meaning? People transferring papers from one to another. Life certainly is confusing. We store away papers in little metal boxes. But the practical part of me replies, "Yeah, and if you get hungry you can exchange those pieces of paper for potatoes."

Lucas graduated from Officers Training school,
Northwestern University, in Chicago, in spring 1943.

RECRUIT IDENTIFICATION CARD
U. S. NAVY RECRUITING STATION

OFFICE OF NAVAL OFFICER PROCUREMENT (NEW ORLEANS)
217-227 CAMP ST. **TO IDENTIFY** NEW ORLEANS, LA.

Name LUCAS, George Blanchard 551-24-74

Rate A.S.V-7, *U. S. N. R. Color of hair* Dk.Brown

Color of eyes Blue XII *Height* 69$\frac{1}{4}$ *in. Weight* 139 *lbs.*

Prominent marks ANT:S.$\frac{1}{2}$"rt.jaw;P.M.rt.hypochondrium;M.

lt.jaw;P.S.1/8"d.lt.lower leg;POST:S.1"lt.occipital;

VSLA.

Countersigned: *C. E. Word*

C. E. WORD, Lieut.D-V(S),USNR.

(OVER) 4—5097 V-7 *Recruiting Officer.*

"You're in the Navy now!"—Ensign Lucas's dogtags and official recruit identification card

In May 1943 ensign George and Betty visited her aunt and cousin in Long Beach, California.

Betty Boyd Lucas in 1943

Ens. George Blanchard Lucas, U.S. Navy, in 1943

BILL OF SALE

Know all men by these present, that I, Emerson Hogan Atkinson, party of the first part, a Kansas anti-prohibitionist, do this day sell, transfer and set over unto George Blanchart Lucas, party of the second part, a Louisiana prohibitionist, all right, title, use and benefit of one mongrel dog, named Pluto. In consideration whereof the party of the second part has agreed with the party of the first part to assume any and all debts of the party of the first part outstanding with the wardroom mess of the U.S.S. TERN; and in further consideration whereof the party of the second part hereby agrees to keep a man of the ships company of the U.S.S. TERN on extra duty for the purpose of acting as valet to the aforesaid dog named Pluto. In the event that there is no man eligible for the aforesaid extra duty, the party of the first part hereby agrees to furnish a man from the ships company of the U.S.S. TURKEY; and it is further agreed by the party of the first part that any such man furnished by him will be clean and respectable, to conform with the standards of the aforesaid U.S.S. TERN.

In witness whereof we have this 18th day of March, 1944 set our hands and seals.

_____ (seal)

_____ (seal)

Witnessed by:

Bill of sale for a mongrel dog named Pluto who was to become the *Tern*'s mascot.

A close friend of George Lucas, Emersin is seen here feeding the ever-present and loyal Pluto.

A crewman's sketch of a fleet tug of the bird class built during World War I. These durable workhorses saw extensive duty in the Pacific theater in World War II, with their normal complement of six officers and sixty-six crewmen.

Officers and crew of a fleet tug off Pearl Harbor in 1944. Pluto is featured prominently in the front row.

To celebrate their reunion, Betty sewed her own hat, purse, and suit "to look nice" for the occasion.

Many sailors on board the *Tern* carried good luck charms. Betty sent this five-leaf clover to Ensign Lucas for St. Patrick's Day 1944.

Ancient Order of the Deep

This is to certify that

......Lt.(jg) George B. LUCAS......, U. S. Navy, R.

Was duly initiated into the Solemn Mysteries of the

ANCIENT ORDER OF THE DEEP

HAVING CROSSED THE EQUATOR ON BOARD THE

U. S. S. T E R N , ATO 142

LATITUDE .OO=OOAT LONGITUDE .WAR ZONE.......

Davy Jones   Neptunus Rex

His Majesty's Scribe   *Ruler of the Raging Main*

Ensign Lucas was proud of this testimony to his having "crossed the line," a Navy ritual at a sailor's first passage across the equator.

31 July 1944

Last Will and Testament

I, George Blanchard Lucas, being of sound and disposing mind, memory, and understanding, do hereby make, publish, and declare this my Last Will and Testament, hereby expressly revoking all other wills or writings in nature testamentary by me at any time heretofore made.

FIRST: I direct that all my just debts be paid as soon after my decease as may be found convenient.

SECOND: I give, devise and bequeath all my property, real, personal, and mixed, of whatever nature and wheresoever situated which I may own or have the right to dispose of at the time of my death, to my wife, Jennie Elizabeth Lucas, absolutely, and in the event that my wife, Jennie Elizabeth Lucas, be not living at the time of my death, then to my sister, Nancy Jane Lucas, absolutely.

THIRD: I hereby nominate, constitute and appoint my wife, Jennie Elizabeth Lucas, as executrix of this, my Last Will and Testament and if she be not living at the time of my death, I hereby nominate, constitute and appoint my sister, Nancy Jane Lucas, as executrix of this, my Last Will and Testament.

FOURTH: I direct that neither of my said executrix, as the case may be, shall be required to give bond or other security in any jurisdiction, wherein proceedings may be had in connection with my estate.

IN WITNESS WHEREOF, I have hereunto set my hand and seal, this 31st day of July 1944, A.D.

George Blanchard Lucas (seal)

Signed, sealed, published, and declared by the aforesaid testator, as and for his Last Will and Testament, in the presence of all of us, who, at his request, in his presence, and in the presence of each other, have hereunto subscribed our names as witnesses, hereby certifying that this attestation clause has first been read to us and that the acts herein named actually occurred in the order specified.

1. *Denny Ray School.*
2. *Robert W Baxter*
3. *Norris J Stogerbo*

Under the pressure of wartime duty, Ensign Lucas drew up his last will and testament on July 31, 1944.

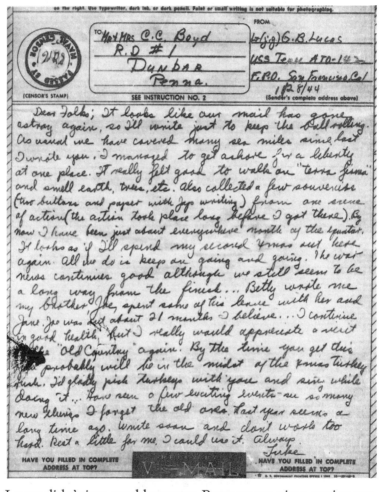

Lucas didn't just send letters to Betty on wartime stationery. Above (and following) are samples of his correspondence with Betty's parents and from his own.

No. _____

To
Mr & Mrs. C. C. Boyd
R. D. #1
Dunbar,
Penna

PASSED BY
NAVAL CENSOR
EHa

From
Ens. G. B. Lucas
(Sender's name)
USS TERN AT 142
(Sender's address)
F.P.O. San Francisco
3/17/44
(Date)

Dear Folks,

Betty sent me your letter to her about the secret of Pork sausage, & new innundated, continuity in writing, and birds. I can see now where Betty gets her loves of animals and flowers. It seems the more woe-begone a dog is the more she likes it. (I hope I did not impress her that way) Betty wrote me that u. will probably visit her in June. I hope so 'cause it will do them both good. If things work out properly I may get some leave this summer but I can't be too sure. I'm due for a promotion in May or June... Had a pretty rough trip a week or so ago. Very bad weather (I felt green inside for a week) and it was a pretty important job. However, everything worked out swell and it's all over now. We are getting sort of a rest the last few days... Wish you could see some of the sunrises and sunsets way out here. At least during my naval career I am learning something of the immensity and profoundness of sea, sky, earth & heavens. Stars are like old friends to me now, I know 'em well... I'm glad to hear your teeth problem is being solved. Your general health will be better as a result... I surely would like to do some farming for a coupla weeks. I betcha I could hoe more corn than anyone in Centre County (at least for the first 15 min)... You probably will have to use a magnifying glass to read this but they asked us to use V-Mail for the planes are over-loaded with mail.

As always Luke
G. B. Lucas Ens.

V-⋯-MAIL

To	From
Ens. G.B.Lucas USS Tern, AT142 Fleet P.O., San Francisco, U.S.A.	Ens. D.S.Humphrey USS SC-503 [Sender's name] %Fleet P.O.,N.Y.C. [Sender's address] December 10,1943 [Date]

(CENSOR'S STAMP)

Dear Luke,
    I received you card the other day. The family sent it to me and
it almost made the journey by Christmas. I was sure pleased to hear from
you. We had some cards for our ship, but the number was rather limited, so
I only sent out cards to members of my family. I'm rather amazed at seeing
your address, what's the story behind all that? As for me, much has happened since I last wrote you. By the way, did you ever get that letter? I
wrote it from Miami.After getting out of school in Miami I had four days
travel time and was able to get home for a couple days. From there I went
to Norfolk and stayed there for a while- about a week I'd say--and then
had transportation across to North Africa where I am now. I found my ship
over here. The trip across was very enjoyable. I came with a flock of other
officers and we had the best quarters available. We ate in the ship's wardroom and had very good food. We didn't do anything but sun ourselves and
read, or play cards. We couldn't have had a better setup. After getting into
North Africa we had to travel around hunting for our ships. Most of us
caught up with them at the same base so I had lots of friends around to keep
me company, which helped a lot. Most of us were in the invasion of Italy.
Our ship was right in the thick of things for a while.I've been through
a lot of air raids and once we were shot at. Lately, though things have been
fairly calm. I don't mind the calmness a bit. Got a short look at Italy,
but as yet haven't had tome to get a real opinion. From what I saw it is
a lot better than North Africa. I've seen Vesuvius, and at night it is
quite a sight. Also, saw the Isle of Capri which didn't appear to be all the
song cracks it up to be. I've(that is the ship) changed bases recently,
and although there isn't too much in the way of amusement, there are some
good movies here that make spending free time more enjoyable. I keep pretty
busy aboard the ship; there's a lotto do as you can well imagine. We play
a lot of gin rummy and the people at home send me all the old magazines
they can find, so I keep pretty busy and am seldom bored. Also, there are
a lot of books around to read if I ever get the urge. I like this duty oke.
[illegible]; our little cracker box bounces around a lot, but after a couple trips
one becomes accustomed to it and thereafter doesn't notice it so much. I've
gotten along well with the other officers aboard, and that helps. Saw Truly,
Clardy, and Mahoney at Norfolk. At Miami I saw all the lads who were scheduled
to go there, and whom I mentioned in my letter to you from there. Bill Boding
went to sound sound school as did Dick Cullen. Ralph Fields went to commissary
instruction class in Miami. I forget what happened to the other guys.
Well, Luke that is about the works for the time being. OH, yes, did I tell
you that Haydell wound up in Miami? At school with us. Best of luck to you
Luke, and give my regards to Betty. Drop a line if you find the time, I'd
like to know what you've been doing, as much at least as you can say. Haven't
heard from Harry as yet, have you? Hope you can read this attempt at typing--
no matter how bad it is it's better than my long hand,

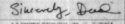

Sincerely, Dud

Betty and then-lieutenant (junior grade) George celebrated his assignment in May 1945 to a new ship—whose home port was Cape May, New Jersey—at the Copacabana in New York City.

5/28/44

Dearest wife,

You may remember back in December when I wrote you of meeting Henry George, former ag student from my class at Penn State and now a torpedo bomber pilot. Well today we got the May 1, 1944, issue of *Life,* and by golly, there were pictures of Air Group 9, to which Henry belonged. He sat at the same table with us and drank beer. A jolly fellow! The only other one I remembered meeting was the squadron commander, Lieutenant Commander White, shown with his wife and two kids. He is an Annapolis man and impressed me deeply as a capable, quietly spoken and efficient fellow. I got a kick out of seeing their pictures. I'm rather envious of them getting leave like that, but they deserve it and even now they are probably out here again "doing battle." We who are on the working ships do not get nearly the opportunity to return that the fighting ships do. But I guess those shore-based lieutenants, former psychology majors, who parcel out rest and recreation leave figure our prosaic existence does not inflict such a strain on the nerves as much as battle conditions do. Still, monotony can be more enervating and depressing than most people imagine, especially when one does not know how long this wearisome boredom will last.

By the way, I just saw in the paper where some gal was arrested for posing indecently for a picture with enlisted men. Another racket here is the little nook-and-corner curio stands which specialize in selling pictures that just barely pass the limits of decency.

It is easy to see the urges and conflicts which the hormones and pent-up energies create. Speech becomes coarsened, smutty and suggestive; tempers become short; drunks become more frequent; homesickness more noticeable. Also, it becomes apparent how much of an animal man is, and it is no wonder that crimes of passion increase and morals decrease in such times.

5/30/44

Dearest wife,

Last night Mr. Skogenlager drew up a will for himself (he is a lawyer just like Stoneburger). He is going to have it witnessed and sent home. Just to be on the safe side, I believe I will use the same form and make up a will for myself. So don't be surprised, amazed or alarmed if, in the near future, you receive a letter with my will in it. It is something which every man in the service should have.

6/1/44

Dearest wife,

Today I was the only officer to receive a letter. It was from you. I believe that is the first time I was the only one to get a letter. I clutched it like a gold nugget and hastened to the solitude of my tiny cabin to open it and devour its contents without interruption. To say the least, letters create a peaceable state of mind, even though not gratifying.

It will be difficult to get more pictures of Pluto. The pictures I sent you were taken by a regular Navy cameraman as a favor to us. Otherwise, cameras are restricted and hard to get, let alone find film to use in them.

Lately, he has learned how much adventure there is on the dock. Whenever we come in, he always puts his front feet up on the rail, waiting for someone to lift him ashore. He is a real "whorehound" now, too. The other day one of the chief firemen took him for a walk and he met a little she-dog, whom he quickly wooed and won.

The chief fireman was dumbfounded. When he came back he told me all about it in detail, and he said to me, "Mr. Lucas, he screwed like an expert. Now I ask you, where did Pluto learn to fuck?"

I said, "I don't know, are you sure he actually mounted her?"

That made him mad. His eyes grew big. "Goddamn it," he snorted, "Don't you think I know fuckin' when I see it?"

Anyway the word quickly spread and everybody looks at Pluto differently now. His good fortune is the most talked-about subject on the ship. There is continuous discussion about it. And the big question is "Does a man have to be *shown* how to do it?"

Of course every sailor aboard couldn't wait to tell about his first piece, where it was, how skillful he was, and so on and on. Myself, I didn't say much, but I thought a lot. I look at Pluto differently now.

6/5/44

Dearest wife,

Last night Mr. Skogenlager and I went into town late in the afternoon. One of our crew had been picked up by the shore patrol for drunkenness, and we went to the station to get him out. Oh yes! The patrol had a drunken (and thoroughly scared) soldier who had walked up to a maiden right on the street and familiarly grabbed a handful of the back of her lap. She screamed and the MPs stopped him before he got any farther.

After we finished our rescue, we went out to the famous beach to have dinner, the same place Bob Mack and I went to. It was grand with the cool sea breeze, the sound of waves, excellent service and tasty food.

Yesterday too, I had a talk with Bosun Puregold. He is

back after a trip south and west. He was glad to see us and has some interesting stories to tell. He invited me over to his ship tomorrow evening for dinner. He likes his job as navigator, and his captain is capable.

Perhaps I may be assuming too much, but I believe Puregold and I are kindred spirits in more ways than one. Someday maybe he and I and you and his family can meet somewhere under more normal circumstances.

6/7/44

Dear spouse,

Today at the picnic, an enlisted man from another picnic group came up to me and said, "Aren't you from Pennsylvania? Philipsburg?"

I didn't recognize him at first, but then I knew his name was Lownsend—Jim Lownsend. I hadn't seen him for five years. He has been married, has a little girl about two (he showed me her picture), and is separated from his wife. He has been out here only since March and is an electrician third class in the Seabees. We talked to each other about home and all the gossip. He says all the boys have gone from home and the town is a dead place. In the last few months, he said, they have taken the men out of the town by the bunch. I guess like every other town, there are few men left.

At about 11:00, Pluto followed two of our men out on the road, and be damned if a jeep didn't clip him. I heard the brakes screech and heard Pluto yelp. Fortunately, he wasn't hurt bad. It knocked him down and hurt his rear starboard leg, and cut him a little. So they took him to the sick bay and had him painted, and soon Pluto came limping back to the picnic. By golly, after that he wouldn't get more than 5 or 10 feet away from me all day. Tonight he is a tired dog. Right now he is lying by the wardroom door on the deck trying to catch any cool breezes that may meander by.

I musn't forget to tell you about my powerful body. Continually I am plagued with thoughts of you, and wrasslin' is always in the back of my mind. God, what an appetite and what restraint it takes to restrain it. But I know you burn with the same discontent and I bear my burden patiently (or try to), for I know that someday a delightful, non-ceasing solution will take place. I love you so much that I guess I would lose weight if I didn't force myself to eat a great deal just to be in good shape for all the future tussles I must participate in with you.

6/9/44

Dearest Gretchen,

In the years to come when you and I look back on past events, I have no doubt that Wednesday, June 7, 1944, will stand out as an eventful day. On that day, Lieutenant (j.g.) Himmel was informed he was relieved of command of the *Tern*. Today, June 9, 1944, the new captain came aboard, and I guess the actual transfer will take place tomorrow. I cannot tell you the story now, but the past four months were sorry ones. Things finally came to a head last week, and I might mention the fact that Pluto was a major contributing cause.

One thing is for sure. Navy regulations are not to be taken lightly. Now the days will not seem so long and the separation from you can be endured with less anxiety and pain. The new captain is an older man, close to 50, I guess. He is a j.g.

We have been busy getting books and accounts up to date for the transfer. I can tell you now that I am no longer communicator, but navigator and commissary officer. The captain switched Skogenlager and me and our jobs, and I have been navigator since June 1. So Skogenlager and I had to get all accounts up to date for our change, and now we (each of us in an unfamiliar new job, but we help each other) must get our accounts up again for the change of command. It's a long, long story and I suppose I will have forgotten most of it by the time I see you again.

6/11/44

Dearest wife,

Valuable Pluto continues in good health. Our mess cook must have overheard some of the wardroom discussions, for he has been feeding Pluto steak for the last four days.

6/13/44

My beloved Gretchen,

By the time you get this, you will probably be a few days beyond your 23d birthday. (I almost had to stop and figure your age.) When I first saw you, you were just a few months beyond your 18th birthday. There were many people round and about, but as soon as I saw "that girl from Fayette" in the yellow blouse and plaid skirt, I started navigating my way through the dance-hall crowd, preparatory to cutting in. And one of the first impressions was "how blue your eyes are." Now you are 23 and almost 5 years have come and gone. We have been married about 42 months and have lived together 20 of them. In one way it is so little time, yet in another way the delights we have shared have been bountiful indeed. Certainly we have shared ecstatic moments that some people will never know and have never known. Every time I see a picture of some good-looking gal I mutter to some unseen person, "You think she is nice, you should see what I have waiting at home."

Someday soon our time shall come, and when it does, oh boy! Did you hear the story of the gal who didn't like the light in her fella's eyes? He said, "That is love light." She said, "Mebbe so, but looks like tail light to me."

6/15/44

Dearest wife,

My new duties as navigator and stores officer keep me stepping. One reason I am so tired is because I must be on the bridge for long hours. Regulations require that the navigator be on the bridge whenever the ship is entering or leaving port, or operating in dangerous waters. I am still a novice with the sextant, but there are many other aspects of navigation which are becoming old stuff to me.

Life has ceased to be a drudgery, for this morning I once again got a thrill out of the sunrise (something I hadn't noticed much for the past three or four months). The water was placid and still and like gray silver. The sun behind the mountains turned the clouds pink and the island foliage was a light, attractive shade of green. The breeze from the island carried the delicate scent (exotic, appealing and almost too sweet) of some flower—say a mixture of the perfumes I sent you. Oh, I felt good, and once more at ease with life!

6/17/44

Dearest wife,

The other day I was running down the dock. I bent over to cuff Pluto a little and the Eversharp pencil that Spencer gave me fell through the crack between two planks. I surely felt bad, but still the pencil was gone in 30 feet of water.

Why are people surprised that I took up with Pluto? Somehow and sometimes I can't quite figure out just how he got into my good graces, but now I am glad he did! By golly, he performed one great, good deed for the ship and ship's company. I don't like useless dogs, but Pluto is not useless!

6/19/44

Dearest Gretchen,

Now the days are passing quickly. I guess it is because I am so busy. It seems I have been on this ship all my life. I do know that gradually more responsibility has been shoved onto my shoulders and I try to imagine how it would be to not worry about this, or has that been done, or are all reports in, did I forget something, how will we get this done, how to arrange for that and on and on? Christ, there is a lot of housekeeping and paperwork to running a ship!

I must close now, but I cannot close my heart or thoughts to you. Always you are with me, every minute, every day. Wait for me, Gretchen, I'll come walking up the hill to your house someday.

6/21/44

Dearest girl,

There is a destroyer out here that does *not* lead the fleet in shooting accuracy. They have a dog for a mascot. His name is "Misfire."

Enclosed is Pluto's ID card. It will be proof of his reality when people dispute my word. Did I tell you Pluto now raises his leg? Yes, he is really a man. We intended to have holiday routine aboard ship the first time he lifted his leg to expel certain liquid wastes, but somehow it slipped by. Of course, Pluto has to think a little bit to get the proper sequence of stop-lift-squirt-go, and sometimes he forgets one or the other; his aim isn't so good, or he puts his leg down without shutting off the faucet, but generally speaking he waters objects quite well. He is mightily pleased with himself, too. I can tell by the way he trots off at the finish. However, he hasn't learned the trick of keeping a reserve supply on hand. Often he comes to an inviting post and assumes the position, but has no liquid ammunition. In such cases he seems slightly surprised, but he loses none of his nonchalance. Verily, yea, verily, Pluto is a man among men!

Somehow or another our cook got hold of a fresh cucumber. It was big and fat and green. I don't know how or where he got it, but he served it with onion slices and vinegar. Just like we used to have at home and the way you made it. Boy, if ever I were transported across sea, mountain and plain to the scenes of my youth, the smell and sight of that cucumber salad did just that. I recalled Sunday evening suppers in early fall. A whole army of recollections were revived and trooped their way across the windows of memory. Fortunately none of the other officers knew what nostalgia was evoked in me, and the momentary homesickness did not deter me from taking a little more than my share of the salad (the other officers didn't care much for it). I chewed it thoughtfully and slowly to make it last, and to derive the last grains of olfactory, gustatory and mental images caused by it. I suppose I should make a list of things I want to have when I get back. The item which would be at the top of every page would be "You." And as long as I could have you, the others wouldn't matter so much. I like you, wife.

Dearest wife,

Yesterday I received your letter about the heat, bugs and sweat. It brought back memories of Louisiana in summer. Annoying memories, too! Remember how those little black bugs would come through the screen and drop on the book or fall on yours or my bare back? I like warm weather, but not all the time. I want a place to live where we can have a home with a fireplace and weather to use it. I figger seven months' warm weather and five cold is just about right. Say like Kentucky, North Carolina or Tennessee. And then too, you mustn't forget California, where we can meander up in the hills for our cool weather. One thing about genetics, research on it can be performed most anywhere, so one thing I am keeping in mind when choosing (or being given the choice) a university is the climate. I dread long winters. Also we should be within half a day's trip to a large city for shopping excursions and for us to sneak away some weekend for a short clandestine honeymoon. Oh! You would be surprised at the amount of time I spend with my thoughts of the future.

More and more I find myself tormented by the thoughts of 30 days' leave. Jeepers, what heaven that would be! I guess the excitement of the past few weeks has worn off now and the nervous letdown is setting in. Anyway, the drabness is more and more apparent, and I am so keenly dissatisfied with it all.

Also I must give you warning of possible forthcoming events. You say Madeline hasn't heard from Emersin in three weeks. Well, don't take it too hard if the same happens to you. It is only natural that I might go on a fishing trip (not toward but away from you). After all, we have been away some time, and I won't be surprised if soon I can't mail my letters to you regularly. I know how you must feel, but we just have to face it.

6/25/44

Dearest spouse,

Someone told me recently that in *recensoring* mail, the Navy has found that officers are by far the biggest offenders in writing on forbidden topics. So I must be careful and not let my pen slip.

More and more I am becoming an old-timer on the *Tern*. Few of the crew are left who were aboard when I got duty on her.

We now have a movie machine aboard. It's really quite an asset, for now instead of going to the other ships every night, we can see our own selection. More important than all this, however, is the boost it gives the crew, for to them (and officers, too) it is a valuable contact with a familiar pleasant aspect of hometown joys.

Our sound-gear operator has been designated and appointed movie operator. He is a quiet, shy, tall, blond boy from Indiana, not tough at all. It will be interesting to see how he withstands the verbal attacks from an impatient crew some night when it is raining during the movies and the film keeps breaking. Either he will get mean in a hurry, or we will have a battle-fatigued movie operator to ship back to the States.

Pluto is overjoyed that we have a movie machine. Creepers, I've never seen a dog that gets such a kick out of a crowd. During the movies, he is everywhere, under chairs, around the captain, up and down the deck, on the gangway and all about. He likes to get right up in front of the screen with some other canine companion and tussle and play. Then if everyone laughs too loud, ol' Pluto starts barking imperiously as if to ask what all the noise is about. Also, if any visiting sailors come aboard, Pluto meets them at the gangway and informs them in no uncertain tones that he, Pluto, knows they don't belong on this ship and that he disapproves of them. But I suspect most of his barking is just bluff. He really comes alive at movie time. I guess he suspects that crowds gather for pleasure, so he gets all excited and full of pep.

6/27/44

Dearest Gretchen,

I am convinced that cigarettes will never cease to irritate me. Especially when at sea, if it is the least bit rough, the smell of them can really nauseate me. The smoke seems to penetrate my nostrils right to my temples, and there it sets up a malicious headache, which I detest. No, wife, you will never have to worry about me smoking, for I am thoroughly conditioned against it. And something else which amazes me! If you ask someone not to smoke in your presence, they immediately think you are infringing on their rights and that you are being temperamental or touchy. So now in the wardroom, when they start lighting up cigars and cigarettes after the meal, why I find some excuse to get up and leave. Like the other night, I was working out the star computations with the quartermaster. It wasn't too rough, but we were pitching, and when I do paperwork at sea it doesn't take much to give me a headache. So I asked him not to smoke. He looked at me so queerly, as if I asked him not to eat or something.

My one big aim in life now is to be with my wife. God, how I would like to look into your eyes again and hold you in my arms. Maybe it will all come true someday.

6/29/44

Dearest Woman,

It seems as if I have been on this ship forever. We haven't started out on our fishing trip yet but we are expecting it. Despite all this, we are putting in our sea time with weary, long hours. All I do is sleep, eat and spend my time on the bridge.

Often I muse as to the reason and meaning of things, and now in time of stress I am concerned that I cannot accept the belief of a divine being. Everything seems so meaningless to me. I can figure out no sensible reason why there should be war, why some guys get killed and their buddies do not. Jesus, several times I have said to myself, "Well, this time isn't for me." Actually, in time of danger I catch myself saying or thinking to myself, "I'll get through this one okay." It seems you can sorta pick out the close calls beforehand. And yet I have no feeling of some omnipotent one or thing dealing the cards to determine who shall be dropped out in the next hand.

Sometimes I wonder if there was a beginning and will there be an end. All things move in cycles and nothing is ever finished. We never get caught up. Few people are ever completely satisfied. And the way humans scrabble and scrounge, bicker and quarrel to get all they can, sometimes seems the most useless of pursuits. Life is a mystery to me. I suppose it will be solved only by death.

Don't let the seriousness of this letter suspend you.

7/3/44

Dear wife,

Evidently Captain Crement must be out of practice in ship handling. The other day he brought the ship in to the dock too fast, and we really banged it. Didn't hurt the bow of the ship, but there will be a sizable repair job on the dock. We busted some big timbers.

Well, we really have been working lately, and I am a tired person each night. I am on the bridge all day long and it really gets weary. However, the labor is very, very interesting (and also nerve-wracking) to say the least, and I am learning seamanship fast—very fast. I have seen some remarkable things lately, and I feel as if I am really helping a bit to carry the war to a successful finish. Never have I realized so completely how much labor and planning and long hours it takes to prepare supplies and ships and material. It is work, work, work, and the only thanks we get is a bawling out if it isn't done quickly and with dispatch. If ever I longed to be alone with you in peace and quiet away from responsibility and tension and suspense, I really want it now. The normalcy of life as I knew it in Baton Rouge is a remote, dim thing. If ever people should be thankful for a serene life, the folks back home should be. I would like to take some of them with us for a day's work and put the responsibility on them for performing some of the duties and tasks we have to do. The sea is an old son of a bitch and she makes men age quickly.

I sure am glad I got you. I know now that life is only lived fully when one can be in complete accord with another kindred spirit. The satisfaction and comfort that comes of relaxing completely and sharing intimate confidences with a woman who loves you, and wants to be near you, is one of the most gratifying sensations a man can experience.

7/13/44

Dearest Gretchen,

Another minor mishap with the ship. We got out of the channel, even though it was clearly marked, and the ship touched bottom. Fortunately we didn't get stuck in the mud. We backed off with no trouble, but that afternoon Operations sent a diver down to examine the keel to make sure no damage was done.

My life is a round of one administrative job after the next. As stores and commissary officer, I don't get much done but supply the ship, check the accounts and check the men. It would be great to be somewhere with you; to worry no more about reports, liberty lists, invoices, ledgers, requisitions, charts, watch lists, inventories, and on and on.

I watch the night retreat westward at dawn and the day retreat eastward at night. By day our ship is in the center of a huge flat blue dish of ocean. At night our ship is in the center of a huge black disk of ocean under a vault of black sky pricked with stars. But as long as *Time* magazine is not pessimistic, I know things are going well, and in the last few issues they have even been a bit hopeful. This is a sure sign the war is going well.

7/10/44

Dearest wife,

I am afeared I will not be able to keep up my record of a letter every other day. There are so many things I could tell you but they are forbidden topics. So I will talk about navigation. Life to me is star sight after sun sight, after moon sight, after star sight. The moon is not so good to navigate by, for it moves so rapidly. It is difficult to "shoot" it accurately. But the others I can do medium well and I am getting better all the time. You would like navigation and using the sextant. Last night I was taking sights, and one of the lookouts, a young kid who hasn't been around much, said to me, "What do you call that gizmo?"

He sure regarded me with wonderment and awe as I gazed around the horizon calling out such names as Vega, Antares, Capella and Polaris, like I used to do when I taught Magellan and Columbus the rudiments of astronomy.

Professor Hilton sent me a prepublication copy of our paper on genetics. It seemed well written (a little changed from the composition as I knew it), and there were clear illustrations. However, I couldn't get excited over it, although it did make me anxious to get back home again, to teaching and research, and the quiet routine of our campus life in the early 1940s. I'll be so glad to doff my khakis and resume the garb of a civilian.

I have just made a deal with the chief engineer to go partners in the laundry business. He will wash 2 suits of my khakis a week if I will iron 2 suits of his (1 suit = 1 shirt, 1 trousers). I think that is a fair deal till we get somewhere we can find a laundry.

You will notice that lately sex has been mentioned not at all. But if you listen closely to the tone of this letter, you will realize that the rumbling sound you hear is the latent power held in firm check till the one and suitable release is encountered. All I say is prepare to be taken by storm of many hours' duration. Now I must go shoot the sun again, so as soon as I get to the bottom of this sheet, I'll close. What better way to end an epistle (billet doux) than to say I love you.

I have an unexpected chance to mail this. I'll send it winging home to you with all my love.

7/15/44

Dearest girl,

Five days have gone by since I started my last letter. That is a true measure of the scarcity of news. Admiral Nelson used to write in his diary every day, and he wrote letters often, even though he was seasick, scurvy-ridden and depressed. So even though I feel fine and am not an admiral, I'll still try to write you a little something.

Today is Sunday, and we have holiday routine. It is a day off for the hands, and they really enjoy it.

The *Tern* now has a newspaper. Every night our radiomen copy the news dispatches of importance, including the ball games, and publish them each morning. The rag consists of five onion-skin sheets and is called the *Tern Times*. Its masthead slogan: "We burst with the worst or last with the best."

It is strictly a communiqué paper with no editorial policy. Occasionally some propaganda appears, for in the baseball scores I noted Cornell Intramural Team, Sophomore Class 17, Penn State Varsity 0. Of course the radiomen had been paid by the new communications officer to sully the glory of old Penn State.

The *Tern,* named after a bird, is herself a haven for birds. The other day just before sunset, a little bird, something like a killdeer, used one of our canvas awnings for a landing field. He stayed there all night and got a good rest before he took off in the morning to fly "o'er the waves." We were at least 50 miles away from the nearest land. Where did that bird come from, and where did he go?

I don't know.

But I have been told some birds in their migratory flights fly across thousands of miles of ocean. The golden plover flies from Alaska to Hawaii nonstop over the ocean, then back again six months later.

7/21/44

Dearest Gretchen,

The other day, two of our seamen had a contest to see who could chew the most gum at one time. One guy got 4½ packs (22 sticks) in his mouth at once. But his jaw locked on him, and they had to pull the gum out, bit by bit. He had a sore jaw for two days.

Anything to pass the time.

Last night it was hot. After working out the star calculations in the blacked-out chart house that has no ventilation I was dripping wet with sweat. So I took a shower in the dark. I couldn't find my pajamas so I went to bed raw. Slept like a log!

7/24/44

Dearest wife,

Another trip and a new destination. Sleepy lagoons, and beaches and palms, and blue, blue sky and sea. The sand is golden white, and over all hangs a murmuring stillness which seems to be the very essence of endless time itself. I was profoundly affected when I first saw the low line of palms and surf bulging over the horizon as I looked through the binoculars. It was early morning, and I could tell from my emotions that I was entering a new and eventful chapter in my life. The utter aloofness, distance and loneliness of these places gets into you and makes the mind rush with many thoughts all tangled and swift.

The crew was as excited as birds, and lined the rail like crows to look at the scene. The air is very, very clear, and one can see long distances. It was the first real lagoon I ever saw, and I was not disappointed. Even one of the islands (a little one) was typically Hollywood—small, and with a tiny beach and palm trees. I saw some strange birds, too.

We had fresh fish for lunch. It had a rather strong flavor but was tasty. I saw the native boy catch the first fish. It really was a pretty sight. The blue lagoon, the silver flashing fish (about 28 inches long), the bright sunlight, and naked brown and glistening bodies all seemed like a scene from some movie. Somehow I can't escape the feeling that this is all a dream.

Romance and adventure, but above all a feeling of loneliness, endless time, and insignificance of man. Christ, these islands and palms will be here millions of years after all the Japs and Americans have vanished into fertilizer, and coral animals are the most highly evolved forms of life!

Yesterday I received six letters from you. One took only nine days to get to this place.

I guess Mrs. Lendbody Snodgrass must be getting worse and worse as a gossip. If she steams open this letter, her eyes will bulge with surprise (won't they, Mrs. Snodgrass?). Most people with no definite aim in life devise some means of passing the time, and I guess gossip is the device most universal of all. Even I gossip more than I should. It is an easy habit to get into. However, as long as it doesn't get vicious, it is best to ignore it. Anyway, as you said, it is probably all over town now that you dated someone else while your husband is away. But you and I know there is nothing to it.

Endlessly, I think of you and want to be with you. I always think of you when the sun comes up, for I know in that direction is home and happiness. My longing for you is a dull hunger that is never satisfied, just as I will not be completely content till I am with you again. I count a lot on you as my home port, my anchor, the rock of foundation for my faith, raison d'être, and I love you deeply and with all I know. I surely will hurry home to you just as fast as I can. I love you.

7/26/44

Dearest Gretchen,

Life aboard ship during a long sea voyage soon develops into a routine that is almost mechanical. The word is passed, the watches are relieved, chow is eaten, drills are held, watches set, ship is darkened, turn in, turn to, and then start the same routine over again. Still, there is enough gossip and anticipation of the morrow to prevent the monotony from becoming too pronounced. Most of the men aboard this vessel are under 30, many are under 21, and young healthy bodies with energy to expend find all sorts of ways to fight monotony.

Remember once you told me how much you enjoyed Spike Davis and his gang with assorted instruments and noisemakers? Well, one boy on here has several records by Spike Davis, and every so often he breaks them out (unwraps them) and plays 'em. I never saw anyone get such evident enjoyment from such music. At certain passages where the noise reaches a crescendo and the air is full of the sound of dishpans, washboards, whistles and drums, this guy just sits back and roars. Christ! That music really pleases him. He plays the records over and over and his joy in them seems to never cease. I get as much a kick out of watching him as listening to the music.

This morning on the bridge (it was just after sunrise and warm already), I was leaning on the rail looking across to the horizon (always on watch, one unconsciously scans the horizon endlessly, endlessly) when I noticed the breeze. It was cool, and clean with a tangy smell. Immediately I thought of you and how I used to associate you with sea breeze.

Tropical heavens have a multitude of bright stars, made brighter by the exceedingly clear air. I'm glad stars are bright for it makes shooting them with the sextant easier. This morning, I was really tickled for I got *six* star lines, out of nine shot, to cross inside a five-mile triangle. For once I knew definitely and exactly where we were. Now, you musn't tell folks how exuberant I am when I do such things so well. The captain just grunted when I showed him our position. But to be truthful about it, I am surprised myself at the excellent results I am getting. Navigation is not nearly so hard as I thought.

Last night, there was a beautiful sunset. Rich, rich gold and burning red colors caught between a blue-purple sea and a blue sky. Yes, there is beauty here, when one stops to realize it. But most of all, there is loneliness and empty space and a yearning that is never filled.

7/29/44

Dearest Gretchen,

Well, here I am again struggling to tell you something interesting without breaking censorship rules. First of all, I had a glimpse of Emersin. I didn't get to talk to him. All I did was to wave my hand as they went by. From the looks of things, I won't get much closer to him for a while, either. I am far enough west but Emersin will be farther.

Censoring mail is quite a chore these days for, despite

the rules, the boys unconsciously break them. And we have to turn back many of the letters. As I have mentioned before, most of the letters are conventional and dull to one who has to read them every day. But now and then, the unconscious poetry of some of the expressions is very touching.

For instance, one fellow begins all letters to his wife by saying, "First of all, darling, I love you." And another boy made excuses for his poor writing and errors by asking his girl to consider every mistake a kiss. There is humor, too. One guy was telling about some woman "who was pregnant six times in six years and her old man is a no-good asshole, anyway." The words come out so brutally at times. And one time we had quarters so the captain could tell the men where we were going and what to expect and what was expected of them. Later one boy wrote home to his mother, "Don't worry about me, Mom, the captain has promised to bring us all home safely." Well that put it candidly but not quite truthfully, for the captain said he would *do his best* to bring 'em home. Don't let me give you the wrong impression, wife, for if ever a Navy controlled the seas, ours controls the Pacific and I can truthfully say there is little danger as yet.

Our fishing trip was uneventful and unexciting except that we saw so many new things. And navigation made it particularly enjoyable and profitable to me. I have confidence in myself, now.

The hardest part of navigation is using the sextant and I have mastered that. A sextant is much like a microscope. At first they are difficult to manipulate, but now I handle ours with ease. I can bring a star down to the horizon and shoot it with no strain at all. In fact, if I was the boasting type, I would boast you right off the doorstep. Wife, you must not be alarmed at my nautical terminology, for these days I am really a salty Jack Tar. I have shed the schoolroom manner and colloquialisms for the concise, unusual terminology and idiom of the sea, and it is only when I forget myself that I call the deck the floor, the bulkhead the wall, and so on. But be not alarmed; deep down inside I am the same Luke who fell overboard for you at Penn State almost five years ago. I wish I could convey adequately to you how much I count on you. How deeply and greatly dependent I am on you as representing the happiness and comfort and peace that I long for, once all this nightmare is over.

7/31/44

Dearest wife,

Yesterday we had a recreation party on the beach. First time the crew had been on solid ground for some weeks, and they needed relaxation. It was strange! The water was warm and salty. We collected seashells by the hundreds. They are similar to the ones I sent you last year. Some are beautiful.

I have never seen such dazzling sun on the sand. It actually hurt my eyes. The sand is golden white, and the reflected sun is blinding. I never quite believed the sun could be bright enough to blind a man, but I do now. I was grateful for my sunglasses and pith helmet. These islands are near the equator, we are in mid-summer, there are no clouds in the sky. So I would like to measure the sun's intensity at noon someday on one of these beaches. I bet it would be more than 10,000 foot candles.

I have finished reading *Sun is My Undoing*. It really affected me. It is about six stories in one, but powerfully written and well linked together. There are some violent pages that chronicle the slave trade, lust and passion, and murder. Marguerite Steen must have done a tremendous amount of research before she wrote it. If possible, you should read it. I know you will find it absorbing. Which reminds me, we should be getting *A Tree Grows in Brooklyn* as soon as the mail catches us.

We haven't been paid in a month. I have $90 coming. I can send most of it home for there is nothing for me to spend it on.

8/2/44

Gretchen, m'love,

It is a cold feeling to realize you are the only officer aboard who knows how to navigate. And God knows I am new at it! What if we should get lost?

Any afternoon we are not working, we have swim call. The captain is reluctant, but Karol tells him the crew needs it. Everyone gathers on the fantail to frolic and jibe at each other. The water is warm and salty, but refreshing withal.

Swimming in a lagoon is different from what I imagined. But it is still romantic after a fashion, and I am glad I have done it. But I would sacrifice this gladness to be home with you!

Mr. Shoal, our chief engineer, swears we will be home for Christmas, and we have a standing invitation to have dinner at his house. He seems utterly confident that we will be back by then. I hope his expectations come true.

Enclosed in this letter you will find the original and a copy of my will. Don't pass out when you read it. It is something I should have drawn up a long time ago, and I just kept putting it off. Mr. Skogenlager, former lawyer, drew up one for himself and told me I could use it as a pattern, so I did. Show the will to my sister Jane and then put it in our safe-deposit box. I felt kinda funny when I read the will, for it sounded as if I had vast estates and huge sums of money. But, anyway, what I got is yours and this piece of paper might save a lot of red tape just in case something does happen.

Each day I am away is one day closer to you. That is the way I console myself with our separation. And, by God, I hope it ends soon. I need you wife, just as you need me. Good night, and all my love.

8/4/44

My dear wife,

Wife, you should see me iron shirts and pants! In the first place, I don't give the shirttails more than a lick and a promise 'cause nobody sees the shirttail anyway, and it gets wrinkled soon as you put it in your trousers. As for sleeves and cuffs, Jeez, they are hard to iron, and since I always wear 'em rolled up, I don't iron them. But I never like to do a halfway job, so I cut off the lower two-thirds of the sleeve, which eliminated that problem nicely. (It is easy to iron the stumps left on.) I can do the collars and shirt fronts pretty good, and besides, no one ever sees us out here anyway, and we get all sweated up right quick, so our clothes always look rumpled. But ironing clothes gives me something to do (I iron 'em down on the carpenter's bench below deck. It is swell ironing board and there is a big air blower there to keep me cool) and enables me to retain some of the conventionalities of civilization (you know, like an Englishman dressing for dinner in the tropics).

Recently I heard of a Navy custom which I think is swell. It seems that after a ship has been away from the States 18 months or more, it is entitled to break out a "homeward bound" pennant when it gets orders to sail for home. The pennant is usually a long streamer flown from the main mast. It is conspicuous, for the length is determined by the number of men in the crew. The pennant is 1 foot long for each man in the crew; thus, a ship with 75 men in the crew would have a pennant 75 feet long. At this rate, a battleship would have a pennant more than 1,000 feet long (and then some). Not many ships get to fly homeward-bound pennants, for few of them are away 18 months at a stretch. However, yesterday I saw one fighting ship with a pennant on her. It was so long, it trailed in the water. Some ships use small balloons to keep the pennant airborne.

So, wife, on the *Tern* when we fly our homeward-bound pennant, it will be a happy day for me. I will bring my share of the pennant home to you, and we will display it in some conspicuous place, and if ever we get to arguing and fighting, why one of us can point to the pennant to remind us of the 18 months when we didn't even have to talk to each other, let alone "argy and fite."

The work we do here is tangibly contributing more to the war effort than the things we did at the old locale. There is little red tape. We receive a blinker message telling us to do a job, we go do it, then report back and get another assignment. I have seen several examples of Yankee ingenuity, organization and cooperation, which do my heart good. Yes, I still have faith that there are people trying to win the war.

The crew seems to be disillusioned about the South Sea Islands. One guy said, "Stick a few palm trees on some coral sand that's about all there is to it." But I find it more appealing than that. These places are so lonely and secluded that the loneliness itself makes them unusual. Then the ceaseless, beating surf, the sea and sky are always changing. And yet always the same. Sunsets and sunrises are tremendous, and right now there is a big fat old moon, as big as a barrel, framed in palm-tree silhouettes. And to feel that one is seeing history made, in fact helping (in a small way) to make history, adds to the reverence.

But all these things are considered and written only to lessen the ache of homesickness and nostalgia that is ever with us. Going home is the perennial topic of all bull sessions. Talk about it is as ceaseless as the beating surf itself.

8/6/44

Dearest wife,

Today I received three letters from you. It was the first mail we have gotten in two weeks. You should see how I gobbled it up. The shortest time was 17 days' delivery, so I suppose we may as well resign ourselves to being two to three weeks behind on news of each other.

A few days ago I saw Stoneburger, and I went aboard his ship. His baby is now eight months old; he has never seen it. He eagerly showed me pictures. When I gave them back to him, he stopped talking to me for a few minutes and looked at the pictures before he put them back in his wallet.

8/10/44

My dear wife,

The other day we drew provisions from a cargo ship. As you know, Coca-Cola is a delicacy out here. So whenever we have a chance to get some for the crew, we always do. I was down in the hold of the supply ship, just looking around to see what stores they had that we could use, but might have omitted from our list. I saw these crates of Cokes—stacks of them. You know, those wooden crates that hold 24 bottles of Cokes. Those heavy bottles made of thick glass to withstand the pressure of the carbonated Coke (so I've been told). So I asked the supply officer to give us as many crates as our ship was entitled. We have approximately 72 men on our ship, so we got 2 Cokes per man, or 6 cases. Then I got to thinking. My Gawd, they shipped those heavy crates and heavy bottles full of water, a little flavoring, coloring and carbon dioxide, all that weight, clear from the States, thousands of miles out here to our ships. Now, why didn't they send the Coke mix, the carbon-dioxide cylinders, and a load of empty bottles and crates, set up a bottling plant on a barge out here, and use the same bottles and crates over and over again? Shipping Cokes in crates and bottles 5,000 miles seems stupid to me. I mentioned the above to the cargo ship's supply officer, and he said he would relay my suggestion to his commanding officer. Who knows? Something may come of it.

8/12/44

Dearest Gretchen,

The mail service spurted into high gear, and I got a letter from you two days in a row. I enjoyed the letter about your ma and the eggs. Don't let the rundown condition of the farm bother you. After all, if, at the present, you and I can do little to remedy the situation, there is no use worrying.

Most of all, don't feel depressed, it *don't do no good.* We can't let down in the "third quarter," as football coach Bob Higgins would say. Now is the time when we must bear up. As for your pointless existence, let me recommend hard physical exercise and work. Drive yourself! Keep busy! When you go back to school this fall, take a full schedule of credits. It will keep you busy and put you closer to graduation. Wife, don't ever let your feelings overpower you to the point where you become apathetic. Get a kick out of life, even it's weary, boresome exasperation. Live for life alone!

After you've been out here awhile, if you are not careful, you spend too much time feeling sorry for yourself. So after a while you figure out that you just must do the best you can with what you've got.

8/14/44

Dearest wife,

Emersin walked in on us today, so you can pass the good news on to Madeline. He is coming over to the movies tonight if he can, and I guess I'll get to see him again. But he is due to go fishing again soon, so he won't be near me long. You should have seen Pluto when Emersin came aboard. Emersin didn't even recognize the dog, but ol' Pluto 'bout went crazy! He wagged so hard he almost fell apart, and he jumped up on Emersin and tried to get on his lap and whined and grinned from ear to ear.

Bob Mack is here, too. I didn't get to talk to him or see him, but we passed close aboard. I don't even know if Bob is aware we are here, but it is good to know we are together for a while. If possible I will try to see him, but I might not be able to arrange it. You see, we must be ready to get underway any time on five minutes' notice; we keep steam in the boilers at all times. It would take me at least half a day to make the boat trip and visit with Bob and get back—it is too risky. But I'll try to get off a private message to him.

A private message is when a signalman on watch on the bridge of a ship at rest or at anchor sends an unofficial semaphor or blinker signal to a signalman on watch on the bridge of another ship at rest or at anchor. The signalmen are supposed to be on the lookout for official messages from other ships. But there are long, vacant stretches of time with nothing to do, so these kids start up conversations by blinker or semaphore. Oftentimes an intervening ship (B) will relay a message from ship (A) to ship (C), if people on A and C want to contact each other, and the masts or superstructure of other ships are in the way and impair vision. I have seen these kids send a private message between friends all the way down a line of anchored ships, perhaps a distance of 5 to 10 miles. So I will have our signalman try to send a message to Bob on the B that we are here. I just hope the chief signalman on watch on the bridge of the B will be kind enough to transmit the message to Bob.

8/16/44

Dearest Gretchen,

The blow has struck. Pluto has gone! Yesterday the captain gave the word to get rid of him. He claimed Pluto was unsanitary and had to go. I knew it was coming sooner or later, for I believe the captain has disapproved of Pluto from the beginning. We gave him to some fellows on a small ship and they were glad to get him. When the ship came alongside us I said, "Do you fellows want a dog?" They answered right away, "Sure, you bet, we just lost ours." So we passed Pluto over and gave them his collar and service record (Pluto was up to mast once for urinating in forbidden areas), and identity card. Those fellows surely were pleased with him, but the idea didn't go over so well with members of our own crew. I am learning lots in this Navy. Not so long ago someone told me, "Beware of a man who doesn't like dogs." I can see it is the truth, too. But anyway, I'm sure Pluto has a good home, and maybe I'll get to see him every so often. Already I miss him, but it doesn't pay to buck authority.

The other day we were supposed to help Bob Mack's ship go alongside a repair ship. But we really socked them, and Captain Crement had to go over to the flagship and report what happened.

Henry George's ship came in the other day (you know, he's the kid from Penn State that I saw last December). I'm half afraid to try and contact him, because I don't know if he is still alive or not. His ship has been in plenty of action since I saw him last, and Henry would be right in there among them. But I'll check on him, if I get the chance, and let you know.

Wife, the more I think of it the more enthused I become about fixing up the old place. What I need and crave is the actual work, like choppin' weeds, mending fences, puttin' in lights and water, painting and building. Maybe I am just rambling, but I am tired of the sea. I want the feel of solid earth beneath me.

Last night I had a most satisfying and yet tormenting dream. I dreamed we were kissing. I was bare from the waist up and so were you. Of course we were hugging each other, but the strongest remembrance of the dream was and is the vivid recollection of the feel of your cool, smooth breasts. Jeepers, I was never gonna let you go, but the dream went anyway. I wish I could convey to you how good it felt, to feel your bare body enclosed in my arms and how smooth you were. Ah, that was good, very good!

8/19/44

Dearest Gretchen,

I guess it won't do any harm to tell you we are towing a concrete ship down to one of our secret harbors on an island near New Guinea. The concrete ship has no engine and is used for storage only. They tell me the ship has 1 million gallons of fuel oil in her forward storage tanks and 1 million gallons of drinking water in the rear storage. This is a lot of weight to drag across the ocean. Our best speed on a calm day is about six knots. At this rate, it will take us at least two weeks to get there. The other ships with us are similarly loaded. There isn't much danger from Jap subs. They are too busy looking for big ships to sink.

When we get to the new anchorage, any of our ships that need fuel or water can go to this concrete ship and pump it out. Our big tankers will replenish the supply as needed. It's a long way to haul oil from California to some island in the southwest Pacific.

Since I am navigator, I stand the 4-to-8 watch in the morning and 1800-to-2000 at night. As soon as I get off watch at night, I hit the sack—about 8:30 or 9:00 P. M. Then I have to roll out at 3:40 to go on watch again. During the day I have to shoot morning, noon and afternoon sun, so my life is strictly routine and it gets deadly monotonous. No matter how much sleep I get, when I am awakened at 3:40 I am still sleepy. Goddamn this life anyway! It sure gets me down at times. But I take refuge in the thought that it can't last forever, and someday I am coming home to you, and if I ever let you out of my sight I'll be surprised. I never realized how big this bastardly old ocean is till I started driving around on it. As Admiral Nimitz said, "It isn't the Japs that's holding us up, it is the size of the Pacific!" I am headed in my brother Joe's direction, but there is so much ocean where he is, it will be a coincidence if I get to see him.

Before, I used to look on fishing trips with a feeling of adventure, but now they leave me apathetic—I got filled up with adventure quick enough.

How I dream of fresh vegetables and milk, and water

that doesn't taste of the ice box and evaporators, and good bread, and a newspaper, and an easy chair, and good solid earth!

8/21/44

Spouse, m'love,

Yesterday we crossed the equator. The captain had Stolbur standing up on the prow with a boat hook. Stolbur was supposed to grab the line of the equator and lift it up so the ship could pass under. Poor Stolbur stood there an hour or more with the boat hook in his hands, gazing intently ahead of the ship, looking into the water, looking for the equator. Of course he couldn't see it. When he realized that everybody on the bridge, including the captain, was laughing at him, he slowly carried the boat hook back to the motor launch on the boat deck where it belonged. I didn't laugh much.

When Stolbur served supper that night in the wardroom, he said nothing—not a word. In fact, it was three or four days before I heard him laughing and joking with the other sailors.

As you probably know, crossing the equator calls forth quite a ceremony on board naval ships. When one has crossed the 180th meridian (I have), one becomes a member of the Golden Dragons. But upon crossing the equator, there is usually an initiation, reminiscent of college fraternities. Shellbacks (those who have been across) prosecute or try the Pollywogs (who haven't been across) before the court of Neptunus Rex. Of course, there is the royal baby, and royal lawyer, etc. I don't know much about it yet, but I suppose I will learn. There is one slight catch to the procedure.

When the *Tern* crosses into southern latitudes, we, the Pollywogs, outnumber the Shellbacks about four to one, so I am afraid the tables will be turned on the Shellbacks, and the Pollywogs will take over the ship for the day. Once when the aircraft carrier *Lexington* crossed the line, the Pollywogs took over and I guess they had some fray. Anyway, when the ceremony comes off, I'll tell you all about it. Might prove interesting.

It has been a long time now since I have received any mail from you (or you from me, I imagine), so I feel sadly out of touch with you. In fact I have felt out of touch with you for almost 16 months. Jeepers, sometimes I wonder if it will ever end. We haven't had any radio news for several days, too much static.

Besides, we are on the wrong side of the world to get broadcasts from the USA, unless there are some freakish atmospheric conditions that let the radio waves bounce off something and come in clear. Like the stories they tell of the guy next door in Pennsylvania, with a two-bit radio, who on certain nights hears broadcasts from South America.

I imagine the Yanks are in Paris by now. I hope so. For when the Nazis capitulate, the war out here will accelerate and be over that much sooner. If it doesn't end soon, I will be a bald-headed man with no moustache by the time I introduce myself to you. It gets tiresome at times, more so than it would have 10 months ago. Last night we got a glimmer of news on the radio—that which could be picked out of the static. It seems the boys are doing right well over in France. I sure am glad they are going ahead so fast. The sooner it is over, the better I will be pleased.

8/26/44

Dearest girl,

The initiation is all over now, we have passed the equator; the ceremony wasn't much, in fact it was pretty drab. Of course, it was the same as numerous other initiations so maybe they pall on me now. One thing, Pluto sure would have enjoyed the initiation 'cause there was lots of excitement and yelling and tussling, and water splashing. Anyway, the guys got rid of excess steam and no one was hurt, so I guess it is okay.

Frequently now, when on watch, I turn my thoughts inward and try to find out what I believe. Surprising how clear the mind is at 5:00 A.M., when I am suspended between ocean and sky on the bridge of this ship, during those long silences, and the only sounds are the throb of the engines, the rush of the bow wave, and the humming wind in the rigging. That's when a man can probe deep inside.

I don't want life to be boring, monotonous, empty, trivial and meaningless. I want there to be purpose in life. I want to search for the meaning. I don't want life to be as Shakespeare said (one day when he was discouraged, or had a stomach ache, or felt bad, or had his favorite theory uprooted), "It is a sound and fury signifying nothing."

8/30/44

Dearest wife,

Every now and then, we run across Bob Hope and his troupe out here. We got to one place a few days after Hope had left, and then we came to another place the same time his troupe was there. We were anchored a few miles offshore, and I saw the crowd with the aid of a pair of binoculars 'neath the coconut palms. But the captain wouldn't let anyone go ashore to see them. He has been mad at everybody the last week or so.

Mr. Skogenlager is no longer with us. The lucky dog got detached. He was delighted to go. Even though he may not get to go back to the States, he figures any change is for the better.

The other day we had to make a wooden float about 3 feet wide and 6 feet long. We made it out of 2-×-4 pieces of wood. It was pretty heavy. One sailor tried to lift it and couldn't, it was too heavy. So he stood off in disgust and said, "Hell, that thing won't float!" Another sailor said, "Sure it will!" The first sailor said, "I bet $5 it won't float." So they tied a line to it and heaved the platform into the water. Sure enough, it floated. The guy stood there scratching his head looking puzzled. "Christ, it was too heavy for me to lift, so how could it float?"

These guys get into the worst arguments. Like, can crocodiles live in sea water? Where are (or are there) teats on a whale? How far to the nearest star? Is Boston a better town than Los Angeles? It sure is amusing at times and sometimes rather pitiful, the things they don't know. One kid tried to tell me that fleas on a dog must travel to the corners of a dog's eyes to get water or else they will die, so to rid the dog of fleas, dip him all but his head. The fellas use these arguments to pass away the time.

I am reading the book *The Rainbow,* by Wanda Wasilewska, by snatches. It is the Stalin prize novel of 1943. It is much like the book *The Moon Is Down,* only there is more detail of Nazi atrocities. It is powerfully written but saddening and disgusting, too. I bet you that the Poles, Russians and Jews will track down, ferret out and kill Germans for years after the war is over. Boy, how they hate them, and with just cause, too! No animal is more of an animal than man, and none is more cruel or can sink lower in the state of bestiality.

We finally received some press news. It feels good to know how well our troops are doing in France. Maybe the war will be over sooner than we imagine. I hope so, for I am deadly tired of it all.

9/1/44

Dearest Gretchen,

At sea again. Sometimes the sea is very calm. Our young helmsman likened it to a "gently waving sheet of glass," which I thought was a good simile. When the moon shines down on the sea like this, it is peaceful and lonesome.

One night when I went on watch, the sea was so smooth the stars were reflected in the water, where they danced and shimmered. This is the first time I had ever noticed this phenomenon, and I found it entrancing. It was about 0350 when I got on the bridge, and I watched the stars till morning twilight. That morning the stars were hard to shoot with the sextant, for the horizon blended directly into the heavens. The sunrise was all hammered gold and flaming reds that delicately changed to dainty pinks and ethereal silvers filigreed in space.

It seems that during our last stop, one of the men acquired a *Time* magazine for August 21. He lent it to me and I pounced on it like Sheila's [a neighbor] kitten going after a mouse. It was the first time I had seen one in about three weeks, and I read it avidly. Boy, Germany sure is in a bad way. Jeepers, I hope they crack soon. Maybe by Thanksgiving. Hooray! One thing discouraged and displeased me, and that is so many people think the war is about over. Jesus, I wish they had to work on this old bathtub for about two weeks. Then they would soon realize how far we are from winning. We have a long way to go, and people at home must not let up. Not until we have troops in Tokyo and battleships in her harbor. Then the war will be over and we can relax, but not until.

So far I have heard of no demobilization plans for the Navy, but if and when I do, I am gonna take every opportunity to get out as quickly as I can. Golly, I wish that time were now.

I figure it will take 9 months to clean up Japan and for Germany to collapse this year. If Germany hangs in till June, then it will take 12–15 months additional out here.

Those overseas editions of *Time* are different from the ones we read at home. I guess the write-ups are the same, but the format isn't. First of all, they are smaller, pocket-size and thinner, and the paper isn't as slick. There are no advertisements. I never realized how ads fattened up a magazine. Jeepers, they are mostly ads. And I never realized how much I enjoyed reading ads till we got one of these ad-less overseas editions. So at first glance the overseas edition of *Time* is skinny, limber, with smaller dimensions, no ads, and no color. When you pick it up, it is light and it doesn't feel right in your hand. I said, "What the hell is this, a joke?" But the write-ups and pictures are there, and we are glad to get them.

9/15/44

Dear Gretchen,

Here I was all set this morning to get a package of mail from you, but we got none at all—no one did. Everybody kept a sharp lookout for the motor launch. It's a long ways to the island where the local fleet post office is. As the motor launch approached the ship, someone hollered out, "Where's the mail?" And the mailman, his name is

Queegly, hollered back, "No mail." The crew would hardly let him aboard. One boy shouted, "Take your ass back to the beach and write us some letters!" The sailors grumbled and grouched as they hoisted the boat aboard. Queegly slunk off to stow away his mail pouch.

But when there is mail, Queegly stands up tall in the motor launch and signals how many bags he's got. Then the crew is the best-natured bunch you ever saw. Today Coxun Queegly is a wonderful person. They help him aboard, as tenderly as they would Jane Russell (and everybody wants to touch him, but not the same way they would Jane), and they help carry the mail bags full of precious cargo. They remind me of a pirate crew who has just ransacked some tropical town and now prepare to sail away with their stolen treasures. There is nothing like mail for the men's morale. It is more precious than gold.

After being at sea without seeing land for some time, it is fun to watch it reappear. As navigator I usually pass the word as to where and when to expect land. And long before we can hope to see land, the men on watch scan the horizon hoping they will be first to see it. Then the guy who first sees it shouts, "Land, two points on the starb'd bow." And everyone rushes to verify and see for himself. Sometimes a guy is too anxious and reports a low-lying cloud— then he is scorned, ridiculed and made the butt of harsh remarks. It's hard to see land way off (many sea miles). Usually it appears as a tiny blob or shadow, or haze on the horizon, and you have to have keen eyes to see it.

Once when we had swimming call, I pretended I had to abandon ship. The scene supposed that I had been caught completely unawares; all I had time to grab was my life jacket, the kind you inflate. I got both kinds, just in case— the Kapok-vest one and the air-inflated one. The Kapok one protects you somewhat from underwater explosions, but the inflated one keeps you afloat longer (if it isn't punctured by a splinter or piece of shrapnel). So here I was with only a deflated life jacket. I jumped over the side and treaded water while I blew the bastardly life jacket up. Christ, I struggled and kicked and blew in water and swallowed water. I finally got the thing inflated, but I was plenty tuckered out when I finally used it to float me. Several of the crew were watching me and they laughed at my antics and red, puffing face. But it sure did surprise me, what a job it was.

9/16/45

Dearest spouse,

Out here the tropic rain squalls come up suddenly. Just like in Louisiana, the heavenly bucket empties in about 10 minutes, then the sun comes out again. I always take my foul-weather clothing to the bridge. I have an oilskin jacket and overalls and overshoes. Then I have a regular, floppy, shapeless rain hat, called a sou'wester by some. When I get them all on, I look as if I weigh 190 pounds. No matter how hard the wind drives the rain, I don't get wet. Rain storms at sea make me feel odd. Water falling on water, or something. It is odd to watch the rain come marching across the waves and then, after enveloping us, pass on.

Remember those Vitamin B1 pills we bought in Chicago? Well I am using them up, and to good advantage. As long as I can eat hearty, I know I am okay. I believe the B1 capsules help me, for I eat lots. The food is none too tasty, fresh fruit is scarce, and the diet is a little starchy, but I drink lots of canned fruit juice to keep me well balanced. Anyway, the B1 pills won't last much longer (a month or so), so for a Christmas present to me, how about sending a bottle of them?

As Christmas approaches I will think up other things I need which you can send me. However, wife, don't buy anything expensive for there is absolutely nothing I need at present. I have plenty of clothes, get substantial food, and can get what I really need from ship service. I would rather you save the money ordinarily spent on my Christmas present till I come home. We will go out some night and spend it together. Besides, I hate to think of me still being out here at Christmas. Maybe if the gods are kind I'll be with you. Boy, what a Christmas present that will be; almost too good to think about!

9/18/44

Dearest Gretchen,

The other day the sea was calm and, by golly, we saw three whales. They seemed to be very friendly and upon closer inspection, one of them turned out to be a small one. So I guess you could say we saw a family of whales! Anyway, they swam almost side by side with companionable ease. I looked at them through the glasses. They were only a coupla hundred yards away. The biggest one seemed about 30 feet long, but I couldn't tell exactly, they lie so low in the water. This is the first time I have seen whales in several weeks.

9/22/44

Dearest wife,

I suppose you have read of the recent Palau landings. Of course the old *Tern* ain't a frontline vessel, but we did our bit to help make the push possible, even if it was beforehand and from a safe distance.

When an attack task force comes into a secret anchorage, as soon as they drop anchor they must be refueled, rearmed and reprovisioned, in that order. All the aircraft carriers anchor in a row, the battleships in another row, cruisers and destroyers in a row. This group of ships might occupy a sea space of two by five miles. Then us tugs and the other service ships go to work, round the clock, night and day. May take us two or three days before we finish. One night about 9:00, we were loading 16-inch shells aboard a new battlewagon. Their whole crew was watching movies on the deck, but we were transferring shells from barge to battlewagon. Their sailors didn't even notice us. But they deserved the respite.

One job I don't like is refueling aircraft carriers with aviation gas. That is a nervous job and I am always glad when it is over. During such operations, all ships involved fly Baker flag. It is a red one and means danger. Everybody in the Navy knows what it means when Baker is flying alone at the yardarm. Some of the refueling hoses are eight inches in diameter and made of limber, flexible rubber. When transferring fuel they pulsate like palpitating pythons.

After the task force is refueled, rearmed and reprovisioned, you wake up some morning a few days later and they have gone. The lagoon is empty save for us, the repair ships, storage ships and other auxiliary vessels. But in a few days or a week, another task force will come in and we start all over again, round the clock night and day.

I have seen many of the ships that are making history, and I have talked to some of the men on them. I haven't seen nor heard of Henry George since Christmas. I don't know if he is or is no more. Oddly enough, I am almost afraid to inquire of his shipmates, but I will next time I see his ship.

A couple of weeks ago I thought Germany was on the verge of collapse, but the way things look right now she may hang on till Christmas or later. I certainly will be glad when they fold up over there, because then it will only take as long to defeat Japan as it takes to move the stuff from Europe to China. I talked to a fellow who had been at Guam, and he said he was surprised no end to see some of the inferior equipment the Japs had. Yes, out here the only thing holding the boys up is the size of the Pacific.

9/24/44

Dearest spouse,

As you can tell from this letter, we are back in serene waters after a recent trip. We are anchored in a lagoon in company with other ships.

Today is Sunday and we got a day off. The first day off in some time, and it surely came in handy for me. I ironed clothes (a big ironing, too, and my feet are killing me), and washed my overseas hat and wrote letters to the folks at home. Now I am writing you and listening to transcribed music. Schubert's Unfinished Symphony is playing. It fits my mood. The lagoon waters sparkle and dance in the sun. The white breakers foam over the gray-green reef. The perpetual wind makes little choppy waves, and the bright blue sky is strewn with tumbled masses of fluffy white clouds (in describing them for the log they are cumulus with some cirrus, but then Navy log books are far from being poetic). Most of all, I am far from home in a strange land (or strange sea), and I long for my wife, and other scenes most dear to me.

At one island we visited, the crew went ashore for a short liberty. I didn't go, I was too tired. They saw some Jap prisoners, a big Jap graveyard, and got a few souvenirs. What tickled our sailors most was to see our Army men using their canned-meat rations to catch fish.

I guess the problem of supply is a monstrous one, and it is just impossible for all ships and bases to get fresh vegetables, meat, and other stores as often as they wish. Objects assume different values. For instance, money ain't worth much but the crew would give $50 for a quart of liquor. Also, we are very careful to keep adequate supplies of toilet paper and soap aboard at all times. Both are essential and once you run out, you don't walk to the grocery store and get it. And we are very careful with fresh water. All ships evaporate sea water to get fresh water, and if anything happens to the evaporators the ship is in a bad way.

Our mail is all fouled up again, so we sent two men in the motor launch to go look for it. Where? Why to the flag ship, to the mail ship, and to the fleet post office—which is a Quonset hut on a sandy beach on a small island with only three undamaged palm trees—to any place or any ship who might have *our* mail and fetch any they find. Why, I have seen only one *Time* magazine in 10 weeks, let alone all the letters from you, which I miss most of all, which are still due me.

The captain isn't too much concerned about the lack of mail. He seldom gets a letter. In fact I have never seen the mailman take any personal mail to the captain's cabin. The captain seems to be pissed off at the Catholic Church and his wife. I think he wants a divorce, but the Catholic Church won't permit it. I don't know if he has any relatives who would write him.

9/26/44

Dearest spouse,

Did you know that all the big new fleet tugs have Indian names such as *Chicasaw, Arapaho, Sioux, Potawatomie, Molala* and *Tawasa?* These tugs can go much faster than we can. They trail the task forces and help in case any ships get in trouble. One time the commander of a task force turned the entire flotilla around so that the doctor on a destroyer could remove a metal splinter from the eye of a sailor on the *Tawasa*. The tugs have no doctor aboard so they had to use the one on a destroyer.

9/29/44

Dearest Gretchen,

The other day while waiting for chow, I picked up *For Whom the Bell Tolls*. I have read it once, just skimming through, but the dialogue so impressed me that I resolved to read it again. I know it will take me a long time for nowadays I am busy!

I never saw a ship any busier than ours. As soon as we get to a port, they send us off again. One thing is for sure, the busier we are kept now, the sooner we get to come home. A ship can stand only so much time at sea; then it must be overhauled. And this is exactly what will happen to us.

Just the other day I heard over the radio (we managed to hear a garbled broadcast) that the supply problem in the Pacific is three times that of Europe. And being on a service fleet tug, I can certainly see it for myself.

The crew is full of scuttlebutt that we are going to be home for Christmas. I don't know where they get their information. Maybe they have intuition. I think they are just wishful.

10/2/44

Dearest Gretchen,

Just came back from a trip ashore to get provisions. First time I have been on land since the first week in August. The island is well known and many marines got killed there last year. I saw the graveyards (white wooden crosses, many inscribed "Unknown"). To tell you the abject truth, I was quite overcome—to see these sandy graves, on a coral island 5,000 miles from home, of men my own age who died for some abstract entity which they could not even express in their own minds. Sometimes I become horribly afraid that all this fighting is senseless, just suicide.

On one plaque was inscribed a little poem, the last line of which was, "And all shall perish but the truth." Yes, there were tears in my eyes (which I was careful to hide from the men of the crew with me) as I stood there looking at the graves of the men who died for me and for you, and that all mankind may know the "truth." And I hope the truth shall never die. I hope we are not just fighting for fine phrases and platitudes. And I hope I do not become cynical, because I have seen so many ugly things out here.

I know it was a terrible battle, for the pillboxes were everywhere and very thick-walled. I saw the palm tree where the first American flag was raised. Perhaps I was a bit maudlin, but I did not ask the tears to come. First thing I knew they were filling my eyes and my vision blurred. I shall never forget that trip ashore.

The other day I had a letter from Skogenlager. Lucky dog, he got transferred and is now a communications officer on board a big ship where part of the staff of a flag officer is located. He can get milkshakes every day from ship service. He likes his new ship! Every officer who has left this ship since I came aboard has gotten a better deal. Maybe my chance will come soon!

I am anxious to see *your* dog. I warn you, if he is mentally the equal to Pluto, I will appropriate him to fill the chimney corner of my heart, where Pluto dwelt. It always saddened and puzzled me a little that I couldn't tell what country Pluto came from. I knew it was way out, that's why

I called him Pluto. But I am sure that he lived, in his trans-migrated form, in a land of laughter and kindness and sympathy. I am not lying when I say that Pluto had the valuable attribute of harmonizing his mood to that of his companions. He was quick to sense my feelings and then adjust his accordingly. When I was happy, so was he. When I had to be stern with him, he asked no questions but did as he was told. And when I put on my tie to go ashore and called him to come along, he was the happiest, proudest dog in the tugboat fleet.

It was a bad day that I had to give him away.

The other day, Mr. Karol went ashore at one of the islands here and brought back two "real" newspapers. One from Oakland, California, and one from Honolulu. Evidently they were flown in by plane. They were worn and tattered and three weeks old, but I enjoyed reading them, even the advertisements, before I passed them on to others.

I wonder how many different guys have read those two copies of newspapers?

10/6/44

Dearest wife,

Here I go again, ready to write another page to my wife. As per usual, interesting news is still scarce even though we are working hard every day. In these little frequented waters, fish are quite plentiful and some of the crew have caught some nice ones. Also there were three sharks around the ship yesterday. The water was blue and calm and they were easy to see. Golly, they sure are arrogant. So one boy got a big hook, put some bacon on it, and caught him a shark. Boy, he was ugly! About eight feet long. They hauled him up on deck and hit him with an axe. Of course everyone wanted some of the teeth, so I didn't bother trying to get any. Catching the shark sorta gave the crew a little diversion, and God knows they need it, as hard as they have been working. I gotta hand it to the fellas, they surely do their share with the minimum of complaining. They get a big kick out of listening to the World Series (when we get a chance to tune in).

I found an excuse to go ashore again [to the island where so many marines died], and there I knelt before the plaque in the sun-scarred sand and ceaseless wind. The hot sun, the white glaring sand, slanting palm trees, the incessant wind, green-blue water lapping foreign shores—that feeling again of strangeness, loneliness, lost, forlorn. Oh, where does it all end, and why am I here? Is there no peace, no surcease from strife? Will I ever rest and in contentment be free? Or is life just an aching, a void and a lacking? I don't understand; I am confused. I am puzzled, whimpering, searching. For what? Why? The smell of damp salt air and marine life and the endless horizon. Where does it end, and why am I here?

It would be hard for me to describe to anyone what true patriotism is, but I guess I got some of it now. More than that, seeing those rows of white crosses in symmetrical design, I came to appreciate much, much more fully just how dearly we owe those people who gave everything so that we might live as we want. I know this may sound foolish to you, but if ever I loved my fellow man, I did then.

Sometimes I wonder if the main thing in life is to find or fall in love and have that love returned in kind. Sometimes I wonder if that isn't the acme of a happy life. Certainly those who have never been in love cannot appreciate how marvelous it is, and those who have had their hearts broken know there is no greater pain. I suppose I never will get it all straightened out, but at least there are some things clear in my mind, not the least of which is a true appreciation of wife, home, and country, and the price young men pay that we might have such bountiful properties.

10/10/44

Dearest wife,

Recently we have had the opportunity to catch fish, and some of the boys have done well. I haven't even tried to fish, but I have had some of the eating! The fish taste good, especially since our chow of late hasn't had too much variety. The fish are tender, flaky and sweet. Guys catch 'em at 9:00 and I'm eating them at 10:00. They catch enough that everybody who wants some gets a piece to eat.

Today, we were able to get field shoes for most every man aboard. Jeepers, you should see the guys dig in when we got "them there" shoes aboard. I have been trying to get them for some time for the men. They are general issue for all hands in advance areas, and this was the first time any shoes were available. Some of the guys really needed shoes, and as I dished 'em out, you would think I was giving them each a personal gift. The shoes are untanned leather, ankle high, with heavy rubber soles. They are regular GI, and marines and seabees wear 'em all the time. They are durable but a little warm and heavy for this climate.

One of the men aboard is Stanislau Kokksavage. He wears size–14 shoes. None of the shoes were big enough to fit him, and he really needed shoes. So I told the mailman next time he went ashore to go see Marine Sergeant Sasser at the supply depot located next to the big, demolished Jap pillbox where the two palm trees were leaning against each other. You see, they have more than one supply depot, and

I wanted him to get the right sergeant who had recently been given a bottle of Navy whiskey. Sure enough, next day our mailman brought a pair of shoes with him. He had stuffed them in his leather mail pouch, but the toes stuck out. When Kokksavage tried those shoes on and they fitted perfectly, he started grinning and talking to himself in Polish!

Did I ever tell you of the sailor we have on board who reminds me of Pluto? Every time this sailor walked down the deck, he reminded me of someone I knew. After seeing him walk by a few times, I suddenly realized he reminded me of Pluto. Pluto was little and compact, and this guy is, too. Pluto sorta wiggled when he trotted. This guy has a suggestion of a wiggle, and he takes little, short steps like Pluto did. Furthermore, Pluto always reminded me of a child seriously trying to be grown up, and this boy is serious that way, too. Also, on top of his hat this sailor had sewn a little red fluffy yarn ball which wiggles jauntily. And if I had made Pluto a little hat with a red yarn ball on top to wear between his ears, why ol' Pluto would have busted with delight and proudness. I never told anyone this kid reminds me of Pluto, but now every time I see him, I make some excuse to talk to him.

10/12/44

Dearest wife,

Even though I am able to get letters off to you, we are not so located to be able to get any mail. It's over two weeks now and everyone on the ship (except the captain) is sort of touchy about the mail. How they grumble! What makes it worse is the crew doesn't know whom to blame. They cuss "them" out at bull sessions and over coffee, but it frustrates the crew that they don't know whose ass to kick.

Maybe it's the fly-boys, or some lunkhead on the beach, or some stupid reserve officer in the post office. One guy said, "Well for sure Eleanor doesn't have anything to do with it." And another one retorted, "Don't bet your ass. She tells FDR what to do, and she could fuck up the mail service, too." If it wasn't so pitiful, I would have to laugh.

The other day a native canoe with three men in it capsized in the lagoon near us. Our boat picked them up and the natives were very grateful. One seemed to be the native doctor (not witch doctor, but trained in medicine). He spoke English well and told our boat crew if possible to look them up and the natives would give them some souvenirs.

Also, a wrecked Jap plane is furnishing pieces of metal which our boys are making into bracelets and other souvenirs. I asked one of the machinist mates to make me a bracelet for you. He is seeing what he can do about it. Some of our men are good craftsmen, so don't be surprised if I bring you a bracelet.

10/14/44

Dearest wife,

The crew has gone casino crazy. It's a card game where you match cards and the one who gets all the cards first wins. There isn't much to the game so far as I can see, but the sailors play it all the time.

It probably is a little early to begin thinking of Christmas, but it looks as if this is to be a barren one. Of course it is useless to predict so far ahead, but we might as well assume that I'll be far from home. Then if it works out otherwise, we can be happily surprised. I probably won't even be able to buy Christmas cards this year, so to dispose of that problem I won't send any. Also, I won't be able to buy any gifts, so I won't have any shopping to do. But you can bet your boots I won't forget you, and no matter if my gift is two or three months late, I'll manage to get you something. As for me, don't bother to send me anything unless I ask you specially to get me something. Since we move around so much, the package probably would never catch me, and when it did, it probably would be compressed and battered. No, Gretchen, our best bet is to put this Christmas on ice and save the money usually expended for a later date when we can be together and spend it for some good things.

We get paid erratically out here, so to provide for emergencies I drew $120 (now in the ship's safe). The rest of my pay I will let accumulate on the books and then draw it when I get back to civilization. But this $120 I will keep with me just in case I get transferred (oh happy thought), get leave (oh happy thought), or some other unexpected good fortune.

10/18/44

Dearest lover,

Yesterday we got mail! Hooray! Hooray! I received 24 letters from you. Only one or two are missing, and they ought to show up anytime. I just finished reading the last of your letters. Some I read twice, and I will read them again and again to glean all the harvest I can from them. Reading your letters was like reading a book. There is much I have to answer, and it will take several letters to do the job, but I will write every day till I get it finished.

Since I got your letters, I sure cheered up. I could tell Dr. Stafford what is wrong with you. All you need is your husband and some good, hard wrassling. (At first you scared me, you witch, 'cause I thought you might be getting

TB, but it is separation that ails both of us.) I cannot help but feel, Gretchen, that right now you and I are experiencing the dark period before the dawn. If we come through this, we can weather any storm.

This ship offers a splendid opportunity for one to observe men living in continence and how they get consumed with powerful desire. I bet every ship in the Navy has men aboard who possess typewritten stories, pornographic to the nth degree. You can't forbid the guys to have them 'cause it's just like trying to make them stop gambling, but you can make the men keep the stories out of sight. To be frank, I have read some of them. I don't know whether to be disgusted or not. They are lewd and shocking, and often ignorant as to anatomy and physiology. But they leave nothing to the imagination and encompass all situations. If ever I get the courage, I'll tell you one sometime if I can remember all the shocking details.

As surely as Sirius is the brightest star in the sky, my love shines for you steadily and constantly. I love you tremendously all the time. I'll be home as soon as I can.

10/20/44

Dear one,

That Penn State alumni news casualty list sure got me down. There were lots of guys I knew. Steve Black was a swell guy, I knew him well. Christ, I feel bad! What a stinking, terrible price we must pay in war. Goddamn! Gretchen, it doesn't take much to get me riled these days. I suppose I will carry my own soapbox when I get home and make speeches at the drop of a hat. But I feel some things so intensely and deeply, and the ignorance, unjustness and double-dealing really make me sore. I know one thing, when I come home I will say what I believe whether it embarrasses people or not (maybe I'll modify that under your influence). But I have seen men die because of the selfishness and ignorance of people who should know better, and it scares me to think that 25 to 30 years from now we will have to pay the price again.

10/22/44

Dearest wife,

This will be a really puny letter, but I wanted to mail it because the next trip will be a long one. We will probably end up at some longitude west of Tokyo. It may take us a week or more.

Somehow since I got your last batch of letters, I have been immeasurably cheered. Maybe it's because I realize our separation can't last much longer. In a couple of weeks, 18 months will have passed, and then it is only logical that they must give the *Tern* a rest.

10/27/44

Dearest wife,

The other day Captain Crement thought his executive officer, Lieutenant Karol, had hidden beer. At the last islands where we stopped, our crew had been ashore. We sent a recreation party to the beach (the captain wasn't enthusiastic about it), and each guy got his two-can ration of beer. Well, as you know, alcohol is forbidden on Navy ships. Somehow the captain got the idea that Karol brought a case of beer back and hid some of it in the radio shack in the decoding machine. But there wasn't room inside for any beer. The space was all occupied by electric machinery.

Also on one of our trips we lost the barge we were towing. The towline was fastened improperly. We had to go back and look for the barge. It took us all day to find it. This is the first time we ever lost one.

Did you see in the paper the size of the operations in the Philippines? Boy, when we can muster a 600-ship convoy that far from home in the Pacific, you know the war can't last much longer. And you bet your boots some seagoing tugs were among the 600. They couldn't operate without workhorses like us.

Today I heard the news of the Jap fleet taking a licking. Boy, I surely am glad to see it. The quicker our fleet knocks off their battleships and carriers, the quicker we can land on the China coast and, most of all, I'll get home quicker.

10/29/44

Dearest wife,

Now for some semi-serious joking. Aboard ship I have learned how necessary it is that all gear be stowed in its proper place. So, I feel it only fair to warn you that when I come home, I will be awful picky and fastidious about our personal gear being stowed and secured properly. In other words, I don't want no silk stockings and brass earrings adrift about the deck, and I want your makeup bench to be squared away at all times. The same applies for the head, galley and the main decks. I shall hold inspection every morning, and if I find things snafu, I will take the end of a line to you, and make you get on deck and heave around and turn to with a clean sweep down fore and aft. There is no excuse for our cruiser not looking shipshape with all bright work polished. I'm serious, sailor, not just battin' the breeze, either. But in any weather I want you for a ship-mate. I guess my ship would sink if I couldn't have you.

Something else I have been pondering. If, as is extremely possible, the war is still on after you get your degree and I have to be away from home (after my 60-day

leave coming up, ahem!), I want you to get a full-time job.
But instead of spending the money, you save every darn
penny and use your salary for fixing up the farm. I will still
send you the allotment, and you can live off it and save
what you can for us. But we will use all of your salary to fix
up the place. What do you think of this scheme? I know
your mother and dad do not like to accept money from *us,*
but surely they would have no objection to borrowing
money from you personally, especially since they intend to
leave the place to you and your sister anyway. One of the
problems you and I must face after the war is: Can you and
I afford to keep up two homes, our own and the farm?

One thing for sure, wife, I need to get back to the land.
Don't be surprised if, before I start to work at LSU, I pack
you off to Pennsylvania and spend a month just working. I
want to prune, and spade, and milk, and cut grass, and pull
weeds, and smell the earth! I need a place where I can look
up from my work and see familiar things—the blue mountain ridges against the sky, solid things, security and peace.
In other words, I need to get rid of mental unease and stop
watching out for something always unexpected to happen.

10/31/44

Dearest Gretchen,

It is surprising (and a little terrifying) how rigid a routine I
follow from day to day—2030–0330 I sleep; 0345–0705
on watch, shoot stars; 0745–0815 eat; 0815–0900 check on
galley force and menu; 0900–0945 shoot sun, figure out
local apparent noon; 0950–1115 free time, write you, read,
do paperwork; 1115–1230 shoot sun, noon position; 1230–
1300 eat; 1300–1530 free time; 1530–1930 on watch, shoot
evening stars. That is my day with minor variations. You can
see how much leisure I get and how much recreation. On the
morning watch it is usually quiet, and I can do lots of think-

ing when I am not too sleepy. When we get in port, the routine is sometimes easier, sometimes harder, depending on the jobs we get. But it seems there is always something on my mind, something to get done, or check up on, the cooks, or the commissary steward, or the signalmen, or the charts. Jesus, I get so weary of it all at times. It really gets tiresome and continues on, day after day. Golly, I wish I was home. Yes, 1944 has been the worst year of my life!

11/4/44

Dearest Gretchen,

Yesterday as soon as the anchor dropped, I got in the boat to visit Mr. Puregold. I had seen his ship so I went to visit him on both business and pleasure. He hasn't gotten back to the States since he left us (March), but he keeps on hoping. He gave me lots of news. Emersin is here but I haven't had a chance to talk to him yet. Probably he will be over to visit us shortly. Mr. Puregold told me that Emersin has had some exciting experiences, not dangerous, but sorta funny.

Mr. Puregold also told me some news of Bob Mack, which wasn't good. His ship really had some excitement, and not the humorous kind. Of course the crew didn't have to do any swimming, but don't be surprised if you get word from home that Bob has been injured. Of course I can't tell you all the story, and *don't write to your folks about what I've just written you.* Let them give you the news or let his mother pass the word when and if she is informed. I have no definite information that Bob has been hurt, but I just wanted to give you a little advance information to prepare you. Remember, keep mum about this till you get definite information from home.

As I've told you before, many things become clear to me out here. For instance, you are the dearest thing on earth to me. But I have actually found out that as long as one is honest with himself and does what he thinks right, well, life isn't such a burden even if his ship does go aground now and then.

To me, my love for you is one of the immutables of life. One of the granite rocks on which I build. I'm counting on you (and me) to pull through. I *am* coming home someday, you know. Maybe sooner, maybe later, but I'll be there and then life will begin again.

11/6/44

Dearest spouse,

There is something exciting about going to a big ship for materials. The booms are swinging and voices shouting and cargo nets and activity and excitement and strange smells and exotic odors. I'm sure it would appeal to you. I know ol' Pluto ate up such stuff. Boy, he thrived on activity and doings and crowds and excitement.

Then when we get the stores back to the ship the word is passed, "All hands turn to and unload stores."

So everybody on the ship gets in line, and we get the stuff out of the boat or landing barge and walk it up to the deck to the fo'c'sle to stow it below. Stores are taken aboard any time, day or night, whenever you can get 'em, cause no tellin' how long till you get 'em again.

Yesterday I worked hard, but even so I got awake at 0615 this morning (I guess I am too used to getting up at 0330). I lay there and did a great deal of thinking. Wife, I want you to buy me an hourglass for Christmas. That will be your present to me. But I want you to take special pains and get a nice one. Better yet, could you make me one or rejuvenate one? Don't buy the first one you see, and don't spend over $5. Get one which runs anywhere from 15 minutes to an hour.

Gretchen, this is a very special gift I want you to get me, so use extreme care in purchasing it. It will be a symbol for us (me, especially) and a part of our philosophy of life. Now I don't want some knicknack or plaything. I want a good, substantial, attractive, souvenir piece which I can place on my desk. In the hourglass, I will use sand from all (if possible) the atolls and islands I have visited.

Throughout the past lonely months during my pre-dawn thinking, I have come more and more to know how valuable life is. Time is precious, and the hourglass before me shall be a constant reminder that I have little time to waste—there is much, much for me to do—many things to accomplish, much truth to seek.

To know that you put in time making a gift for me—that is what makes it valuable. The pj's you made for me, I would rather have than a trip to a night club. Any person can buy a gift, but a true present is one which a person has fashioned with his own hands. I know this is a tough assignment, Gretchen, but I hope you don't fail me.

11/7/44

Dearest Gretchen,

The other day we censored mail. We have an actual mailbox fastened to the bulkhead in the crew's mess hall. The crew writes letters and puts them in this mailbox. Just before we get to the next port, the officers gather round the wardroom table and one of us unlocks the mailbox, fishes out the letters and heaps them on the table. Then we wearily go through them. After the letters are read and stamped with the censor's mark, they are put back into the mailbox. As soon as we get close to a mail ship, or island post office, our mailman puts a postmark on them and takes them in the boat to the post office.

One boy wrote, "If we keep heading away from home

much longer, it won't make any difference which way we go because we would be heading home any way we went." I laughed about that. It is almost true, but not quite.

It seems our troops have struck a snag over in Europe. I hate to think of the war lasting till spring over there, but I guess it will. One reason it grieves me is if they need supply ships in Europe, that means they keep using barges out here, and we know how to drag barges around.

One thing I do know, once I get home I'm gonna sleep for a week (maybe) straight and try to get some of this weariness out of my bones. I wonder if being tired all the time makes me think of such deep subjects as freedom, honesty, the next war, how we got in this mess, death and sad songs. I wonder if it does.

When I was a kid and we were gonna have a corn or wiener roast, it seems we never made any plans about who was gonna get wood for the fire. So we ended up at the wiener roast in the grove on the hill at the edge of town at dusk, and no wood found. Of course someone had to go stumbling and fumbling in the dark to find wood. And I was always one of those smaller kids who was sent by bigger kids to stumble and fumble for the wood. Well, it seems to me that the guys overseas (unfortunate bastards) are the same fellows who stumbled around in the dark looking for wood so their companions could have a safe and successful wiener roast and not be chilled by the cold autumn night air.

11/9/44

Dear spouse,

As I mentioned before, fresh water is scarce aboard ship, and valuable. On long trips, Pappy Shoal (our engineer) really babies the evaporators and condensers, those instruments that take the salt out of sea water by heating and

then condensing the steam into potable water. He doesn't
want to overwork them or have them break down. The
ship's sewage system uses sea water for flushing. To con-
serve water, only the water fountains have water available
24 hours a day. Water for washing or showers is rationed,
and the faucets are turned on only at certain times during
the day. Some of the crew take salt-water showers, but that
leaves one sticky and uncomfortable. Sometimes they take
a bath out of a bucket. Shaving is an ordeal, too. However,
the crew always has someone on the lookout for a rain
squall. When he sees one approaching, he passes the word;
the men off duty gather on the fantail and set out buckets
and dishpans to catch fresh water, which they use for bathing and shaving. And if it looks like the rain will last any
time at all, they will soap themselves and take a shower in
the rain. Only sometimes the rain stops abruptly and they
are still covered with soap! Then they must borrow some
water from one of their buddies to rinse the soap off.

Spouse, you got me all wrong about liking dogs. Of
course I like 'em and I always did. Dogs are like people.
There are useless ones, arrogant ones, selfish ones, dirty
ones, sullen ones, dumb ones, ad infintum. It is only occasionally that one meets a dog, or human, who is truly interesting and has personality. That is the big reason Pluto and
I got along. Pluto was a character. He took an interest in
things, and he wasn't afraid to let people see how much he
enjoyed himself. Wherever Pluto was, there was laughter,
activity, and excitement, 'cause Pluto hunted these things.
And when he got all played out or tired out, why he came
into our room and slept. I never saw Pluto downcast, or
sullen, or mean, or selfish. Hell, he liked to do things! And
he had the capacity of making people perk up and be jolly
and feel better. Christ, when he came into a group, the conversation immediately brightened, and laughter was near

everyone. And he always gave, he wasn't a taker. Pluto would select someone and then sit at his feet and look at him as if to say, "Let's do something. I'll help all I can. Let's go!" Hell, he helped put up the movie screen, and bring stores aboard, and stand gangway watch, and tie up the ship, and sweep the decks, and play ball, and distribute mail. Pluto was a good dog. I wonder where he is now? It was a bad day in my life when we had to give him away.

Now to finish up this letter, and whether you like it or not, I am gonna talk about us. In reconstructing the fun we have had, I find that we were much too hasty. Just like in drinking wine. To really enjoy it and the flavor, wine must be sipped, and good wine needs to be prepared properly before it is drunk. The proper glasses need to be used, proper temperature obtained, and the best circumstances in which to drink the wine. A cozy room, soft lights, and music. Good wine must be seen at all angles to be enjoyed: the color, the body and the form are to be felt and appreciated. And the actual drinking is an art in itself. No hasty gulps, and sink back exhausted. But fondle and caress the precious drink, make it last as long as possible, and then drain the glass together, but get every drop of enjoyment possible out of it. And even if we didn't have any wine to drink, I love you with all my heart.

11/10/44

Dearest wife, m'love,

Today I received letter 252 from you. It made me laugh. All those questions you asked about the *Tern,* when you know and I know I can't answer one of 'em. But the *barnacles* are not that thick on the bottom, and ships don't have to go all the way back to Uncle Sugar Able to be repaired. The crew is betting now (either way) that this ship will not get back to the West Coast until the war with Japan is over. As for you guessing where we are, it ain't no use. You never heard of the place, and neither did I till a short time ago. Besides, the *Tern* doesn't stay anywhere long enough to recognize the place when we get there again. This ship is just steaming from place to place doing her bit. And the crew is learning some geography and lots of lies to tell their grandchildren.

I think you will be glad to know that your husband thinks Roosevelt deserved to be elected for a fourth term. Only God knows what will happen if he dies and Truman takes over.

11/12/44

Dear woman,

A quiet Sunday afternoon and a good time to write to you. It was just 18 months ago that I sailed away. And I don't truthfully know when I will get to sail back. All of which makes this opening paragraph an uncheerful one. I just finished reading in the press news about the V-2 rocket, "which travels faster than sound and goes to a height of 170 miles." What a gloomy forecast that makes for the next war. I bet the next war will last only a few weeks and will devastate all large cities in the world that the opposing forces wish to devastate. Isn't it pleasant to look into a future like that?

I see where the Japs are landing more troops against MacArthur. Maybe we should go out there and help him. I guess he can handle things, himself, though.

In relating events to you after I get home, I know now that Pluto will always take precedence over my horror stories or sad stories or events, or any bitterness felt toward certain officers. I also know that probably in my old age, I shall frequently think of him and recall vividly many of the happy moments Pluto and I shared.

And, when I do get home, and we resume our lives together, I hope there will be other Plutos (human and otherwise) with whom we can share our days and help us find life's meaning.

11/14/44

Dearest Gretchen,

So many fellows I have met seem to think that because they have been out here a year or more, they have the right to go home and raise hell in general and get away with it (just as drunkards think their drunkenness gives them the right to be rude and nasty and then not have to pay for it). Well, I for one believe that we who are out here are just unfortunate and unlucky. The thing to do when we get back is not to see how "devil may care" and blasé we can be, but to govern our words, deeds and actions and make goddamn sure that our kids don't have to come back in 15 years. Christ, the past is gone—only the future can be planned and met.

11/15/44

Dearest Gretchen,

Yesterday I had a long talk with Mr. Puregold on his ship. He has good duty and I am envious of him. His executive officer used to have duty on a fast troop ship like the one Russ in on. He says it is the best yet; good chow, nifty quarters, return to the States every three weeks, good movies, and all. I guess when I got stuck on the *Tern* I "done got stuck smart."

I have met the captain of Puregold's ship several times.

He is an Annapolis man, and returned to the Navy from a successful business when the war broke out. He seems to be a splendid person and is my idea of what a naval officer should be. We are old acquaintances now, and talk of many things. When I salute him he returns my salute with ease, snap, and efficiency. Sometimes I think I see a slight twinkle in his eye when he salutes me, for he salutes much better than I ever will.

Emersin told me the whole story of meeting Bob Mack. They sent Emersin's ship out to tow Bob's in. Emersin said the rear of Bob's ship was beat up pretty badly by the dive-bomber. There was big hole in the rear of the ship. It took them two days to tow Bob's ship back to here. Then they used Emersin's ship to ferry the wounded to the hospital ship. Before they started transferring the wounded, Emersin went aboard Bob's ship and asked for him. They took him to one of the stretchers. Bob was lying on his stomach; he was conscious. Emersin stooped beside Bob, told him who he was and that he had been on the same ship I was. They were at GQ, then suddenly a loud bang and he felt something sting his back. Soon the ship slowed down and the guns stopped firing. Later the doctors told him it was either shrapnel in his back or little pieces of steel from the ship. He was hit in several places but not desperately wounded. Bob was lucky, Emersin said, because there was one gun turret that burnt up and nobody came out alive.

Emersin helped put Bob's stretcher on Emersin's ship, then stayed with him during the half-hour trip to the hospital ship. Emersin said Bob didn't seem to be in any great pain but the only time Bob smiled was when he said, "Tell Luke I'm gonna get home before he does."

11/16/44

Dearest wife,

I have seen not one woman in over four months. Is it any wonder I am restless when I know there is a treasure like you at home waiting for me? Yes, I am, have been, and will be a lucky guy to be yours. Golly, I go for you. Did I tell you that on Mr. Puregold's ship I saw a picture of three girls? They were good-looking gals, too, only they were completely naked and all had beautiful breasts. I have often wondered about these gals who pose in the nude. Are they naturally exhibitionists, or do they do it solely for the money, do they enjoy it, and are they loose morally?

11/18/44

Dearest Gretchen,

Just now as commissary officer, I am busy planning the Thanksgiving menu for the crew of the U.S.S. *Tern*. I don't know how much you have heard of the "stretched supply lines" in the far Pacific. Anyway, we have been promised turkey (when we get it aboard I will feel better), and in case we don't get turkey, I guess we will feed steak. I haven't mentioned food problems much to you. Fortunately, Mr. Puregold helped us out, and we needed it. We have seen him twice since we left the mid-Pacific, and each time he passed the word to the cargo officer on his ship to take care of us. Outside of that, I can say that the fresh fish we caught in the lagoon off one of the Gilbert Islands surely came in handy. I was also able to draw (thanks to Puregold) some plum pudding and hard candy. So with mincemeat and pumpkin pie, the pilgrims on the *Tern* should make out fine on Thanksgiving Day.

Now I know how the pilgrims must have felt. To cross a wide ocean, go to utterly new and foreign shores, see new and awesome sights, not know what the next day may bring, to have fear reside within you. Truly, without faith in something man could not have survived this long.

We got the turkey . . . Hooray!

11/24/44

Dearest Gretchen,

As you know, from time to time we haul barges from place to place. Sometimes these barges have men on them to care for the barge. Occasionally, too, living conditions on the barge are not of the best, with lack of space, tedious duty, no refrigeration, and dullness. Well, recently I had the opportunity to observe a barge crew. The crew was composed of a chief and five sailors. The barge was anchored just offshore of a beach that our troops had taken and secured. Our ship was gonna pull the barge to another forward beach that our troops had recently taken. They hadn't been ashore or off their barge for several weeks, and when we went alongside them, they were glad to see us. You should have seen their faces when they found out we had *cold* water in our scuttlebutt. Jeepers, did they go for that! Then we invited them to have dinner with the crew and, when they saw fresh meat and butter and bread and other things they didn't have, it was a pleasure to watch them eat. And when we told them they were welcome to come to the movies that night, they were overjoyed. Just like telling a farmer kid you were gonna give him a ride in an airplane or some other unheard-of treat.

Wife, it is things like the above that get me. They twist my heart and make me swear little curses. Here these men out here, and in France and all over, live like dogs in many cases. The monotony is worse than a disease. And the work is very hard at times. Worse than that, these kids have no idea when they will be allowed to go home. All they do is take orders, work hard and put in one weary day after another. And yet people back home go blithely on their way, seemingly entirely unconscious of the sacrifices others are making for them. I read in an old copy of *Life* of Elsa Maxwell's victory party on the liberation of Paris. Jesus Christ! She's wastin' money on a drunken party and young men all over, fightin' like hell so she can have her party. By Gawd, they oughta put Elsa Maxwell and all her guests on barges and let them do duty out here for six months or so.

It's a good thing I can maintain my objectivity (sometimes I lose it), or I am afraid I would become bitter. And I am more mild in my attitude than most of the men I talk to. Many of them, in spite of themselves, become resentful when they see, hear and read the stories of what goes on in the States. They loathe anyone with shore duty (even though the guy may honestly have tried to go to sea). They sneer when they read, "Notre Dame loses *heart-breaker* to Michigan." Or "Liquor scarce in the USA." Ah, yes, it is truly interesting to observe men and their attitudes. And these men will carry their resentment home with them and there will be arguments and fights, and perhaps political effects. However, Gretchen, I can truthfully say I am trying to think with my head and not my heart.

Mr. Shoal got some Christmas cards. He gave me two, so I will send one to you and one to my entire family. As for the other people I know, I will send them a nice V-mail letter and wish them a Merry Christmas.

11/25/44

Dearest wife,

We are now at a place where you thought I was once, only we weren't there then. We left the place where you knew I was and went somewhere else. Then we left there to come

here, and before long we may go back to the place we were
first, but I don't figure we will stay long 'cause they will
probably want us at the place we just came from. Emersin
has been to the place where we are now and then he came
back to the place where we were. This is where I saw him
the first time since he left the real old place where we were
together. Later on I saw Emersin at the place where we just
came from. He may not be there yet, and if he gets back
first to the place where we were together, I sure will be
mad.

So, now since you have a good idea where I am, I will
proceed. At least this place has some mountains, which the
other places do not.

As usual the record player in the mess hall is going full
blast. I believe I can name every record aboard. Some night
I am going to go in there and bust up a few that have been
played 90,000 times or more, such as "It's spring again and
birds on the wing again," and "Don't get around much
anymore," just to mention two.

We haven't received any air mail in a week, although
Christmas packages are coming in. Jeepers, it's a scream to
see the packages. Christ, are they battered! One guy got a
box of cookies and fudge. When he opened it, all that
could be detected was a brown and creamy colored candy
mixture. So the kid ladled it out by the tablespoonful to
be put in cups, added a little condensed milk and hot water, and a fine pastry broth was the result—but it tasted
good. One guy got a box of chocolate candy and it turned
out to be a sticky mess, the consistency of warm chewing
gum. You see, the mailbags are dropped 20 feet into the
hold of a ship. Then they jump on them to pack 'em tight
and so the cargo won't shift. Also it is hot down in the
holds. So between the temperature and pressure, we have
Boyle's law of reduced volumes (sometimes a change of

properties results, too). Very probably the fruitcake you sent me will turn into a pancake, but we got plenty of syrup aboard.

Life on here continues the same as before. I now whistle to keep up my courage. But it can't last much longer, of that I am sure. Something will happen soon!

We have an Irish seaman named Kelly aboard. He is from Brooklyn and is at least 40 years old. One of the oldest enlisted men aboard, never finished high school. I don't know how they could logically draft him, but they did. He drove a taxi in New York and is plenty savvy and tough. He is at least six feet tall and heavyset, but is getting paunchy. He loves whiskey. One of the greatest deprivations he must suffer is no whiskey to drink. But I noticed in censoring mail that periodically, at least every two weeks, he asks his wife to send him "another can of her wonderful pickles." Notice he writes "can," not "jar." Now Kelly is one of our helmsmen and frequently has the wheel for a two-hour shift on the dawn watch, when I have the bridge. It is a custom among the crew when they get food from home for them to share it with other members of the same watch. But Kelly never brings any pickles to the bridge! So I asked him one morning, "Kelly, do you enjoy the pickles your wife sends?"

He looked at me astonished and stammered, "Yeah, I sure do. How did you know?"

Now I was waiting for him to offer me some next time on watch, 'cause you never ask a shipmate for some of his personal stuff. If he wants to give you some, he will, and if he doesn't offer, then there is a reason. Well, he didn't offer so I didn't say any more. But a day or two later, during a lonesome pre-dawn stretch, one of the signalmen and I were leaning on the rail looking at the horizon and chatting desultorily in low voices, and he asked, "Mr. Lucas, did you ever hear of drinking pickles out of a quart can with a straw?"

I waited awhile, then said, "No, where does he get any straws on this ship?"

The boy said, "Why he uses some aluminum tubing from refrigeration repairs."

Long pause, then I said, "Doesn't anybody ever steal his pickles?"

He said, "No sir, he has a $10 steel padlock on his locker as big as a turnip."

Another pause, then I said, "Does he drink his pickles all at once?"

"No sir, he just sips some every night before he hits the sack."

"How do you know?"

"I bumped into him one night in the dark and knocked the can out of his hand. You could smell the pickles. Kelly was mad as hell at me. Not for knocking the can out of his hand, but because it spilled. He called me a clumsy bastard. I thought he was gonna try to lick the stuff off the deck, in the dark yet. The can was almost empty anyways, 'cause you could hear the slurping noise as he sucked in air from the bottom."

Long pause, then I said, "Well, I hope he can handle the stuff."

The kid said, "Hell, he could drink a quart all at once and you couldn't tell the difference."

Somehow or other, Kelly had rigged a deal for his wife to send him "pickles" in sealed quart tin cans like condensed milk or tomatoes. Kelly must have known some guy in Brooklyn who owned a cannery and a distillery. I wonder if he was an Irishman, too?

11/28/44

Dearest Gretchen,

We are headed east back to one of our old anchorages to pick up another tow. This old ship is jumping like a bucking horse. My seasickness is not so intense as it used to be. Now I get mild headaches and a sour stomach. Last spring I got very sick and very weak. I bet if I had duty in the North Atlantic, I would be sick all the time. I know some fellows who have gotten shore duty because of chronic seasickness, but I have not been lucky enough to get that sick.

And we on the *Tern* are more fortunate than those on smaller boats. For instance, when we go out to retrieve torpedoes, we are accompanied by a sampan, which is a small boat about 15–20 feet long, with a gas engine and crew of two. It is their job to go alongside the spent torpedo, which is floating vertically with only the tip out of the water, and hook a line through a ring in its nose, and tow it to us. Then we come alongside and use the line to hoist the torpedo aboard. Well, one time we were out and the sea was too rough for the sampan, we had to call off the practice. That little boat just bobbed around like a cork. The two crew members got sick and had to hang on for dear life or be thrown overboard.

I am glad I am not a crew member of a sampan.

As the *Tern* approaches within 50 miles of an anchorage or harbor toward the end of a trip we always guard the radio wavelength on which instructions to harbor tugs and local service vessels are issued. This circuit is under the jurisdiction of the operations officer or harbor master and is always monitored and controlled from his headquarters. The monitor polices the circuit, maintains order, sees that conversants use proper broadcast procedure and identification, tells certain ships to be quiet while other ships are talking, and bosses the whole deal in general. He can even indict offenders and they can be court-martialed, busted in rank, or otherwise punished. Even so, things get messed up at times with static interference, several ships talking at once, misunderstandings and some broadcast operators acting cute or just plain goofin' off.

Just before Thanksgiving, one morning we were approaching this harbor which contained many ships loading, unloading, tugs going back and forth, barges moving and everything in a bustle and hustle. The circuit was busy. From the squawk box on the bridge we could hear one voice say, "Tug Charlie, this is harbor control. Please move barge 109 from berth Able to buoy 6, then pick up floating derrick and take to beach 9. Over."

Then the reply, "This is tug Charlie, please repeat, please repeat."

So the guy gave his directions again. About this time another voice breaks in and says, "Gobble, gobble, gobble, happy Thanksgiving all you draft dodgers."

It's just some seaman first class on a harbor tug messin' around. But the monitor ignores the gobble and keeps giving orders to other tugs. Much traffic. And every now and then this interruption of, "Gobble, gobble, gobble, Happy Thanksgiving all you SOBs."

Pretty soon another voice says, "This is tug Able, did you tell me to take barge 109 to beach 9?"

"Tug Able, this is harbor control. No, I told tug Charlie to move barge 109. What are you doin' over there?"

"This is Able. I am moving barge 109 to beach 9. Over."

"This is harbor control, come in tug Charlie. Over."

"This is tug Charlie. Over."

"This is harbor control. What barge do you have? Over."

"I have barge 39, moving to berth Able. Over."

At this point the third voice says, "Gobble, gobble, gobble. Boy, are we fucked up!"

Then the harbor control says irritably, "This is harbor control, last user identify, identify. Who transmitted that last message? Identify, identify." You could tell he was mad.

After a few seconds a voice says, "We're not that fucked up!"

"This is harbor control. Last user identify. I repeat, last transmitter identify, identify!"

Silence everywhere.

12/2/44

Dearest wife,

We heard radio news for the first time in a week this morning. I can't understand how the Germans hang on so tenaciously. They must be groggy from all the stuff we throw at them. What makes me more impatient is that the longer they hang on over there, the longer we must plod across this endless wasteland of water out here.

When I wrote you recently that I didn't get seasick anymore, I was a bit hasty. For the following three or four days, I was quite indisposed. Nor was I the only one. One fellow wrote his wife that the ship was moving like a corkscrew, with numerous bounces, quivers, shivers and poundings, so you understand how it struggles from one wave to the next and plods from one port to another. We are now back where Mrs. Shoal wrote you about in September. But we won't be here long. We are due to sail west. It really gets monotonous and tiresome.

The other day I was reading *The Mirror of the Sea* by Joseph Conrad. I have seen such a sea in a typhoon. Our ship rolled and tossed sickeningly. The waves were enormous and all colors were gray. The rain came down in horizontal sheets, and the wind roared in the halyards. I saw a destroyer roll so far on her side that her red bottom showed. I was scared—truly fearful—for we seemed so little and puny in comparison to the magnitude of wind and sea.

Streamers of white spray ripped across the tops of the waves. All was a leaden gray. Gray rain. Clouds hung low. There were little waves and big waves. And then there were the big, high-rolling swells which could swamp us quickly. It was wet and miserable, windy and violent, and I was seasick and afraid, truly afraid.

And now I will close so I can go look at the ocean. I haven't seen it in the last five minutes . . . it still looks the same.

12/3/44

Dearest wife,

Tonight for the first time, I heard a rebroadcast of the program "It Pays to Be Ignorant," with Tom Howard, Red Skelton and others. Boy, I really laughed. They had some nifty gags and the conversation was fast and witty. The woman on the program has an odd voice. Boy, it sounds rough! The program is a takeoff on those quiz programs. I enjoyed it immensely.

Saw a Jap rifle today. It surely doesn't match our rifles for appearance, quality and machine work. Also heard that whiskey sells anywhere from $20 to $50 a quart. Which is about $50 more than I would pay!

But how about you, Gretchen? Here I go rambling on and on about me and never a question about you. How are you standing the strain? Do you ever think how exquisite it will be just to see each other again? No mail for a long time now. That makes the days worse. I have found the only way to bear up under the strain is to just grit your teeth and hang on and don't think about it.

12/6/44

Dearest Gretchen,

I told you how we got combat shoes for the crew. Now, every time I see a certain seaman wear his, I feel good inside, because I know I made it possible over someone's silly objections. I wear my shoes all the time. The thick rubber soles and heels act as efficient shock absorbers against the steel decks. My feet don't get as tired as they used to. I believe they are supported better than my low-cut shoes.

One letter from you in over a month. I hope we get some the next port we hit. We surely have covered a lot of sea the last few months. Haven't heard any radio news in a week. Wonder how the war progresses? I keep fretting over the slow progress in Europe, but when I realize how many guys have to die to make such progress possible, I stop fretting!

Mental Inventory

Since we have been apart for almost two years, I have devised a means by which to hold "inventory" on you and to see just how much you have progressed. Accordingly, I "thunk" up some questions.

1. What new skills have you acquired this year? Name them.
2. How aware are you of world events? What is Nimitz's strategy in the Pacific? How does it affect your husband? What is the GI Bill of Rights? What is the connection between Harry Truman and the PAC? What is the PAC? Have Gandhi and Chiang Kai-shek ever met?
3. Name one new good habit formed and one bad habit broken.

4. Name the five best non-fiction books you have read this year.
5. What preparations have you made to cope with any possible emotional crises that may occur?
6. What was your greatest act of kindness during the past year? Have you ever deliberately gone out of your way to help someone?
7. How much have you saved? Name one instance where a specific act of yours enabled you to save $10? $50?
8. What physical shape are you in? Is your figure as good as last year? Do you exercise regularly? Are you careful of your appearance?
9. Have you made any plans as to how to reap full benefit from every minute of time the next leave you spend with your husband? Aside from the obvious, what special entertainment and recreation have you planned?
10. How much thought have you given to that home we are going to build?
11. Are you a better cook this year than last? Housekeeper? Dressmaker?
12. Have you progressed mentally? How much self-analysis do you carry out? Do you ever investigate the reasons why you like certain things and people and dislike others?
13. Is your correspondence up to date? How many letters do you owe?
14. Name 20 new words whose meanings you have learned.

12/14/44

Dearest Gretchen,

Day before yesterday, a new officer came aboard (after Mr. Skogenlager had been gone three and a half months). He is an ensign and a big fellow. He is a graduate of George Washington University in Washington, DC. He came from Indiana and went to midshipman school at Columbia. His name is Stover. I am glad he is aboard for it really was a grind to navigate and stand four hours on and eight hours off every day in addition to being supply officer. Now I have only one watch a day to stand, and the navigating. Stover seems intelligent and has traveled quite a bit. We are well on the road to becoming friends.

The captain and Mr. Shoal, our engineer, now speak to each other only when they have to. We were operating in difficult waters, and the captain called Shoal to the bridge and chewed him out because the engine room crew wasn't answering bridge commands promptly. Shoal said the engine room crew was doing the best they could, and if he was unsatisfactory, "let the captain relieve me." Then the captain simmered down in a hurry. He knows Shoal does a good job. It was not a pleasant sight to see these two Navy officers arguing in front of the bridge crew.

Shoal told me several weeks ago that the condensers and evaporators need overhauling badly. Every additional hour the evaporators run makes them cake up with salt that much more. One thing about it, when they stop operating, we will have to get them fixed. The boilers can't operate on salt water.

The next port we get to is a secret anchorage for the task forces and there is a floating fleet post office there. Then I will feel closer to you, for without mail I seem to lose all connections with the happy days I knew.

12/16/44

Dearest Gretchen,

I am now with Emersin again in the same secret lagoon. Today I received two letters from you. Both were blue ones.

And you mentioned the word "cheated." There is no doubt that during the last 19 months, you and I have been cheated—yes, definitely. And before that, due to lack of money, we had to share an apartment. So we were cheated of privacy. And our wedding—well, I get heartburn every time I think of it—due to money (lack of) we were cheated again. So the only thing we seem to have garnered from our days together is the happiness we ourselves manufactured. And the joy we found in each other. I love you wholeheartedly and I have never committed a shameful or undercover act since I have known you.

As you know, soon it will be January 1. And I will have been out 20 months. By then, I am sure there will be developments. If not, I will put in a chit for new construction. I do know it cannot last much longer. I just hope we both can last it out.

Here is one of the poems I wrote. The less I say about it the better!

Inconvenient Death

> *Death picks no convenient time*
> > *To visit us.*
> *His thin cold scissors probe our midst,*
> > *And snip the cord that binds us,*
> *At awkward hours.*
>
> *Man's bright logic does not know*
> > *Why this is so.*
> *Today he has no time to die*
> > *Tomorrow he may start to plan for it.*
> *But today is not conven—*
>
> *Snip, go the scissors!*

12/17/44

Dearest one,

I had a letter from your folks today. Your mother told me
of Bob being injured. I am glad that he got through the
deal. Someday Bob can tell us the whole eyewitness story
and someday I can tell you the accounts I heard. I can say
now that Emersin gave Bob a free ride shortly afterwards.
They used Emersin's ship to carry the casualties to the hospital ship. Yes, wife, I see so many things happen that I
have to think prodigiously hard to give accurate accounts
of what happened three or four months ago. Today's events
drive yesterday's excitement from my mind. After all, our
physical receptive powers can only record and absorb a
limited amount of the irritations generated by the external
world.

However, I am glad to say that memories of my joy with
you never grow dim, nor does the realization of how dear
you are to me grow less.

12/18/44

Dearest Gretchen,

Today I was glad to receive Bob's letter. I didn't know just
how serious the show was for him, but now I can rest easy.
Bob is at a hospital on the same island where Jimmy Tur-
nipseed is, but probably not at the same hospital. But I am
sure they will ship Bob back to the mainland as soon as he
can travel. I will write Bob a letter tonight. By the way, he
is now electricians mate first class, which is only one step
removed from chief.

The new ensign is a cheerful fellow. It seems I had all
but forgotten the carefree banter so typical of young officers full of life. (Don't be alarmed, I am not taciturn or

moody, just on my guard around certain people.) As you can guess, the crew named him Smoky Stover. He is good company—cheery and happy. Just the sort of person I need to offset some of the unnecessary unpleasantness that envelopes us. I like Smoky more each day.

Almost every magazine I pick up has some article in it about the people back home who don't even know there is a war on. Wife, do you believe the folks are letting the boys down? I read about horse-racing scandals, black-market cigarettes, purses selling for $100, and neckties for $25. I tell you, wife, there will be some awful barroom arguments and fights when the boys come home and see some of the stuff firsthand. For my part, I will just keep my mouth shut, but I can think silently, and actions always speak louder than words. To say the least, wife, we are living in interesting times. But Lordy, how much more interesting they would be if we were together!

12/20/44

Dearest wife,

We are supposed to move soon so there may be a gap in the mail. Boy, if ever I felt like a "bird of passage" or "ships that pass in the night," I do now. We are as homeless as the wind, and probably cover as much ground, or I should say ocean.

The men on here are really saving their money. They are anticipating getting back to the States. For my own part, I have a few bucks on the books myself. This we will use for our honeymoon and leave. Of course, we won't spend indiscriminately, but we shall not hesitate to have a good time.

When you wrote me about your friend paying $102 tax on a diamond ring for his girl, my first reaction was "poor business on his part." He could get exempt from the tax and use the $102 to increase the size of the diamond. Men in the service can purchase articles free of tax if they take the necessary trouble to fill out the proper forms.

Enclosed find our Christmas menu. I copied the idea from someone else. I ain't very original.

12/21/44

Dear sea wind,

First of all, spouse, I love you. Don't be amazed that I begin a letter in such fashion. I copied the idea from a letter I censored. So I used the same phrase just in case you might have forgotten the extent of my affection for you. This to you is four letters in four days, and it is getting closer to Christmas all the time. The second Christmas away from home. What a dreary prospect! Thank God it can't last forever. Soon it will be two years out here.

Finally started to read the book *Chad Hanna.* It is good escapism. After the Barrymore story, I decided that from now on I will read no depressing or sad stories. I will read humor and straight non-fiction, philosophy, and so forth. I am too susceptible to sorrow and hard luck in my present frame of mind. So I will use the device many people do and avoid thinking about the topic perennially on my mind. (I fooled you. The topic isn't sex, it is *when will I get home?* Sex will be later!)

I saw in a December 22 newspaper where Governor Jimmie Davis will not interfere in the dismissal of a coed at LSU who wrote an article on sex and kissing. Leave it to LSU to get in the news!

And now back to topic A. There is no doubt in my mind that topic A is you! My libido pesters me with its cycles, but it always cheers me to anticipate the bliss to come.

What I need is reality and reality is you. Boy, I would like to face bare reality soon!

Christmas at sea, 12/25/44

Dearest Gretchen,

Today is Christmas. And what a day it is. Why, I don't even count this as a letter, it is just a wailing lamentation! We are bucking the wind and waves, and some are sick. I, among them. The password is "Misery Christmas." The idea behind this staggering attempt at penmanship is for you to preserve this letter. Then in years to come, I can read this factual account of my hours of travail and realize how lucky I am. What a day! Here we have a big menu planned and few to eat. I know some fellows who will taste their dinner twice—going down and coming up. And, of course, my stomach tries to keep up, little realizing the belching and retching it causes me. Anyway, Gretchen, I hope you have a good time this Christmas 'cause it will have to be for both of us. What a day!

Smoky Stover is really an asset to this ship. Of course the lucky dog doesn't get seasick. He is disgustingly healthy, and eats tremendous quantities. And all the time he admonishes me (between hearty mouthfuls of pork and potatoes) to not be bitter, for I will feel better soon. He is full of pep, cheerful, and friendly, and altogether a beneficial person to have around. He has a ready laugh and bluff good humor. I am sure you will like him. I hope you can meet him soon. And I hope I can meet you soon, too.

12/30/44

Dearest girl,

This is my first attempt to write you for a week, unless you wish to count the Christmas letter as a letter. I really believe that was the worst week so far, still there were a couple of times I remember that were as bad.

We forget awful easy. Last year I met an ensign who was in the Alaska operation. He told me how he was in a foxhole for several days. You may ask what an ensign is doing in a foxhole, but in assault operations the ensigns go ashore for certain chores. And a sniper had his eye on him. The ensign told me how miserable it was in the sand and dampness with that Jap sniper laying for him. Then he said, "But you forget awful easy the miserableness of it."

12/31/44

Dearest Gretchen,

This is the morning of New Year's Eve, and never have I been farther from celebrating or felt less like celebrating. We are having right now a few days' respite from the broad ocean (that is why I am writing you every day while I can), but soon we will be back on the bounding main, resuming our chores which seem never to end. Still no mail for anyone, and it is now 10 days. And no Christmas packages. I am just now catching up on the news from Europe. I guess the men over there have had an especially tough time of it the past few weeks. I sure am glad I am not in a tank outfit. How brutal a price we have to pay! How very, very expensive!

I have (among other problems) thoroughly dissected myself and my libido. Deep down inside I am very, very moral. I don't know where my morality came from, how it grew or developed, but I know this: Wife, I could no more cheat on you than I could shoot your mother.

Now to the topic forever with me. There has been no change since yesterday in my homecoming status. Every month or so, we send one to three men home on "rehabilitation" after being out 18 months, but so far I am right where I was before. I am stuck. Sometimes I feel like I am in a blind alley. You see, I am the only one aboard this ship who knows how to navigate. So I am now reduced to three chances: 1) when the *Tern* comes back (God knows when!); 2) if I get orders straight from the bureau; 3) if we get a new captain and, oh yes; 4) sick leave, which is remote, since I am lean but healthy.

That is the situation as it stands, for I have had all other doors closed to me by reasons beyond my control. Can't even put a request in anymore. This is the story, wife, I must sit back like an implacable statue and wait. Then, too, the picture is not so grim as it sounds, for when the word does come, I can be off this ship and in the States in four to seven days. The white, hot, brilliant flame of joy at being with you again. God, I miss you!

1/1/45

Dearest girl,

Before Stover came aboard our conversations were dull and drab. All we did was discuss the obvious and commonplace. However, Smoky, with his business and economics and enthusiasm has given me a shot in the arm, and once again we have mental duels which keep the mind agile and quick. Mr. Stover not married—is a good man to know. He asks me about you. How often I write, etc. I discuss you with uxorious pride! When I told him you were an A student in math, his eyes widened in amazement. And someone must have told him I was "teaching" at LSU 'cause he asks me about that and I reluctantly, oh yes, reluctantly, tell him of my varied and copious skills and accomplishments as a professor, which I ain't!

Dragon Seed turned out to be good entertainment and

mediocre propaganda. Mediocre because to us out here, we need no movie to tell us how serious is the menace of Japan. In fact we live with and in that menace every day. I enjoyed Miss Hepburn, in fact I have always liked her portrayals. She reminds me of you in some ways. I also enjoyed the refreshing manner of conversation they used, very proper and formal with no contractions.

After the movie last night, I had a small dish of ice cream made with synthetic constituents, and then to bed. That constituted my New Year's celebration. Before I slept, I vowed that in my return to civilian life I would attempt to welcome in all the new years to come with some honest-to-God recreation and sincere good times.

One thing about having no recreation except movies and books, it gives me a splendid opportunity to catch up on novels and non-fiction I have missed. I probably will never again have as much free time to read in my life as I do now. So I am endeavoring to read all the worthwhile tomes I can. I have piled up quite a heap of non-fiction. Between reading and thinking, I feel almost like a monk in his cloistered cell. However, I have no illusions that I shall uncover anything as profound as Gregor Johann Mendel did with the pea experiment in the cloister garden, when he formulated the Laws of Inheritance. He *chose* to be in his cloister; they *assigned* me to the *Tern.* And I am not sure what a cloister is, anyway.

1/3/45

Dearest wife,

Yesterday, unexpectedly and fortunately, I got to go on the beach with the recreation party. Let me tell you, it felt good to get off the ship for a change. The recreation island was not very big and had few trees, but the beach was dazzling yellow-white under the sun and the water warm. We played ball and the fellows drank coke and beer. In the hot sun it doesn't take much beer to make the head spin, so I drank my two cans slowly, but with relish. There were quite a few sailors around, and of course no women. As there was no danger or need of modesty, of course the guys went swimming naked. Jeepers, I sure did laugh. Christ! I never saw such an assortment! Here, the fellas in the Navy are supposed to be a superior fighting type with good healthy bodies. Well most of them are built pretty good but nothing special. And another thing, it sure is hard for a man to look dignified when he is bare-ass naked! These guys would walk up and down the beach looking for shells, bending, stooping, and squatting. God, what scenes and postures! There is, to me, something almost ludicrous and ridiculous in an awkward, human, naked body.

Now as for me—ahem. I knew what the sun could do to you and how bad the glare could be, so I kept on my pith helmet and my sunglasses. Then I stripped off everything else. Of course, when I took off my khakis, I lost my identity as an officer so I was just a human—a lean one— like the others. When I write "lean" I don't mean skinny! I am not skinny, just lithe—you know me! But I was solemn in my hat and glasses and nothing else. I paddled in the surf, and stooped, and bent in the search of seashells.

I would never join a nudist colony (unless all had figures like yours), for I know how absurd the human body seems. Conversely it really felt good to strip to the skin and run in the waves, and feel the sun on me and the warm wind. I lay on the sand and obtained a nice pink coating. I lay there and thought of you and how far I was from home and the remoteness of it all, and the truth of it all. But it was good to run around unclothed. I hope that someday we can have a private area where we can cavort in the nude with absolute freedom.

1/5/44

Dearest Gretchen,

Recently I met the captain of a subchaser who was formerly an architect (Harvard graduate). We had a good talk swapping stories of our adventures. We also talked of literature, architecture, eugenics and religious philosophy. He thinks religious music is one of the most exalting aspects of worship. And he said he knew an architect who had been awarded a research grant to study "Christian worship and its expression through architecture." These are phases or features of worship which I have overlooked or been unaware of. The urge to worship God is expressed variously by different men.

Isn't it odd how you come upon the truth in strange moments? The two of us sitting in the shade on the deck of a little ship, anchored in a lagoon off a lonely island, far from home and country, trying to convey to each other in an awkward way our concept of a supreme being.

Did I tell you I am devotedly trying to learn semaphore? I have a late start, and I progress slowly. And I know you will cuss when you read this, but I still don't know flags well (except Baker); even George and Love don't impress me (flags, that is). I try and try, but they just don't register. Same way with blinking-light signals. On dull watches, the signalmen drill me and drill me, but somehow I have trouble catching on. Maybe it's a mental block or psychic one. I know some guys pick up signaling real easy, but I don't.

One of our shipfitters on board is an interesting person. He is my age and has lots of ambition. He is a little taller and heavier than I, and he is resourceful, self-reliant and ingenious. Before he came in the Navy, he was a jack-of-all-trades—plasterer, lumberjack, welder, carpenter and ship-builder. And recently I have come to know him well, this Bill Eversen, shipfitter first class. If I were Sinclair Lewis, I would describe him as pioneer type, one of those energetic, hardworking restless men who have made the United States what it is since 1700. Anyway, Eversen and I have had several talks lately on house building. He knows a lot of inside dope on contracting, plastering, and plumbing. So we pass time on the night watches, and other spare moments, building a house as cheaply as possible. Right now I am getting an estimate for a five- to six-room house and how to save money here and there and how to watch the contractor so he doesn't shove off weak or faulty material. You see, I am gonna help you build a house one of these days, and any dope I can get on it will be useful.

Also, dear spouse, I have mentally packed my seabag and suitcase 100 times. Why, I can be packed and ready in one hour. I don't know how soon the day will come when I can leave this old *Tern* bitch, but I sure will be glad.

1/11/45

Dearest wife,

The other day, one of the seamen told me how the folks at home wrote and asked him if he ever heard the special radio broadcasts to men overseas. So he wrote back as follows, "The only radio we hear is Radio Tokyo. According to it, we have been beaten about 10 times. The only thing is the program gets louder and clearer every day. Which probably means we are still in retreat."

Now, wife, I am not going to add anything one way or the other to that story. That's exactly the way I heard it. All

I want to say is I don't understand Japanese and I get tired of listening to it!

Wife, don't send me anything for my birthday. For one thing, by the time it gets to me, I should be long gone from the *Tern,* and there is no use for the package to follow me halfway round the world and back. I have no idea when we will come home or when I will get relieved from this duty, but surely by March. Also, I don't need anything now, and when I do get home I want to go shopping with you and pick out something together for you to buy me.

The other day I decided I would retrace my steps and start with elementary electricity and learn radio. We have some good instruction books on board, and I dug in, but bravely. However, after about 18 minutes by the clock, I began to wonder if I wasn't getting too old to begin anew with Kirchoff's Laws, vacuum tubes, volts and amperes. Besides, my mind wandered and anyway I can buy a radio for $40 or so, and if it goes bad, why you could try to fix it before we sent it to the radio shop to be repaired. I am keeping my instruction books and if I get the time, I will continue with my studies, but I am awful busy, and besides, radio and electricity is an everyday affair. Those damn electromagnetic impulses and generators alternating. Did you ever study electricity? Can you repair an electric fan?

When we get in, we should get lots and lots of mail. I'll write you every day then while I have the chance. Meanwhile keep watching for me and remember how elegant it will be to sleep together again. No more lonesome beds. Just love and companionship and happiness!

1/15/45

Dearest Gretchen,

Saturday was Christmas for the *Tern.* We received a total of 17 bags of mail, which had been due us for some time.

You should have heard the sailors cheer when the working party started throwing the sacks aboard. I received 10 letters from you, Christmas cards from Sally, Joe, and Russ and Ludwig. Also letters from your Uncle Clyde and Milly. Besides which I got your fruitcake. Jesus, they must have piled ammunition on it! It sure was beat up. Anyway, the messboys and I ate it (with our fingers). Your uncle also sent me a fruitcake. It wasn't wrapped as well as yours but came in better condition. I guess yours got on the bottom of the pile. Your package of B1 pills came, too. It's good you wrapped it well, 'cause that can was bent in the middle. However, neither bottle of pills was broken. I got your two books, and also one from your folks, *The Razor's Edge.* I'll read 'em soon as I can. Helen sent me two packages of the *Philipsburg Daily Journal,* both had been on the way for several months.

Anyway I had a good Christmas. But most of all, lover, I want to thank you for the letters. God, they are like nectar to me. They really keep me on an even keel. I have read them all twice already, and will read them again.

Unconsciously in your letters, you answered several of the inventory questions for me, in addition to the ones you answered straight out. I like the reply of saving $30 by not buying the formal dress. That was eggzactly what I had in mind.

The crew wrote Esther Williams for a pinup picture with the briefest bathing suit possible. Well, her autographed copy came back today. It is a nifty picture; she has some body. They fastened the picture on the bulkhead right above the scuttlebutt in the crew's mess hall. Some of their comments are out of this world. Boy are they hard up!

When we brought our tow into this place, a local pilot guided us into the lagoon, for the channel is tortuous and not well marked by buoys. When it was time to leave we didn't go more than 1,000 yards before we hit a coral rock.

Ripped a two-foot slit in the hull near the bow well below
the water line. Fortunately we didn't take on much water,
the pumps worked good and the shipfitters were able to
patch it from the inside.

The hole in the ship made us unseaworthy temporarily
and we had to stay in the lagoon. So Operations sent two
PT boats out to guard us and help protect us from Japs
who might swim out from nearby islands.

1/16/45

Dearest Gretchen,

Now that yesterday's excitement is over and the Christmas
mail is diminishing, I want to tell you more about it. Our
ship was working a few miles offshore from an island
battered by war. We could see the scarred beach with its
wreckage of man's folly. It was a gray, cloudy, dreary, humid
day with squalls and rain. From the bridge, I watched this
LCVP [landing craft vehicle personnel] labor towards us
over the choppy gray sea. Sometimes the spray would
bounce over the top of its upraised ramp. Finally it came
alongside and as it bounced up and down, the coxswain
shouted, "We have mail for you!" Man alive, the word cir-
culated instantly and in a few minutes most of the crew
were gathered at the rail. Our crew quickly put fenders
over the side and secured the LCVP to us fore and aft.
There were three sailors in the LCVP and as they tossed
the first bag up on our deck, the crew let out a cheer like I
haven't heard in a long time. As fast as the bags hit the
deck, someone dragged them up to the mess hall. That
LCVP was unloaded in less than five minutes. Our men
invited the boat crew aboard. We would have given them
about anything, but they said they had to get back to the

beach. Besides, the sea was getting too rough for their small craft.

I had never seen that boat crew before, and I probably never will again, but they surely brought us joy and excitement. What a strange Christmas!

During this momentous event of receiving our long-awaited mail, the captain gave no outward sign of pleasure or anticipation. In fact, he seemed unconcerned. I surely don't understand that man. He must be hiding something inside, or someone or something is hurting him deeply.

It's too bad that Bob's mother is so hard hit by his injury. I don't blame her, but I hope she snaps out of it soon. At least Bob is alive, which is more than many other mothers have. I have found out that you can't close the door on life. You have to live it out to the end, either bitter or sweet, and I have had plenty of the sour end these past 12 months.

Wife, I can truthfully say I believe I will get home soon. It will soon be two years now, and if they do not let me return by then, I surely will be bitter. However, I have not given up hope. Our time will come, and when it does, I shall take advantage of every second we are together. Once I get in your immediate vicinity, what a wonderfully pleasant chore it will be to plant seed in such a fertile body.

1/20/45

Dearest wife,

Once again we are in a place where few people get to very often. This place is secluded, few outsiders have seen it. You guessed this place once, only we hadn't been here yet when you guessed it. The place is practically deserted. The invading forces come and go, but the waves still break on the empty white beaches.

I guess it won't hurt to tell you things are a bit warm now, including the weather and general dealings with the Japs. We have armed guards at night patrolling the deck to make sure the little fellows don't come climbing aboard. Almost every night, we watch the fireworks ashore. I wear my gun on watch, but somehow I don't get excited.

In this letter I want to write about the four sailors we have aboard who are of Mexican descent. To look at them, one would say they are Mexicans, but these boys are proud and conscious of the fact they were born in the USA, and they are careful to tell you they are Americans or American Mexicans. The names of the boys (I always think of them as a unit) are Garza, Gonzales, Garcia and Jacquez (pronouned Hawk-ez). Garza is a big husky guy who will be fat in middle age, but he is a jolly one. He has a slow drawl and lazy grin. Garza is the paternal one of the group and he sorta looks out for the others. Gonzales is the youngest one and the smallest one. He is called Tito and is good-looking. He will always look young. In Hawaii the wahines really went for him in a big way (scuttlebutt says). Jacquez and Garcia are the quiet types. Quick to anger, violent in their reaction. If they hated a guy enough, they would not hesitate to use force. All the boys speak Spanish fluently and in the evening sometimes they gather together to laugh and joke. They are gay and jolly when gossiping. The American Mexicans get along well with the rest of the crew. It is another example of a heterogeneous company so typical of the United States melting pot. We have all sorts of men in the crew. I am proud to say that I cannot think of one man aboard with whom I am not friends. And there are several whom I have helped that I know would do just about anything I asked them to.

I never told you about the time three of the crew and myself got caught out in a squall in our boat in the lagoon at Eniwetok. It rained so hard we couldn't see. We took off all our clothes but our underwear and put them under the engine hood to keep them dry. Boy, the waves got big and the wind blew us way off course. I had to make some quick decisions or we would have been smashed on a reef. I hate to think what would have happened if the boat's engine had cut off on us. After that episode, I could see how those men looked at me differently. You can tell if the men think you know your job, and if you are working for them as well as for yourself. They pay you back in 100 different ways. Several souvenirs I have now were given to me by the men and I didn't ask for them. Yet they make no mention of sentiment, they show you by their actions.

I want to tell you again and again how much I love you. Jeepers, jeepers, how I miss you, how I miss you. My longing for you is probably the fiercest, most yearning feeling I have every known.

In *Life* magazine for September 25 it showed a girl who plays the part of Miss America in the movie. She had a 37-inch bust. *Life* magazine thought that was remarkable. But, shucks, my wife is that good. Votre poitrine etes tres belle! Wow!

1/23/44

Dearest wife,

Yesterday I had a chance to go ashore with a recreation party. We rode in the motor launch to shallow water. Then we had to wade ashore, so I took off all my clothes except my pith helmet and sunglasses. The water was warm and the sand soft. We had quite a few men with us and as we struggled ashore, it was easy to picture what a landing might be like. Only we had no enemy fire to bother us. My clothes were in a bundle on my head with my gun on top.

Arriving ashore, we found a nice coconut grove and immediately some of the men filled a sack full of coconuts.

With typical U.S. ingenuity, the marines and Seabees
who lived on the island had rigged a basketball court
among the coconut trees. The deck was of sand and a bit
rough. Well, anyway, the Navy decided to inaugurate some
inter-service competition. So we chose a basketball team
and challenged the marines. I believe we were the first
Navy team to play against the marines on this island. Our
team consisted of Smokey Stover, myself, Kokksavage,
Graw and Jacquez. We were some crew!

Kokksavage is sandy-haired, red-faced and lanky, with a
long neck and big feet. His first name is Stanislau but the
crew calls him Peter. All he had on was a pair of huge, worn
combat shoes and old white skivvies. All the buttons on the
fly were gone except the top one, which held up the skivvies but did not keep the aperture closed. After the marines
made a basket, we would take the ball out of bounds and
pass it up the court. Each time Kokksavage lumbered up
the sandy court, sure enough the head of his pecker would
emerge from out of his shorts, and after a few strides the
entire ugly instrument would be flopping up and down as
he ran. It resembled a red rubber truncheon with a dingy
red apple at the end. When Kokksavage jumped up in the
air for the ball, the apple would slap him in the stomach.
When he jolted back to earth, his peter would flop back
halfway to his knees, and the big apple would disappear
for an instant between his legs, before reappearing as Kokksavage passed the ball. Of course, at every opportunity, he
would hurriedly shove his magnificent weapon back inside
his shorts. In fact, one time Smoky threw him the ball and
it hit "Peter" in the chest 'cause his hands were busy down
below! But it was no use. Before he was one-third the way
down the court, out came Peter flopping wildly.

The marine audience (some of them were stark naked) were delighted and amazed. As I rested on the sidelines I heard one guy ask our crew, "What about this guy? He sure is a man, isn't he?" Pretty soon the sidelines were crowded with marines who had come to see this monstrous thing. And our fellows grew proud that they were on the same ship with Peter. After all, he was different from the rest. They started to brag about him. One of our men told a marine, "When he takes a shower, he has the place all to himself. Nobody trusts him!"

Well, the marines skunked us badly. I got beautifully tired and sweated out a lot of body poisons. Afterward we swam in the warm water, walked on the dazzling white beach, then took a fresh warm water shower (use all you want) supplied from 50-gallon drums upon a platform. The marines were splendid to us, kind and courteous, and good fellowship abounded. They showed us some of their souvenirs and Jap letters that they collected, and told us stories of what they had done. It was good to get away from the ship awhile. On the way back, a marine gave me a whole sock full of beautiful seashells. I intend to make necklaces out of them to bring home to you.

Recently we have been working with PT boats. Some of the officers are ex-football stars and they carry their college camaraderie over to their Navy organization. They sure are a jolly bunch. We get along swell.

Wife, I wish you could hear the local radio announcers out here. It seems that as soon as we get an island or group of islands well secured, we establish a radio to serve the area. Of course, there are no commercials. Just music, news, sports news and transcriptions of programs made especially for the armed forces. Well, some of these announcers are the berries. They really have a line. For instance, they will satirize a commercial by telling us of "Retaw."

"Drink Retaw and be strong good old boys and girls. Retaw for health! We like it. You should like it, too." And of course, Retaw is "water" spelled backwards. Or they tell us of Bodies by Swisher, which has a double, double meaning for me. Or when Blondie comes on he says, "Uh-uh, uh—don't touch that dial. There is nothing else on. You gotta listen to Blondie." Or they invite you to join their lodge or club—where dust is served with every drink, and on and on. The announcers are given quite a bit of leeway (no obscenity, though) and they think up splendid skits. The guy may be playing records when he will break off and ask all the studio hands to say a few words. Golly, I sure get a kick out of it. As long as they please the men in the area, the monitor doesn't say a word. We really get good entertainment under the circumstances. I wish local radios back home could be as good.

I am still anxious to return to your arms. But I liken myself unto a monk who has so many years of privation and penance to do before he gets his reward. My reward shall be you.

1/26/45

Dearest Gretchen,

Every time our mailman leaves the ship, every time, he carries at least one letter from me to you.

I thought the book *The Razor's Edge* by Somerset Maugham was swell. I don't see why the dirt in it would be a detraction. After all, dirt is everywhere in the world. It cannot be ignored. Maybe the ultimate purpose of dirt is to act as contrast to the beautiful so that the beautiful can be appreciated more. Goodness knows, I appreciate you, wife!

I met another officer from a PT boat. He is Lt. George

Blanchard. When I told him I was George Blanchard Lucas, we were old friends, especially when I realized he had taught ordnance to me at Abbott Hall. So he calls me Luke and I call him Skipper, for he is captain of the PT. We talked of many things. He told me of his wife and showed me pictures of his little boy who was born while Skipper was teaching at Abbott. The baby is handsome. I don't like to talk of children, for it reminds me forcibly of what we are being forced to miss.

Now to set your mind at ease about my request. I have not applied for it because I know the captain would refuse it, and more than that, he would probably use it as a mental whip over me. As I have written you before, this has been the bitterest year of my life. You know, Gretchen, when things are really serious with me, I endeavor to solve the problem as quickly as possible. In my case of the past 12 months I have, through no fault of my own, been the victim of circumstances. Ordinarily officers get to return after 18 months, provided they can get the approval of the commanding officer. And in my case, this is impossible, not only for me but other officers aboard. I cannot write what I think, for some statements are better left unwritten. Someday you will know the whole story and you can judge for yourself. But I can say to you truthfully, don't worry about it. It all falls down to the fact that I just must wait my time until I get back, or the ship does, or orders from the bureau come, or some other unforeseen event. I can wait it out. This life isn't so tough and it will be a big mental victory to me. I want you to know that I am making the best of an unpleasant situation. If I could possibly get home, I would do so quickly.

You were entirely correct about me wearing the pith helmet, sun goggles, and nothing else ashore. I have numerous stories to tell you of such affairs. Also I must admit it gives me a feeling of complete freedom to run naked on a sandy beach in the sun on some pagan island. Is it possible for clothes to confine and restrain the spirit? I know I feel much more lighthearted, buoyant and gay when I cavort about in the complete freedom of nakedness.

But there is another side to these escapes ashore, these short hours spent away from the ship. There is the remoteness, the beauty, the unreality, the strangeness, unconsciously absorbed and impressed on one's awareness. To frolic on the sun-drenched sand of a foreign beach, vacant except for sailors of the *Tern* in varying degrees of nakedness, to have your words mixed and tumbled with the sound of the surf and the ululations of the wind, to feel against your hand the rough bark of a palm tree, to try to remember the name of this place, the time of the year, and the endless centuries that stretched before and after this instant of standing on a foreign beach and the sun-drenched sand with a few sailors who may be the last humans ever to stand on this far away strand with a strange-sounding name.

On this beach, no one is here to see you, few have been here before, and few will come in the years ahead. These remote iotas of sand and coral—alone and empty—surrounded by sea and sky and air with the sighing wind, the beating surf, and the docile, slanting palms.

1/29/45

Dearest wife,

I told you about Lieutenant Blanchard. Well, we are old friends now. He is a nice guy. In fact, all the boys on the PT boats guarding our ship are swell. Just as our ship is strictly regulation, their PT boats are strictly informal.

I hate to think of my tour of duty stretching into two years, but if it does, I really ought to be home by summer.

Just to be free from nervous tension will be a boon in itself. Enclosed you will find a letter Ensign Puregold sent me. He used to be Bosun on here. He got to go back after 17 months, only he had a different captain. I am glad for his sake.

2/1/45

Dearest wife,

The beginning of another month. My God, my God, when is it going to end, and when am I gonna get a break so I can come home? This just keeps on day after weary day with no end in view.

The crew is enthused over the fantastic Russian advance. I wonder how far they will be from Berlin when you read this. I hope they are darn close. Also, the boys in the Philippines are going right ahead. I wonder if I will get to see the Philippines before I get to see you. Now isn't that a lonely thought!

Time magazine says inflation is decidedly with us, that 1944 was the boomingest year yet, that Christmas buying was a mad splurge and nightclubs are doing a bang-up business. Let me encourage you again to think twice before purchasing. I believe the best place for money today is in the bank. Plenty of use for it later on.

By the way, concerning our financial statement, do you realize you let the month of January slip by with no report on the exchequer? Did we hit our $1,000 mark? Can you live on $100 a month, or have prices gone up too much?

And how do you feel, wife? I feel that when I first see you, it would be best to keep a wire fence between us to sorta protect us both until I am used to seeing you. The longing is fierce and deep. Sometimes it frightens me how much I miss you.

These are the nights of the full moon, and although most

of the romance of this part of the world began to pall on me months ago, I must admit there is still loneliness and beauty out here. These specks of land we are near now have a few hills, and the white moon gives them a brooding countenance. Rain squalls are frequent, so the cloud shapes are interesting, too. And there is always the universal ocean which seems to surround everything, and goes on and on. Yes, there is beauty here, but I am afraid it is wasted on me.

2/3/45

Dearest wife,

In one letter, you asked me if I were getting enough to eat. Well, I am happy to report that I am. Once or twice we got pretty low, but of late we have been getting our share of fresh provisions. However, I must admit that long ago, food began to lack taste to me. I believe I am just tired of the cooking on here—same seasoning, same everything. Also the weather is always warm so that causes appetites to lessen. However, I knew I would soon lose weight if I didn't eat and I didn't want to get the way I was the summer of 1942. So I attacked the problem like this. Religiously I take vitamin B1 tablets every day. At breakfast I always force myself to eat. Our breakfasts consist of either eggs and bacon (or ham) or hotcakes and bacon (or ham). Sometimes we run out of eggs or they get a little strong. In any case, I always eat a big breakfast, including butter. Sometimes I almost gag, but a swig of coffee sends it on down. Even coffee I use as a food. I put in lots of sugar and condensed milk. Once the food gets to my stomach I manage to keep it there. Between meals I try to munch on something. I always try to keep something on my stomach (it seems to lessen tension and the adrenaline flowing). At night on watches I have eaten pieces of bread slowly and methodically like a cow with her cud. Saltine crackers are good, too, they help combat seasickness. When we have apples and oranges I always eat lots, even though they have the musty, moldy aftertaste of a ship's storage hold. I always manage to have access to canned fruit. Raw carrots go good when available, and cabbage cores. I use the food as medicine. Eat the damn stuff 'cause my body needs it! Also, when I am sorta seasick, I concentrate on what I might like to eat. Once I think of something which would appeal to me, I have the cook make some, and I keep picking at it all day—like vegetable soup, or pea soup, or some such stuff. Another trick I have is to make hot chocolate—easy on the chocolate, but heavy on condensed milk and sugar. This concoction goes well at times. Of course when I get real seasick I lose ground, but this is infrequent now. I haven't been too sick to eat since November, when it got pretty bad. I am in good health. I weigh about 144, a good weight for me, and I am in pretty good shape.

The other day I realized I would soon be 30. Jesus! So that night I looked at me in the mirror. Without bragging, I am glad to say my body is a healthy temple. My stomach is flat and hard, my posture is better than ever, and my eyes are clear, not bloodshot! However, I must admit I get tired easily, but that is mental weariness due to the monotony and circumstances under which I live. But I sleep well with only occasional nightmares. I sleep lightly, though. Jesus! I can be out of bunk and dressed to lifebelt and gun in 15 seconds flat. In other words, wife, I am standing it well.

2/5/45

Dearest Gretchen,

Had letters from the home folks today. Golly, I guess winter this year in central Pennsylvania is rigorous with extra heavy snow and low temperatures. Remember the creak of wagon wheels on cold snow, with the air so frigid it hurt your nose if you breathed too deeply?

I haven't been too cold since February 1943 at Abbot Hall, Northwestern University, in Chicago.

Things have settled down in this locality, and the duty isn't bad. We don't get under way much and we are usually in calm water, so it is nice. We have movies most every night and the mail service, though not swift, is regular. It could be worse. There is still no sign of coming home. Somehow or other it seems far away, but I am not discouraged. Today I finished reading a book which affected me. It is *Country Cured* by Homer Croy. It is an autobiography of a Missouri farm boy who becomes a writer. He wrote the scenarios for Will Rogers and also worked with Dale Carnegie of *How to Win Friends* etc. fame. Homer Croy is a humorist of the type you would like. He is also a sentimentalist (which of late appeals to me).

2/6/45

Dearest Gretchen,

A favorite occupation of mine is to lie half asleep and picture all the things we shall do once the world is safe for democracy again. I conjure up scenes of us with our children and (ahem!) how dignified and wise they will think I am. I even imagine the process of us making children which in itself may develop into a pleasant avocation.

Much of my time, too, I think of research in genetics. And more and more, I think of eugenics. Maybe my old professor Dr. Hill was too eugenics-conscious, but I agree with him that if we are to progress and overcome war, we must be more discriminate in our breeding. No animal breeds as haphazardly as man does. Between eugenics and education, I believe much can be accomplished. We can breed a good type of people and then teach them kindness, compassion and brotherly love. Ah, yes, wife, you will have to listen to long discourses when I get home. 'Cause if I don't practice on you, who will listen to me?

2/9/45

Dearest wife,

Did I tell you about one of our radarmen? He got appendicitis. They operated on him out here at an island base hospital (which is a group of quonset huts), and sent him back to our ship! He now has 37, count 'em, 37 months in the Pacific with no leave!

Yesterday we were to assist a wounded landing craft (A) bring her cargo of four new light tanks ashore. Another landing craft (B) was already tied up to the first one. When we steamed up to the scene, B cast off his lines so we could take over. But then A capsized. She didn't sink, but she lost all her valuable cargo (four tanks). We picked up A's crew of eight and towed the landing craft (upside down) to quiet waters. In about an hour, the chief salvage officer was on the scene. He is that same commander who backed the *Tern* into the beach to pull off the destroyer. You should have seen the withering look he gave us.

2/11/45

Dearest wife,

In my leisure time, I am slowly making a few seashell bracelets and necklaces. They are not at all like the ones I sent home the first summer I was out. I believe you will like these. I'll bring them home when I come. Maybe it will be soon.

I am so full of plans of things for us to do, plans I want to talk over with you concerning our pathway through the years. I think a lot about money and find I have no burning desire to accumulate a lot of wealth. Smokey says he wants to earn $10,000 a year when he's 35. Why, I never aimed that high. If I hit a full professorship and $4,000 a year at age 45, I won't feel cheated. I guess I see too many goods go up in flames and smoke, or go the bottom of the sea. Ammunition alone is a monstrous expense. Boy I tell you I don't see how the world economy can stand another war, for we deliberately make articles, pay for them and then destroy them, burn 'em up, remove them from the system irrevocably. And we cannot dissipate wealth (and men) like this for any prolonged length of time and expect to survive as a civilized society. That is why you and I must continually raise our voices against being caught in such a trap again.

Recently we acquired a January 29 issue of *Time* (Smokey got it on the beach somehow). Under the medicine section was an article on neurotic wives of servicemen as a result of separation. Be sure and read it, for I am sure you will recognize some of your symptoms (only in the mildest form, though, I hope). They ended the article by quoting, "There is one sure cure," or words to that effect. Check me on it.

2/12/45

Dearest Gretchen,

I am beginning to lose faith in the Navy's mail system. Golly, we get less and less mail the longer we are here. Some fellows are just getting their Christmas packages now, and many packages have yet to come.

2/14/45

Dearest Gretchen,

Do you realize today is St. Valentine's Day and that 21 months have come and gone? My Gawd, sometimes I wonder how we have stood it. I guess no one knows how strong the spirit is until it has been put to the test. I am glad to say I am standing up under the strain, even though a few frayed edges may be showing. Have you started to unravel, wife? If you have, grimly pick up your knitting needles and repair the worn garment as best you can.

Today we sent four more enlisted men back to the States for new construction. We had BuPers orders to do so, so the captain couldn't stop them. The other crew members lined the rail and gave them a cheery send-off, for each man knows his time will come. The crewmen who remained behind even carried their seabags for them. As our motor launch left the ship and headed for shore, the departing sailors grinned and laughed, shouted and waved.

I see where Ernie Pyle is out here in the Pacific now. I have read some of his columns. I like them. It will be interesting to read of his reactions to this godforsaken part of the world.

We had a little excitement the past few days but it's all in the day's work now . . . The *Tern* sailors are picking up souvenirs right and left. One guy has a Jap machine gun. Jap rifles, money, letters, postcards and personal gear are common. One boy has a Jap kneecap. Yes, I mean the bone that fits on your leg. So far I haven't acquired anything. I don't want to get cluttered up with too much personal stuff, for when I get word to leave, I will be off here so quick it will make your head swim!

2/16/94

Lovely Gretchen,

At last I have some good news. Both for you and for me. Finally I have been able to put in a request for change of duty (which means new construction). Certain events transpired; the request was presented and I am sure it will be acted upon swiftly. The request goes off in the morning mail. I do not know how long it will take. Probably anywhere from two weeks to a month, but by Gawd, at least we will have something to look forward to. You can tell I am excited by the way I am writing. The whole picture has changed, and I am now full of optimism. By golly, it was about time I was getting a break. And at last it is now happening. I really feel good. Now, please don't let your hopes soar too high, for there are many things which can happen. But at least I have one good iron in the fire.

Well, the days keep going by but waiting gets no easier. I know that sooner or later I will get word one way or the other, but I really wish I could hurry things up a bit. I have one consolation. I know that if my request for change of duty and leave is approved that I won't be out here 22 months the next time. If I knew I had to spend 22 months the next time, I would say the war would never end. However, I do believe that events will move quickly now. We have so much power out here that the Japs don't have a chance. And just think of the men and material we will have when Germany capitulates. Gee, when I think I may get three to four months back in the States (it is entirely possible) I really get optimistic for I know my next tour of duty will be a short one.

2/22/45

Dearest gal,

Of course we were all excited and pleased about the Tokyo strike, and we listen carefully to all news from the Bonin Islands and Iwo Jima. I know we have to lose men to accomplish our ends, but I can never get used to the casualties. I have met, talked to and seen many of the fighting men. And some of the guys you laugh and talk with today may be absent tomorrow. But I won't dwell on these things now, wife, you can easily tell or will be able to tell my feelings when you see me. Never have I been more aware of each man's right to live, of the dignity due each man as a human being. I don't know, but I meet so many big basic problems out here and see them and hear of them, that I am more than a little confused. What I need is about 30–60–90 good nights of sleep in your arms to heal me. I often dream of walking over hilly pastures of green grass, dotted with daisies and drenched in sunshine.

2/24/45

Dearest Gretchen,

Yesterday I received four letters from you. I read them avidly. I get hungry for the sight of your handwriting and still hungrier for the sight of you! Your letters were long and newsy, and I liked that.

The enclosed letter excerpt is stolen from a love letter written by one of our seamen to his wife. I have tried to reproduce faithfully the spelling and punctuation and grammar. May the good Lord forgive my invasion of his privacy.

When I see you next you better be ready to tussle and take your lickin' cause I ain't in no mood for foolin. Your factory has been idel to long so you may haf to work dubble to catch up. And I meant that to.

I mite as well tell you now that when you git pragnant you will git absolutly no simpathy from me. After all that is what a wimmen is fur and you can keep right on luggin the wood and water same as always and dont expect more than one pair of shoes neither. This is the way I figger. If you have akes and pains and I can help you ease them why tell me. But if I can't help any there ain't no use to tell me cause I got worries of my own. You know that and I know that.

Your legal lovin husband

I think it is a wonderful idea for you to get a job. Then if my leave doesn't come through, little will be lost, and if it does come through you can always quit. Besides, that $140–$200 a month you will earn will be a help to us in our post-war plans.

It has now been a week since I sent in my request. It may take six weeks till I hear from it, but then again it may not. I am impatient, but all I can do is wait, even though life is unpleasant.

2/26/45

Dearest spouse,

Now to answer your question. Yes, I am near the place you mentioned. I am west of Tokyo longitude and you guessed it once. The last time I saw Emersin was at the place where Bob got transferred from his ship to the hospital ship. All this was way back in November. I have since heard rumors that Emersin got to go back, but I have no definite word.

Probably Madeline could let you know as well as anyone. Or write to the Navy Hospital at Great Lakes and ask Bob Mack where he got the hospital ship, and that is where I last saw Emersin. We are south-southwest of there about 300 miles, and that is as much as I can say.

2/28/45

Dearest Gretchen,

When I tell you someday of the jobs we have done and the close shaves we have had—well, at least I think you will be interested. Once, way back in 1944, we towed a disabled aircraft carrier for almost a week. It was off Pearl Harbor. In one of the actions down south, the carrier had been hit near the rudder by a torpedo. The carrier could not steer well. They sent her back to Pearl, where she was temporarily repaired. Just as she got outside the channel at Pearl, headed for the States, the steering mechanism broke again. It was stormy, rough weather. Maybe the heavy seas broke the steering gear. Well, all she could do was steer straight ahead. We were on duty at the time and were instructed to leave Pearl, catch up with the carrier (traveling at reduced speed), take her in tow (out of sight of land), back and forth till the weather abated and she could be pulled back into Pearl and fixed up again. Well, you should have seen us going alongside that monstrous carrier trying to put a line on her so we could take her in tow. The waves were high and we rolled back and forth. The top of our main mast came just above the carrier's flight deck. We rolled as we came alongside. Our mast caught on a life raft and just wiped it off the side of the ship (and broke our radar shield). But finally another fleet tug got her in tow. The towing cable was fastened through her hawse pipes to the anchor chain. It took some good seamanship to do it, and coordination on both ships. When they did get her in tow, the other tug could pull her in a straight line but did not have enough power to turn to left or right. So we were instructed to tow the tug towing the aircraft carrier.

We tried to get a 3-inch manila line aboard the other tug, but it slipped and got tangled up in our propeller. Boy, there was some cursing and swearing then. So we cut the manila hawser and finally got a steel tow cable onto the tug and proceeded to pull on it. The only time our ship really had to strain was when we tried to make turns left or right. We would pull her southeast for 10 miles, then turn and go southwest for 10 miles, then back north for 10 miles, just out of sight of land, so that no Jap spies on Oahu would see our predicament and send word to a Jap sub to come by and sink her.

We were out there at least four days till the weather finally calmed down. Our ship was rolling and tossing and everyone seasick. Yet the carrier was barely rising up and down. Every morning some of their crew would do calisthenics on the flight deck. At the same time I could hardly walk down the deck we were rolling so badly.

When the weather calmed down, we pulled the carrier back to Pearl. At the harbor entrance, there were at least a dozen yard tugs waiting to push and shove that monster carrier up the channel to a drydock where her steering gear was repaired again. We were glad when they cast our tow line off her.

Next morning they sent a diver over to our berth. He went down and cut the manila rope away from our propeller. It was a brand new line. It had never been used before.

Most people picture a sea tug as some sort of squatty little boat that helps dock ocean liners in New York City harbor. Not us. We get most of our jobs in bad weather, for that is when ships get in trouble. Oh well, it ain't glamorous, but is often monotonous, and I am thoroughly tired of the whole lash-up.

Battle plans and wrasslin' holds are being developed daily, ready to put into instant operation. Every contact, every melee, every hand-to-hand combat will be a pleasure with endless delights. And the forays into the blissful mountains with skirmishes on the happy hillsides will leave memories that will never be forgotten.

3/4/45

Dearest wife,

Unexpectedly I had to give up using the typewriter and return to my trusty pen. Each system has its few faults completely offset by tremendous advantages, as you can see.

By the way, did I tell you that one day I bent over to grab a line to help "heave around" and my Parker 52 Eversharp fell into the blue ocean? Never before did I realize, so acutely, how definitely something is lost than when it sinks into the ocean. I watched that pencil sink deeper and deeper—removed completely from the economic system, my use and personal wealth. I started to cuss but realized how futile it was. However, one "goddamn" slipped out 'cause I had paid good money for that pencil. It was a beauty and wrote so nicely and efficiently (better than a typewriter). Even now I have pangs of regret when I think of my beautiful pencil lying in the ooze at the bottom of 500 fathoms of water—bastard!

3/6/45

Dearest wife,

Another indication that I am undergoing a character or mental change—never before have I really enjoyed Shelley's poems, but last night I picked up a paperback pocket-book of verse and read "To a Skylark" and "The Cloud." Oh! They were good! They really struck home. Maybe it is because I have been so long deprived of terrestrial visions, sensations and images, but those poems excited my imagination and the singing lines took me back again to peaceful countrysides I have known. Before, when I was in school, I read Shelley and Keats and other poets because they were assigned reading, but now I shall read them again as therapy.

I have been restless lately. No literature seemed to hold my attention, but that poetry surely did soothe and calm me. How would you analyze that, wife? Does one have to go through ordeal and privation before one can appreciate deeply the written emotion of the poet?

Yes, I must read some more poetry. I will remember the best passages I have read and will read them aloud to you some lazy afternoon under a maple tree by a brook in a sunny meadow.

3/8/45

Dearest Gretchen,

Enclosed you will find excerpts I copied from a directive we received. It is humorous and literally true in some instances.

In Anticipation of that 30 Days' Leave!

In compliance with current policies for rotation of armed forces overseas, it is directed that in order to maintain this high standard of character of the American sailor and soldier and to prevent any dishonor reflecting on the uniform, all individuals eligible for return to the U.S. under current directives will undergo an indoctrination course of demobilization prior to approval of his application for return.

In America there are a remarkable number of beautiful girls. These young ladies have not been liberated and many are gainfully employed as stenographers, salesgirls, and beauty operators, or welders. Contrary to current practices, they should not be greeted with a resounding wolf howl, hound-dog bay, or Great Dane bark. A proper greeting is, "Isn't it a lovely day?" Or, "Have you ever been to Chicago?" This should be said in a controlled, well-modulated voice.

A typical American breakfast consists of such strange food as canteloupes, fresh eggs, milk, ham, etc. These are highly palatable and though strange in appearance, are extremely tasty. Butter, made from cream, is often served. If you wish some butter, you turn to the person nearest it and say quietly, "Please pass the butter." You do not say, "Throw me the goddamn grease."

Americans have a strange taste for stimulants. The drinks in common use in the Pacific such as underripe coconut "kava," wine "ulcers," pineapple "swipe" or just gasoline, bitters and water (commonly known by the Hawaiian term "Okolehau") are not ordinarily acceptable in civilian circles. These drinks should not be served.

Upon leaving a friend's home after a visit, one may find his hat misplaced. Frequently it has been placed in a closet. One should turn to one's host and say, "Don't seem to have my hat, could you help me find it?" Do not say, "Don't anyone leave this room, some SOB has stolen my hat!"

Whiskey, a common American drink, may be offered to the sailor on social occasions. It is considered a reflection on the uniform to snatch the bottle from the hostess and drain the bottle, cork and all. All individuals are cautioned to exercise extreme control in these circumstances.

In motion-picture theaters, seats are provided. Helmets are not required. It is not considered good form to whistle every time a female over 8 or under 90 crosses the screen. If vision is impaired by the person in the seat in front, there are plenty of other seats, which can be occupied. Do not hit him across the back of the head and say, "Move your head, jerk, I can't see a damn thing!"

All individuals returning to the USA will make every effort to conform to the customs and habits of the regions visited and to make themselves as inconspicuous as possible. Any actions which reflect upon the honor of the uniform will be promptly dealt with.

3/16/45

Dearest Gretchen,

Wonder of wonders! I got to go ashore again with a recreation party, and I really had fun. It wasn't strictly recreation officially, but it was a change for me. We rode in an amphibious tractor and I really got a kick out of it. The AmTracs are bigger than they look. I sat on the hood over the driver's seat. We splashed through the lagoon and when we came to the shallow water, we really rolled along. Our trip ended in a coconut grove near where we played basketball. It surely is a pretty place. After the work was done, we played volleyball and collected seashells. God, it was good to get on solid ground, relax and run around "nekkid."

Recently I met some Army fellows from Pennsylvania, although none I knew before the war. When I told them I was a Penn State grad, they really were glad to see me. And do you know, wife, that a tour of duty out here for the Army is three years? Then they wait for a chance to go back. So even though I did get screwed by Navy custom, it is not hard to see someone who is worse off than I.

3/18/45

Dearest Gretchen,

Today I wrote your folks a letter. I told them that we would have four big expenses after the war (in order of their importance):

1) Getting my Ph.D. (Our cash income will be limited).

2) Children—as many as you want in the next 10 years.

3) Our home in the college town where we finally settle down—including furniture.

4) *The farm.* I wrote them I could take care of the first three and, if you got a job, you could take care of the fourth. Of course, all this is just thinking out loud and everything is subject to change. My main purpose in discussing all of this is to take my mind off the Western Pacific. It is a form of escape and can be a profitable one at that. Write me your ideas on this and let me know if I am going off the deep end.

Twice now, you have mentioned a scheme you are concocting for us. I know it involves considerable money, for you said it would take three to four months' salary. Now what in hell have you cooked up? I try to figure what it will be, but I don't get far. I know it isn't a car, 'cause there ain't no such animals anymore. It can't be a ring, for that would be only for you. What is my wife gonna buy for $400–$800? Is it furniture? So far I have not decided for sure. You must give me more hints.

3/20/45

Dearest Gretchen,

Last night we had the movie *The Fighting Seabees,* with Susan Hayward and John Wayne. I was really disappointed. First of all, what a fake it was. What utter ludicrousness!

They had the Japs landing on a tropical island using *our* landing craft. Absurd! Also, before the Japs landed, they were not preceded by an artillery barrage. Not one palm tree was tattered or defoliated. Jesus! On every island I have seen, there is lucky to be one palm tree *not* injured. Also they had six barges of Japs to land and take the island held in strength by us. After awhile I started to laugh. Especially when the naval officers appeared wearing black ties for tropical gear. Christ, you would sweat to death in 10 minutes with a tie on out here. So I up and left about the middle of it.

Lately my head has been filled with post-war plans. You know I will be eligible for financial educational assistance when I come back, for my education was interrupted. If I can get such money, I will not take an assistantship from LSU, but work full time on my thesis to finish up the damn thing quick.

Did you ever hear Dr. Dutcher at Penn State talk of farm chemurgy? I figure after the war that farmers, to make a profit, will have to use waste products more, such as corn cobs, corn stalks, bagasse, leaves, brewer's grain, even feathers to be transformed into food, plastics, paints, etc.

During my stay out here, I have realized more than ever how much easier and more pleasant life can be if you just have the money to buy a few of the extra things. For instance, when I recall that we had one stinky little electric fan in our apartment to keep us cool during those humid summers, I get sore as hell. Think how much more pleasant life would have been if we had a couple of big fans, Coke in the icebox or a car to go somewhere. It all boils down to what we want out of life!

3/22/45

Dearest wife,

Recently, an official letter came out relaxing censorship rules a little. We are now permitted to mention ports we have visited after we departed from them for a minimum period of 30 days. In this letter I will mention the places we have been and in later letters will tell you something of what I did and saw in each. Since I left you those many months ago, we have been to the following places: Hawaiian group, Oahu (Pearl Harbor and Honolulu), Kaui and Kahoolawe. I have seen most of the other islands of the Hawaiian group, but did not get to go ashore on them. We have also been to the Gilbert Islands. I went ashore at Tarawa and fished in the lagoon at Makin Island, made famous by Carlson's Raiders. (Incidentally, I have a bracelet made from part of the fuselage of a Jap plane shot down at Makin. I am saving it for you.) Around the Gilberts I did some pretty good navigation, if I do say so myself.

We visited the Marshall Islands, too. Majuro, Kwajalein, Eniwetok. I have many good stories of these places. Once in a storm at Eniwetok, I was out in the motor launch with three men and almost did not get back.

We also went to the Admiralty Islands, down near New Guinea. We saw Manus Island, of which you may have read in *Time* magazine. We also went to Guam and Saipan (air raids at Saipan—too many). We saw the new superforts (B29s) at Saipan and I sent you souvenirs from there. Some of these places we have been to several times, some we only stayed a short while, and others we remained for a week or more. One other place I have not mentioned, and that is Ulithi atoll. I doubt if you ever heard of it much, but the Navy knows its worth. The last I saw and heard of Emersin he was at Ulithi. I saw Bob Mack at Eniwetok, and just missed him at Ulithi the last exciting time he was there. Maybe I should have said the "painful" time.

If time permits, I shall in succeeding letters tell you of some of my experiences in these places if I run out of other ideas. Some of the things happened so long ago that they are very dim; or maybe they have been pushed out of my mind by more recent events. Anyway, I shall recall them as best I can and relate them to you with as little exaggeration as possible. However, most of our days were and are monotonous, for we are a service vessel. You might liken us to a truck or dray for we drag equipment and stores around as they are needed. Seldom do we get in on the adventurous jobs; I am just as well satisfied, for I am tired of excitement and danger, and long hours and lack of sleep, and being tired too often.

3/24/45

Dearest spouse,

Since we are not getting any mail (the service has fouled up again), and while I am waiting for my orders, and because censorship regulation has been eased, I will fill my letters with accounts of places I have been.

First of all, Honolulu. I think I wrote you about how crowded it is, and was. While there, my liberties were of two sorts. I would go window-shopping in Honolulu. This also constituted exploring, for I visited out-of-the-way sections of the city. Of course, the population is a miscellaneous mix of all breeds, but the Chinese produce markets were exotic. I used to walk through just to gawk (unobtrusively), listen to the conversation and sort out the different smells. I suppose there are few people in Hawaii who are not hybrids (sometimes even brothers and sisters are different). I found it difficult to distinguish Japs from Chinese, and when they amalgamated with Portuguese, Hawaiian, Filipino, Spaniard, English, Polynesian, Malaysian and Negro, it was impossible. Many of the girls were attractive—mostly because they had an odd-type beauty and contrasting facial features, but many were lemons.

There are many, many curio shops, all charging ridiculous prices. I very seldom purchased things from them, for I could get many of the articles at various ship-service stores for half the price. Many of the articles I sent to you were bought in quiet neighborhoods at stores which did not cater to the tourist trade.

Honolulu is full of service people—too full. Whorehouses did (and still do, I guess) a tremendous business—$3 for 3 minutes! ($1 for the girl, $1 for the house, and $1 for the police). If you are good at mathematics, you can figure out how much they make in a 10-hour day. I pictured a whorehouse as a sinful place full of naked women. Imagine my surprise when a member of the crew told me that most houses have only three or four girls, with two cubbyhole-adjoining rooms as a stall for each. And I used to see the men standing in line for half a block (I am assuming it is needless for me to mention that my acquaintance with this place of tropic lure is solely from reports gotten from enlisted men). Yet, vencreal diseases are much less prevalent than I thought they would be.

I have seen young girls on the street disgustingly drunk, but not often. Of course, drunken servicemen are taken for granted.

Strange flowers and shrubs fill every yard. I also used to go to Waikiki often to swim and lie in the sand to watch the surfboard riders. Of course, all tourists immediately head for Waikiki, so it has lost much of its charm. But the Ala Moana (Moe-ahn-ah) Hotel and the Royal Hawaiian

Hotel are still nice. There are also many quiet seaside hotels which cater to the more expensive trade. Bob Mack and I went to one such quiet place to eat one afternoon. If I remember correctly, it was called the Halekelani (pronounced Hall-lee-ka-lawn-i). By the way, that gown I sent you is called Kikowaena (pronounced kee-ko-wina), which means, I believe, "bare belly."

But I often tired of the journey (10 miles or more) to Honolulu from Pearl Harbor on a bus full of sweating people, so quite often on my liberties, I went swimming at Ford Island (at Pearl Harbor) at the officers' swimming pool. This is a lovely pool with beautiful surroundings. I used to go there twice a week sometimes and lie in the sun and read, or just think of you. Once I took Pluto with me. Boy, he almost went crazy with joy, running around on the grass and digging in the flower beds.

This endless waiting is hard to take. I hate to discourage you, but it may take another month. Christ, I hope not, but that's the way it looks.

3/26/45

Dearest wife,

To continue with an account of my travels. The first tropic island I saw (outside of the Hawaiians) was a little atoll in the eastern Marshall Islands. It was early on a hot, sunny morning and after the lookout shouted, I looked through the binoculars and sure enough, there on the horizon, was a faint smudge.

Later on, we came to the atoll of Majuro. There is a beautiful lagoon here and nice beaches. Majuro was not much ruined by war. However, Namur and Kwajalein atolls were a mess. These islands are all small and they really took a beating. The palm trees were all stripped and battered, and shell craters were everywhere. I didn't get to go ashore here but I looked at the island through the glasses. My lasting and deepest impression is the cemetery. Row on row of white crosses. Then there were pillboxes, debris and litter.

Kwajalein lagoon had many sunken Jap ships in it, some of them quite big. I also saw some smaller Jap ships which had been beached. There are still Japs on bypassed islands in the Marshalls. I got to go ashore at Eniwetok. This atoll has several islands which took a beating, too. I went on the liberty party to Parry Island and that is where I wore my pith helmet and glasses. On Eniwetok Island they have a nice church made out of a Quonset hut. Also a big cemetery. I gathered seashells at this atoll. We had some bad weather at Eniwetok and our ship worked very, very hard.

Later on, we went to the Gilbert Islands. Here again we had some trouble and our chow ran low. Tarawa and Makin were the islands we visited. It was on Tarawa that I copied the poems I sent you, copied from the memorial tablets. Tarawa affected me deeply, especially as I walked over the battlefield and had the story told to me. When we got there, the tanks and other vehicles which had been knocked out were still on the beach and in shallow water.

I saw one skull, too, at the water's edge. We also saw the pier along which the marines crept to get ashore. It was full of bullet holes, and I saw the old Jap ship hull in which the Japs had placed heavy machine guns. Many marines were killed here.

The Jap command center was a concrete building with thick walls. One of our old battleships shelled this building with 14-inch shells. I counted at least 10 hits but only one I remember that completely pierced the wall. A destroyer also shelled this building but took out just little nicks. According to the explanatory tablet, the building was finally reduced by flamethrowers.

Makin Island was not shot up much. (I believe there weren't 10 trees left on Tarawa untouched. At least I didn't see any.) It is a pretty place and typical of a tropical paradise. It was at Makin that we caught the excellent fish, which were a welcome addition to our diet. On Tarawa I saw the native Gilbertese Islanders. I saw only men (laborers). They were without exception tall and husky, well built, with mahogany skin. They had white teeth and were a friendly, happy cheerful group. They really liked the American soldiers and sailors. I saw none of the women, but I understand they are quite attractive when in their teens. It is on these islands that the women frequently appear in public with their breasts uncovered. The native villages in these islands are restricted to servicemen. Strict disciplinary action is taken against any man who molests or tries to molest the natives.

At Manus Island, the natives came out to the ship in outrigger canoes to trade cat's-eyes, a form of shell (I have a nice one for you) for cloth and cigarettes. These natives had holes in their nose and ears, tattoo marks on their faces, and black teeth. They wore tooth necklaces. Rather an unkempt sort, little evidence of civilization. Bob Hope and his troupe were at Manus when we were there but we didn't get to see him. It was on the Manus trip that we crossed the equator. We had one sub warning on this trip, but nothing happened. I guess we weren't big enough game.

3/28/45

Dearest wife,

Each day goes by and still we get no mail. I guess they have other uses for the mail planes just now. But I do hope we get mail soon, for it has now been 10–12 days since we got mail. In anticipation of my leave (will I ever get the word?), I want to recommend to you the following procedure. Wherever we meet, be it West Coast, N'Orleans or B.R., I think it wise that no one but you and me be present. In any case or circumstance, it will be an emotional experience for both of us, so we don't want any friends standing around embarrassing both themselves and us. I guess the ideal situation would be for me to meet you in a hotel room, where we could cry our eyes out and no one to see—but wherever it is that we first catch sight of each other, I believe it best for us to be separated from any acquaintances.

Now to continue my descriptions. Guam is an attractive island. It rains a great deal there and is quite warm, so the flora is luxuriant. I looked at the town of Agana through the glasses and it was really battered. I saw one wrecked Jap plane. At Saipan we underwent several air raids but nothing particular happened. I got to go ashore at Saipan with a recreation party. Officially the island was secured, but there were still many restricted areas because of Jap snipers. I saw a few charming natives and one native (Jap) village, badly shot up as per usual.

I saw one concrete pillbox with four or five Jap remnants in it. Didn't smell good. Also, I saw many sunken Jap cargo ships and one salvaged two-man sub (Jap). I sent you souvenirs from Saipan.

Saipan is a pretty island with mountains and sugar-cane fields. We passed close to the point (Suicide Point) where so many Jap civilians during the invasion committed suicide by wading out into the ocean.

Most of the time out here, the weather has not been too bad except for wind and rain squalls that come most every day. But twice we were in typhoon weather, and I was really scared. I don't mean to be melodramatic, but I was deathly afraid, and sick and weak from fear, and seasick along with it.

I guess one reason why sea duty is no good is because that goddamn ocean is always waitin' for you. It is a relentless, pitiless, unceasing opponent.

3/31/45

Dearest wife

Just came off watch and will continue so this letter can go out in the morning. Tomorrow is Easter, and I am afraid it will turn out to be like Christmas, a day I'll be glad to see go by. I know you will be glad to hear that in all my travels, not once did we stay in a malaria area. Thus, so far, I have had to take no atabrine, for which I am thankful.

If I didn't have you to come home to, and I had a 30-day leave, I would go to some small town in the middle west and get a job on a farm and let solitude and the earth cure me. I have seen too much destruction and devastation and needless work (precautionary measures) and ruin. So that is one reason why I would so much enjoy being at home in springtime.

I tell you, spouse, I have been reading lots of poetry lately—it pleases and soothes me. You know, if I come home in the springtime, let us go away to some meadow sweet, and there I shall read to you lyrics of praise and beauty. The warm sun shall caress us and nodding grasses be our parlor. And a year hence we can return to the happy hillside with our firstborn that he may lie in the nodding grasses, to gaze peacefully at the blue sky above, while I read more to you.

My head is filled with dreams and my heart is full of

desire and need for you. I will be glad to be with you again. I love you.

4/4/45

Dearest Gretchen,

There still is no indication of my orders coming through yet, but I feel sure the month of April could be my last month aboard the *Tern*. I really hope so, but I dare not let my spirit soar too much, for the letdown would be too disheartening. I have enough trouble as it is to control myself now. In your letter, you mentioned you were a "little scared" about us having changed. I interpret that as a good sign, for both of us, because it means you are just as anxious as I am to have a favorable reaction when we meet. Ah! Lord, I do look forward to being with you again. To live again!

To be truthful, Gretchen, I am afraid of my sex appetite, for I have seen what sex-hunger can do to men out here. Sometimes I am surprised that more men do not go berserk when they do return to green pastures. To me, it is a good indication of the civilized state of the average American young man that he can restrain himself so well. I understand that many foreign armies, i.e., German, French, Italian, Jap and Chinese, take official note of the sex desires of their enlisted men by including contraceptives in their gear (or maybe it is preventive medicine). I have seen one Japanese personnel kit. It is a waterproof cloth bag about the size of a ladies' handbag. There were writing utensils, postcards, little pamphlets and three contraceptives. Only God knows what he would use them for in this locality. I understand there are natives here but I have seen none.

When we are together again, wife, I want you to be feminine. I want you to dress up and make up often. I want to watch you brush your hair and fasten your stockings. I want to watch you tango. And in between all these exertions, we can get reacquainted.

And above all, during our lovemaking, we can make glorious plans for the future.

4/10/45

Wife,

In case I have forgotten, let me tell you how pleased I am that you are working at an interesting job and, more than that, contributing a sizable sum each month to our income. Let us assume that your four years of college cost $2,000, more or less. Yet, if you worked only 10–12 months, your college career would be paid for. Of course, I hope you don't have to work that long, but even if you work only three months, that is more than $500. We got a lot of living to do when I do get back.

4/12/45

Dearest wife,

In two of your recent letters, you named a location and asked me if I was there. Well, both times you hit the nail right on the head. As I wrote before, this place has been "officially" secured for some time, but there are still some Japs ashore on this mountainous island.

Now for some more personal philosophy. I have had enough contact the past 16 months with careless, irresponsible, incompetent people (to put it mildly) and the trouble they cause. I have had enough. Maybe my intense feelings on this subject are unnecessary, but I do not like to see anyone make a mess out of his life or cause other people trouble. And, wife, if you ever see me going the wrong way, don't hesitate to tell me, just as I would not hesitate to tell you. Forcibly, during my stay out here, I have been taught ideals and values which I intend to abide by. Everyone has a right to live his own life, but when someone lives in such a way as to cause me undeserved pain, uneasiness, discomfort, worry or worse—if he deprives me of "life, liberty, and pursuit of happiness" then I have the right to speak to him about it. And if he persists, we part company as soon as I can arrange it, or I take steps to preserve my ideals and my life, or take action within the law to prevent him from harming others. I am speaking now of citizens in general as well as naval officers.

4/14/45

Dear Mrs. Lucas,

Who would ever think that in 23 months I would write you 777 letters? That is more than one a day from a taciturn person who has never told a tall story in his life. No, Mrs. Lucas, you must admit I have written you faithfully. I have written almost two letters to your one, so to pay you back I will not *write to you again* until you catch up to me in the number of letters I've written! I figure that is the only fair way.

Yesterday I received a letter from you, and one from Dupree. Your letter, as usual, was one-half page. I can't understand, you who are so talkative can't write much at all in letters. Russ wants me to visit him on his ship. He says he is the fastest runner aboard. Every morning when the crew exercises he wins the foot races. He figures he has run all the way to *California* by now.

As for Dr. Dupree, he is also somewhere in California (*San Francisco,* I think), continuing his studies on genetics.

He says he has a new graduate student coming to work for him in about 10 days. *Lucky fellow!* But, if I know anything about research in genetics, I'll bet LSU steals Dupree's student as fast as they can. I know I would leave California immediately by airplane if I got an offer from LSU.

I must go now. I'll write again when I get the chance. Take care of all of our children!

Respectfully yours,
George Blanchard Lucas

Epilogue

The last letter is a fake. Censorship prevented me from telling my wife that I had been detached from the *Tern* so I used this cryptic letter full of inaccuracies to tell her that I was returning to California.

I left the *Tern* on 4/15/45 and flew by DC3 to Pearl Harbor. I ate at the officers' club mess. Six officers sat at each table. For the first meal there was a large plate of fresh vegetable salad on each table. The table where I sat had only three people eating. I ate the whole salad myself. Nobody but me even noticed. It sure was good! Within the next few days I embarked on a large troop ship for the sea voyage to San Francisco, where I sent the telegram to Betty on 4/26/45.

She met my train in New Orleans, where we spent three fulfilling days before returning to Baton Rouge.

I finished my thesis on fungus genetics in June 1946 and accepted a job at the Tobacco Experiment Station, Oxford, N.C., where North Carolina State University scientists conducted research on tobacco, the principal crop grown in the state. We lived in a four-room house on a quiet street of this small town. Betty had me plant roses in the back yard. They produced beautiful flowers. I can see them now.

Bob Mack died of cancer in 1957. Henry George died of natural causes in 1985. I have lost contact with other shipmates and naval companions.

The years went by so quickly. My mother and father, members of the laboring class of people from the hills of central Pennsylvania, raised 9 children. I helped raise 5 biological children and 2 stepsons. Now, Mary Lib and I are enjoying all of our 19 grandchildren.

Undoubtedly my sense of values and my personality have been deeply imprinted by my mountain heritage, my naval years, and membership in these three family groups. For which I am richer and wiser.

About the Author

George Lucas attended Penn State, where he played football and earned a Phi Beta Kappa key and a bachelor of science degree in botany. He received a master's degree in plant pathology from Louisiana State University in 1942 before serving three years in the U.S. Navy, after which he returned to LSU and earned his doctorate.

Dr. Lucas joined the faculty of North Carolina State in 1946 and was assigned to work at the Tobacco Research Station at Oxford, where he remained until moving to Raleigh in 1951. Among the textbooks he has written or edited, his *Diseases of Tobacco* (Scarecrow Press, 1958), now in its third edition, remains a classic. He has also been the author or coauthor of more than a hundred research papers in scientific journals.

Dr. Lucas taught plant pathology courses and conducted extensive research in the lab and in the field from 1952 to 1980, at which point he retired from the NCSU faculty. Currently, he is a professor emeritus in the Plant Pathology Department, where he continues to work.

The **Naval Institute Press** is the book-publishing arm of the U.S. Naval Institute, a private, nonprofit society for sea service professionals and others who share an interest in naval and maritime affairs. Established in 1873 at the U.S. Naval Academy in Annapolis, Maryland, where its offices remain, today the Naval Institute has more than 100,000 members worldwide.

Members of the Naval Institute receive the influential monthly magazine *Proceedings* and discounts on fine nautical prints and on ship and aircraft photos. They also have access to the transcripts of the Institute's Oral History Program and get discounted admission to any of the Institute-sponsored seminars offered around the country.

The Naval Institute also publishes *Naval History* magazine. This colorful bimonthly is filled with entertaining and thought-provoking articles, first-person reminiscences, and dramatic art and photography. Members receive a discount on *Naval History* subscriptions.

The Naval Institute's book-publishing program, begun in 1898 with basic guides to naval practices, has broadened its scope in recent years to include books of more general interest. Now the Naval Institute Press publishes more than seventy titles each year, ranging from how-to books on boating and navigation to battle histories, biographies, ship and aircraft guides, and novels. Institute members receive discounts on the Press's nearly 400 books in print.

For a free catalog describing Naval Institute Press books currently available, and for further information about subscribing to *Naval History* magazine or about joining the U.S. Naval Institute, please write to:

Membership & Communications Department
U.S. Naval Institute
118 Maryland Avenue
Annapolis, Maryland 21402–5035
Or call, toll-free, (800) 233-USNI.

THE NAVAL INSTITUTE PRESS

Every Other Day
Letters from the Pacific

Designed by Karen L. White

Set in Simoncini Garamond
by Graphic Composition, Inc.
Athens, Georgia

Printed on 50-lb. Glatfelter Supple B-18
and bound in Holliston Kingston Natural
by Thomson -Shore, Inc.
Dexter, Michigan